Virtual
Communities
Companion

Virtual
Communities
Companion

Karla Shelton
Todd McNeeley

CORIOLIS GROUP BOOKS

an International Thomson Publishing company I(T)P®

Albany, NY • Belmont, CA • Bonn • Boston • Cincinnati • Detroit • Johannesburg • London
Madrid • Melbourne • Mexico City • New York • Paris • Singapore • Tokyo • Toronto • Washington

Publisher
Keith Weiskamp

Project Editor
Toni Zuccarini

Production Coordinator
Michael Peel

Cover Artist
Gary Smith

Cover Design
Anthony Stock

Interior Design
Nicole Colón

Compositor
Shady Lane Graphics

Copyeditor
Caroline Parks

Proofreader
Mary Cullen

Indexer
Luanne O'Loughlin

CD-ROM Development
Robert Clarfield

Virtual Communities Companion

Copyright © 1997 by The Coriolis Group, Inc.

Limits of Liability and Disclaimer of Warranty

The author and publisher of this book have used their best efforts in preparing the book and the programs contained in it. These efforts include the development, research, and testing of the theories and programs to determine their effectiveness. The author and publisher make no warranty of any kind, expressed or implied, with regard to these programs or the documentation contained in this book.

The author and publisher shall not be liable in the event of incidental or consequential damages in connection with, or arising out of, the furnishing, performance, or use of the programs, associated instructions, and/or claims of productivity gains.

Trademarks

Trademarked names appear throughout this book. Rather than list the names and entities that own the trademarks or insert a trademark symbol with each mention of the trademarked name, the publisher states that it is using the names for editorial purposes only and to the benefit of the trademark owner, with no intention of infringing upon that trademark.

Published by The Coriolis Group, Inc.
An International Thomson Publishing Company
14455 N. Hayden Road, Suite 220
Scottsdale, Arizona 85260

602/483-0192
FAX 602/483-0193
http://www.coriolis.com

Printed in the United States of America

ISBN 1-57610-156-8

10 9 8 7 6 5 4 3 2 1

To my husband, Bill…who makes every day a joy to live.

To Barb…who keeps me sane.

To Dookie…who gives me her unconditional love.

—Karla Shelton

To two teachers:

Don Williams who inspired me in my youth…

and Kim Whalen who inspires me today…

Kim, will you accept this dedication that I make before all the netizens dwelling within the ether as a declaration of my love for you…And will you do me the honor of becoming my wife?

—Todd McNeeley

Acknowledgments

Many thanks to the folks at The Palace, Inc., who provided us with documentation, encouragement, and help: Ken Arck, Lisa Herschbach, Mark Jeffrey, Mike Maerz, and Tony Storino.

To Mark Pesce for his enlightenment regarding VRML.

To the many community builders who offered sage advice: Auto, Cyberia, Firebird, Gromp, Lisa, Man in Black, Nancy Evans, The Marshfield Family, Saturn, and Turkette.

To the talented individuals who contributed editorial material: Jay Furr, Vince Gelormine, Michael Greene, Kevin O'Connor, and Dr. John Suler.

A hearty thanks to the companies that permitted us to showcase software applications on the CD-ROM.

To our families and friends, who offered tremendous support during the writing of this book: Alec and Betty Osvath, Barbara Stewart, Kelly and Mark Zamonski, Thelma and Sylvester Mowat, Verla McFarlane, Joyce and Glen McNeeley, Kim McNeeley, Michael Capone, Shaunn and Michele Baker, Jordan Baker, Elizabeth Hill, and Diane Phillips.

...and finally, to the good people who make Mountain Dew.

Karla Shelton
Todd McNeeley

Contents

Contents

Part 3   Getting Your Community Off The Ground   277

Part 5   The Future

FOREWORD

By Jon Katz, Contributing Editor for *Wired*

The emergence of the Internet seems to have given much of America and its entrenched institutions something of a collective nervous breakdown. We are constantly being warned about pornography, hate mail, computer addiction, and social isolation. All of these alarms have some basis in truth, but most are so wildly exaggerated that they obscure what this dazzling new culture is really about.

Of all of these many hysterias raised about the Web, the one I find the hardest to understand is the alleged individual dislocation it causes. For me, the Web is a miracle of connection. It brings people together in ways not even imaginable just a few years ago.

The Net is fundamentally about community, as Karla Shelton and Todd McNeeley make abundantly clear in this warm, intelligent, accessible, and useful book.

One of the great hidden secrets of the Internet is the fact that you can't even go online without some sort of community, from the computer conferencing system to the Internet Service Provider to the Usenet group or chat room. Community is the great potential of the Web, one of its most powerful byproducts.

Don't be fooled by phobic political and media portrayals of the digital world as a medium where pornographers and bombmakers dominate. Senior citizens email and support one another on Senior Net, perhaps the Web's greatest example of an online community at work. I've made my best friends online; and learned more things about more subjects than in the previous decades of my life. Had more arguments, too.

The Web can be a powerful emotional, even spiritual, experience. My first online experience five years ago was to help a father survive the death of a young son, along with a group of other men. This was community at its most powerful and fundamental, and the fact that the men involved hadn't—still haven't—even met is almost incidental.

Foreword

The Net and the Web are not about replacing human contact, but finding new ways of building and making it. This book couldn't be more timely. Women are pouring onto the Web in record numbers. So are the elderly, along with the young. All are enthusiastic and inveterate community builders. Bird lovers meet in chat rooms to talk about their cockatoos. Teenagers trade model parts and baseball cards. Thrifty food shoppers trade coupons. Philatelists trade stamps, even show pictures of them. Once isolated gay teenagers can find others and avoid the terrible loneliness many felt until recently. The handicapped can make friends they would never have known. Researchers can share information quickly. Thousands of jobs are sought and found online, as are thousands of mates. A woman in upstate New York stays on AOL 24 hours a day to help rabbits in distress. Thousands of religious communities thrive in the digital world.

Building a Web community can be challenging. I've been involved in that effort for two years now on Hotwired, the Web site of *Wired*. There are complex issues of free speech and access. Should anyone be free to say anything at all times? The emotionally disturbed sometimes message alongside college professors. Aside from the technological issues, there are economic ones as well. How can Web communities be made accessible to everyone, even the poor who can't afford computers? How can these communities sustain themselves in a culture that isn't used to paying for things?

So this is the right book at the right time, done in the right way. And you'll need it. As the Web moves towards becoming a mainstream culture, it will gain influence, political power, and importance as a cultural phenomenon. The questions for kids, grandmothers, politicians, and others in the millenium isn't whether they can afford to go online, but whether they can afford not to. The answer is no.

People need to know how to form communities and keep them working, and the impressive part of this book is that it helps you to start from scratch.

Interactivity is transforming media everywhere, and Web sites are profoundly and intensely interactive. The right for everyone to visit, be heard, and join the fray is so integral a principle it's literally built into the machinery of good sites. The top-down model of information—wise anchors in suits telling us what's happened—

has been shattered. Now, millions of people get to talk to millions of people. No wonder so many people are nervous about the rise of the Digital Nation.

I understand why journalists, academics, and politicians miss the old system. They used to have a monopoly on running it. As a Web columnist, I never get the last word, just the first. I consider myself a spark, an initiator of conversations. When I make a mistake, I hear about it, quickly and forcefully.

We struggle with the right kind of technology and design. To find the balance between freedom and chaos. To tell the truth amid so many conflicting notions about what the truth is.

It's hard to think of a more useful idea than a "companion" handbook to help grow a virtual community from scratch.

The Web is the freest information culture on the planet. You can find, talk about, and see almost everything in the world there. More importantly—and this is unique in media—you can build your own Web community. That's what this book is about. See you there. I'm **jonkatz@bellatlantic.com**.

Jon Katz is a contributing editor for Wired, *and media critic for its sister site,* Hotwired. *He's also written for* GQ, New York Magazine, Rolling Stone, *and the* New York Times. *He has two non-fiction books:* Media Rant: Post Politics In The Digital Nation, *and next year* Magnetic North: Journeys of the Soul, *for Random House.*

WELCOME TO THE WORLD OF VIRTUAL COMMUNITIES

Introduction

There's Nothing Virtual About It

Virtual communities are not new, although the usage of the words "virtual" and "community" together as a computer industry buzz phrase is pretty new. The Internet, long viewed as a so-called "information superhighway," has evolved into a social space. Individuals, organizations, and corporations who want to be on the cutting edge are realizing the value of interacting with Web surfers and are scrambling to add chat and discussion forums to their Web sites.

The Internet has been heralded as a great living encyclopedia, but virtual communities allow us to do more than impart data—we can interact, share, exchange, debate, understand, empathize, learn, grow, and build relationships, both personal and professional. Aside from email, chat is the most popular feature of the Internet, so it's obvious that we want to reach one another and break down the geographical and/or cultural barriers that separate us. That's the power of the Net and the purpose of the community.

Introduction

When is all this happening? Right now. It's already started. It actually started years ago, with newsgroups and electronic bulletin boards, but now, with the Web, it's the rage. Corporations are discovering what early Internet pioneers already knew: that the Internet is a powerful medium for much greater things than just archiving data; that it's a place to interact, to live, to build community.

Where is this going on? We have two answers. First, it's obviously going on in cyberspace, where geography isn't important; where those in California become friends with those in Maine. Where all of the United States is as close to France or Korea or Australia as it is to the next town down the road. Second, in cyberspace, it's happening on HotWired and iVillage, on IRC and AOL, and it's already happened on The WELL. It's even happening at Intel and Compaq. There is hardly an aspect of the Internet that isn't affected by this new universal focus on community.

Why? Because, beyond the byte and the baud, past the silicon, further than the software code, on the other side of the screen, we are humans. And humans want to live together and talk and laugh and cry and feel. The machines we build see only in the digital realm of 1s and 0s, on and off, but these machines can now help us bring distant families closer together, make foreign cultures accessible and more understood, and allow companies to address the needs of their customers directly. And we're just scratching the surface.

How will virtual communities grow? We will be the ones that build them. From a Web site dedicated to cancer research information, to a site that sells laundry soap, to a local online newspaper, to an international dating service, to a site that helps kids learn their multiplication tables, and much more, we will build community tools and features that will add, and in fact are adding, organic communal humanity to the wires and chips that form the foundation of the Internet.

Derived from the phrase "virtual reality," we've come to call this "virtual community." But when you break it down, the communities that are developing online are fostering real friendships, real relationships, and real communal spirit. There just isn't anything virtual about it at all, aside from the fact that these communities are in the bold new frontier of cyberspace. "Virtual community" is a synonym for "real community on the Internet," and that reality is what makes them so compelling and so important to the growth of this new electronic frontier.

How Will This Book Help You?

Now, you may be asking, "Why do I need *this* book to help me build a virtual community?" Whether you're a marketing manager, a Webmaster, a community participant, or a Web designer, you'll find practical and applicable information that will help you in your quest to bring people to your site, such as:

- *Community-building tools*—More than just tried and true Internet applications like mailing lists, community tools allow your community members to engage each other in *realtime* interaction. We show you what tools are out there and the best ways to integrate them into your community.

- *Management issues*—Running a community takes skill and planning. We'll highlight the many issues you will face as a virtual community manager; issues ranging from free speech to censorship to community standards.

- *Legal issues*—The Communications Decency Act, although now resolved, still has implications that you should be aware of. What are they? How will they affect you and your community? We wave the warning flags.

- *Marketing*—We'll not only show you how to bring people to your site, but more importantly, we'll show you the secrets of how to get them coming back.

- *Making money*—Even if you're a hobbyist, you'll want to create a revenue stream to cover your costs—and probably even turn a profit. We'll examine many methods you can use to make money from your community.

- *Finally, we'll show you what to avoid*—Building a community on the Web isn't easy—in fact, some sites have made major mistakes. With case studies, we'll illustrate what you *shouldn't* do.

We hope this book will help you in your quest to bring people into your site, and to bring your site into the larger online world. This is an exciting time for a young medium. It's a time in which we all have the potential to shape and mold the future of the Internet, to take it beyond the encyclopedic nature of simple Web pages and reshape it into a living, breathing world where we meet, talk, and come to understand each other. In our hobbies, religions, politics, businesses, lifestyles, and lives, we can build a place that helps us live together more peacefully with greater understanding.

If you have any questions about what we've written in this book, we'd love to hear from you. You can contact us at:

Karla Shelton, karla@ais.net
Todd McNeeley, indyfilm@donet.com

Thank you for joining us on this journey.

Part 1

BOOKS ∙ MUSIC

The
Basics

Chapter 1

So What IS A Community, Anyway?

Chapter 1

- Understanding Community Conceptually

- The Communications Paradigm Shift

- It's About People, Not Technology

So What IS A Community, Anyway?

Chapter 1

Community Is…

In this chapter, you'll find almost no technical, hands-on, how-to kind of data. Instead we're going to chat about what community is. We have plenty of shiny toys to talk about, like Palace and IRC clients, newsreaders, Web browsers, and HTML editors, but focusing on why we want them in the first place will give us all a common frame of reference.

The idea of "what a community is" is not actually clear. We all think of "our community" as the place where we live, work, and play, and we're familiar with phrases like "the scientific community." A community is a living, dynamic thing. It changes and grows constantly, but its members often share certain common values. Communities are different things to different people. But when we start discussing "community" in the same breath as "the Internet," chances are we're entering unfamiliar territory.

Let's start with the dictionary definition of *community*, and then we'll look at some of the ways computers have affected our global community. Finally, we'll explore communities that are already growing on the Internet.

Throughout the chapter, we'll also listen in on the thoughts of some notable thinkers. The thoughts are as varied as the thinkers, and reflect the divergent views that arise when looking at community from a philosophical standpoint.

Webster's New Universal Unabridged Dictionary

Community: 1) a social group of any size whose members reside in a specific locality, share government, and have a common cultural and historical heritage. 2) a social group sharing common characteristics or interests, and perceived or perceiving itself as distinct in some respect from the larger society in which it exists. 3) a group of men or women leading a common life according to a rule. 4) an assemblage of plant and animal populations occupying a given area. 5) joint possession, enjoyment, liability, etc. 6) similar character, agreement, identity. 7) the community: the public, society.

For almost everybody who's reading this, the so-called Information Age is something that began in our lifetime. The opening up of the Internet to the general public is recent, and the concept of creating communities on the Internet is still more recent. In essence, we're all pioneers here.

COMMUNICATIONS, COMPUTERS, AND COMMUNITY

Throughout the twentieth century, communications technology has evolved at a rapid pace. In the 1950s, television changed the *way* in which we received information, as well as the *speed* at which we received it. But it wasn't until the 1960s that the power of television was fully realized.

November 21, 1963, was a tragic moment in American history. Within minutes, people around the world knew that President John F. Kennedy had been assassinated in Dallas. We saw it on television, and time seemed to stop. Tears were shed. In that moment, a nation mourned together. It was unprecedented. The power of television was quickly understood, and subsequently, the power of mass communication.

In those same years, something else was going on. The Cold War was giving rise to an era of paranoia. The Soviet Union had nuclear weapons and missile technology, making the threat of mass devastation very real. The world was getting smaller, and the need for better and more efficient communication was becoming evident. The military had long since recognized the importance of computers for research and development and for strategic planning, but at MIT and other universities, computer scientists and other researchers wondered if computers could be useful for communications. Their value in this area quickly became evident to both the scientific community and the military, and it didn't take long for business to catch on as well.

At the time, the average person wasn't affected by what was going on in the computer world. Computers were remarkably difficult to build and maintain, and they cost small fortunes. Not only that, they took up enormous amounts of space, requiring that they be built in rooms of their own. Teams of specialists were required to keep the parts working, replacing tubes as they wore out and correcting problems as they arose—and problems arose continually. The idea of a PC on every desk was far in the future. As for us average folks, we wrote letters, talked on the telephone, and gathered in homes and public places, and we all thought that was just fine.

Then everything seemed to change.

The computer science that, in the past, was reserved for national security and scientific research is now not only an everyday business tool, but a personal tool as well. Today, online communications software, graphics programs, word processors, and Internet gaming are all just part of life.

E. L. Doctorow, Novelist

Communities appear temporally rather than spatially. They form as circumstances demand, and when the emergency is over people go back to their semi-estranged mood. Communal expressions that really matter on a day-to-day basis are probably made by people who have no thought of community. A surgeon who only wants to make money and live well and has a lousy bedside manner still contributes. The Korean grocer on the corner who works hard trying to survive may feel a foreigner, but the store is a contribution to the neighborhood. I don't know if you can ask for more.

For the first time, we can talk back to the news, and someone actually listens. Instead of just seeing, hearing, and reading the news (input) we can respond (output). To those of us who spend a lot of time on the Internet, this is the real power: No longer do we just receive information; we can respond, instantly. We can interact, not only with the creator of the news, but with other consumers of media. Later we'll talk about HotWired in depth, but it's a prime example: Internet surfers log into HotWired's Web site, absorb data, spew data back, and interact with each other, eventually forming a community.

Throughout the 1980s, the computer was heralded as the greatest thing to happen to business since the invention of money, and *Time* magazine actually named the computer "Man of the Year" in 1982. Sadly, though, study after study showed that the computer had failed to provide the promised increases in productivity. Databases, word processors, and spreadsheets, the three hallmark applications of the computer, were and are great tools, but too much money was being spent on labor, equipment, software, and training. The bottom line simply didn't show the rewards of this "revolution." The computer industry, it seemed, was really the only business to benefit from computers. Then came the fourth "killer application," email and the Internet, which for business meant communication.

Karla Defines: Cyberspace

Flash back to the 1984 publication of William Gibson's book Neuromancer. *This is the first time the word cyberspace is used. Gibson envisions it as a matrix—a graphic representation of data abstracted from the banks of every computer in the human system— where all types of communication take place, from bank transactions to videoconferencing to game playing.*

Also, a word overused by the media.

Todd Defines: Meatspace

Obviously, it's the opposite of cyberspace. It's reality that isn't virtual. It's a flesh-and-bone universe, where food tastes good and falling down can really hurt. You can't get to cyberspace unless you live in meatspace.

For the business community, the advent of cyberspace has changed the face of business-as-usual forever. No longer limited to local resources or forced to wait for paper-based communications to make their way to far corners of the earth, movers and shakers can make decisions and bring products to market with dizzying speed. Let's take a peek at what this looks like today.

High-Tech Communications At Work

It's Thursday in Chicago, Illinois: The fifth floor of the advertising agency of Sanders, Vannek & Quick appears chaotic amidst the excitement of their latest venture. What was once a warehouse with 20-foot ceilings has been converted into a hi-tech playground for graphic artists, writers, account executives, and a varied crew of other industrious professionals. Computers, scanners, televisions, and VCRs litter the tables scattered around the room. At present, about 75 people are buzzing about this nontraditional office.

James Sanders looks over his staff, almost in awe. Dozens of people seem to be moving in circles, never stopping—but there is method to the madness, and these people have made the agency one of the fastest growing in the country. Right now, though, he turns his attention to the fax coming over the telephone lines. He received an email about it earlier, but now he sees an image of the young model in jeans, and it looks great. "Bobby!" he shouts, "You like this?"

"I can work with that. I can rally with Berlin and San Francisco this afternoon on the Internet."

"Good, I want your team ready. She'll be flying in from Paris on Monday for the TV spots. Let's go talk to Vicki."

Sanders and Bobby approach Vicki's desk. "How's it going?" Bobby asks.

"Great. I have the German team leader on IRC right now. He has a great plan for European magazine coverage, and they have the German Web site up today. The URL is in both of your email boxes. There's a team from PyroTech getting the firewall up, and secure credit card transactions have already begun."

Sanders asks, "Do you have any leads on a new photographer for the San Francisco office?"

"Actually, I was chatting with a young woman on the Internet yesterday. I received her resume early this morning and I FTPed her portfolio an hour ago. I'm very impressed with her, and I think you'll like her stuff."

Susan from Marketing waves to the trio to join her team in the glass-encased meeting room. The monitors on the table, connected to laptop docking stations, are looping through a slick commercial for money-management software. It's set to some very eclectic music. "Listen, we don't like this music for this spot. I'm wondering what you think?"

There is a face on the monitor and it seems to look at James. "Hi James," the face says.

"Hi Hans." James thinks for a minute. "What was that song? 'I know the best things in life are free…' or something…"

Bobby's eyes light up. "'But what money can't buy, I don't need, gimme money…'"

"That's it!" exclaims James, "who did that new wave cover version in the eighties?"

They all look at each other, trying to recall the answer, when the face on the screen starts to talk in a German accent. "That was The Flying Lizards, and I think it was the late seventies."

"That's it, Hans. Let's see if we can use that."

Noam Chomsky, Political Analyst And Linguist

Community is PR bullshit designed in the 1930s by the corporations, when they became terrified by the collapse of their society brought on by the Wagner Act and the labor movement. They developed new techniques to control the population and inculcate the concept of living together in harmony—all Americans, all working together: the sober workman, the hardworking executive, the housewife. And Them—the outsiders trying to disrupt. Community is a bit of a joke. Only labor has succeeded. That's why business hates unions. They can create real community and democracy.

BUT REALLY, WHAT *IS* COMMUNITY?

So we have several notions of what community is, and we've touched on how technology has altered media and changed community. But ultimately, though, the community is just bigger. We humans gather shiny new technologies like squirrels gather nuts, but it isn't the technology that matters, it's the people. It's the people who provide content and data on the Internet. It's the people who have set up virtual communities there, and who open the gates of those communities to allow us to join them. People are the power of the Internet, just like they're the power of a meatspace community. Imagine a town, with a courthouse, a police station, a school, a grocery store, a hardware store, a movie theater, and a park with a baseball diamond. Without people, it's nothing. The Internet is the same way. It doesn't matter how many servers and domains exist; without people to create content and interact with others, it's all pretty much useless.

Computer-Mediated Communication: The Heart Of Your Community

Virtual communities require two key ingredients: communication and people to communicate. "Computer-mediated communication" is a buzz phrase meaning communication facilitated by computers. Sounds straightforward enough, but this doesn't mean just email and Web sites, it includes voice mail, ATM transactions at the bank, electronic Quicken checks, and so on. Basically, anytime a computer is used to transmit data over a network, it's an example of computer-mediated communication (or CMC, as it's often written).

CMC is the heart of the Internet. It was the heart of the bulletin board system (BBS) era, and it was the impetus for the creation of the first computer network, ARPAnet. In a virtual community, most members will never meet face-to-face, but they will communicate extensively and come to know one another intimately. This is all achieved through text, whether in realtime chat, email, or newsgroup posts, made possible by CMC. It's important to remember that you cannot have a community without communication, and you will want to exploit the best tools you can find to make communication easy for your community members. The best tools are the ones that are almost invisible and have easy interfaces. For example, your Web browser of choice will be the one that allows you to best navigate the Web with the least amount of software training and the least technical overhead.

Howard Rheingold, Editor, *Whole Earth Review*

The ways in which people use CMC always will be rooted in human needs, not hardware or software.

If you remember the quote by Rheingold, you are well on your way to creating a great virtual community of your own.

Community Meets Cyberspace

There have been many critics of the Internet, and certainly there are some valid reasons to be critical. One particular criticism that we hear time and time again, however, deserves to be mentioned and debunked. Many Internet champions have compared the Internet to a global community, but some critics have said that the Internet cannot be, and will never be, a community. They say that *community* requires the ability to communicate face-to-face, in order to form relationships. They say that having all this technology between people makes the Net not much more than a distraction from "real" communities.

It isn't often that we'll say that a dissenting opinion is just plain wrong, but in this case, the dissenting opinion is just plain wrong. In cyberspace, we have thus far been able to interact in almost every way that we do in meatspace, short of actually touching physically. (Rest assured, some brilliant researcher somewhere is trying to solve that last limitation.) We've found new ways to meet, to talk, and to share our experiences in cyberspace. People meet in cyberspace, fall in love, and get married. People campaign for political office in cyberspace. Students attend lectures in cyberspace. You can listen to a live concert broadcast in cyberspace. You can file your taxes in cyberspace. There are so many things happening in cyberspace that it's difficult to list them all, or even to scratch the surface.

What more do we need to do in cyberspace to make it a place where communities exist? Nothing. It is a place where communities exist, and it has been since early on. Of course, that doesn't mean that the Internet is finished—quite the contrary. We've discovered a new frontier for community building, and now we can, and should, pioneer new and greater communities. What can we do to continue to break down the natural barriers that exist in cyberspace? How can we move past the simple-text interface of IRC? How can we improve the bulletin-board-like quality of newsgroups? How can CU-SeeMe cameras become powerful tools in community building? It's all just begun, and it's really exciting!

A COMMUNITY OF COMMUNITIES

The Net is not a community in and of itself, but it is home to many communities. These are social groups who gather to commune and share, bicker and argue, meet and fall in love, each in a common place. And yes, the Internet is a place. You'll find it wherever there's a computer attached to a network attached to the Internet. It lives on hard drives around the globe, and communicates over phone lines.

The communities found there have all formed for different reasons. There could be a group of cattle ranchers from South Dakota, a group of sunbathers from California, a group of lawyers from New York, or just a group of people from around the world. These communities are places independent of the geographical location of their inhabitants, and their members develop rules, laws, and hierarchies of authority on their own.

Many Internet denizens have common characteristics, but all share this: they all have Internet access and they all contribute to the growth of the cyberculture.

Community is a word with many definitions, and English is a language that is always growing and changing. "Communities" as they exist on the Internet were not previously an option, so now we must extend our definition to the very place where people meet to discuss politics, buy garden tools, and fall in love, among other things: the virtual world of cyberspace.

Why Hang Out In Online Communities?

Online (or virtual) communities have a lot to offer, information and business opportunities being two biggies. However, while information and business opportunities might be among the reasons why many of us originally rushed to get online, virtual communities are being discovered by more people than ever before, and these newcomers are reaping many of the other benefits of life online. What are some of the benefits we're talking about? Read on. Not all of these items are important to everyone, but it's likely that you'll be attracted by many of them. We all have different reasons for coming together, but communally, these are the reasons we stay.

LOW RISK, NET GAINS

It's sad but true; in this day and age we're often nervous, sometimes even frightened, of forging new relationships. In the cyberspace world of the Internet, forging relationships is easier. You can chat, exchange email, and really get to know your new online friends from the inside out. Your personal appearance, for example, may be something that you're self-conscious about, but online, appearance is not a factor in interpersonal interactions. This gives a warming sense of security to many virtual citizens.

I'M BATMAN! WILL YOU HELP ME FIGHT CRIME?

In cyberspace, you can take on personalities apart from your own. Many virtual citizens balk at this aspect of online life, while others relish it. It's kind of a functional schizophrenia. You don't use your own name, like John or Jane Smith, when you're online; instead you use names like CyberMan, Kookygirl, nIgHtHaWk (yes, some names are downright annoying), or anything else that you feel describes yourself or the personality you're adopting.

Online, you can be anonymous, and in the virtual world, anonymity can be a blessing. If you're prone to shyness, for example, you can adopt an aggressive alter ego on the Web; there, you can conduct interpersonal relationships without fear of serious repercussions for your actions, due to the cloak of anonymity. Why is this good? The feeling of freedom that accompanies anonymous interaction often allows for more frank and open discussion. This all ties in with the low-risk factor discussed previously.

Anonymity can also be a bad thing. Netizens can be deceptive or hurtful because they act with impunity, that is, without fear of reprisal for their words. When you scour the Internet for new relationships, your anonymity protects you. It's a two-way street. You hide your true identity, like your name, your hometown, and other personal data, from those you encounter, unless and until you're comfortable with the level of trust between yourself and those you meet.

Self Defense Class, Lesson One

The following may seem like common sense, but many new Internet users don't think about online security until it's too late. It's true that the hysteria over the dangers of criminals, pedophiles, subversives, hackers, and other potential harm-doers in online communities has been greatly exaggerated by political opportunists, but that doesn't mean that some of these malicious personalities aren't out there. Whether it's you or your children strolling through the many online communities, here are some tips for online security:

- *Never, and we mean never, give any personal information to anyone you don't know. Your name, address, phone number, where you work, even the name of your hometown can be used to hurt you by the extremely small number of bad seeds lurking on the Internet. That information is confidential, so keep it that way.*

> • *When using services that require passwords, don't choose obvious character strings like your phone number. Don't choose actual words. Choose a string of mixed-case characters, including symbols. "Y2%mw3@" may be hard to remember without writing it down, but it's impossible to guess, and very hard to hack.*

Do It Your Way

Rugged individualism and a pioneer spirit are the characteristics that tamed the American western frontier. These are also the traits found in entrepreneurs and free thinkers, and they're the same attributes that built the Internet. If you're hungry for knowledge, outspoken, a free thinker, and independent minded, then the world of virtual communities is for you. Do you have a lot of good ideas? Do you like to debate controversial issues as a fun exercise? Do you want the world to watch as you shine? Get wired and shine online. You'll find personalities that mesh with yours. You can join communities that you'll feel very comfortable in, and that will value you.

Also, the Web is a wonderful home for the independent minded because of the Internet's level-playing-field quality. The Web pages that make up your community are no more or less visible than the pages of your large established competitors. HotWired, Electronic Minds, and YourPage.com are just a click away from any search engine. You can publish anything you like on the Internet, and you can sleep well at night knowing that somewhere, someone is reading your words.

Alive And Thriving On The Net: Romance

With persistence, you could scour the chat channels of IRC, the home pages of thousands of singles, or the newsgroups of postings by single men and women, and eventually find that special someone just for you. Many communities have sprung up with this in mind. They act as forums for singles looking to meet other singles, and the many online singles communities are places where you can meet prospective romantic partners in the safety of cyberspace before you take the big plunge into an offline relationship.

There's much debate about the inherent flaws of online dating. Some are concerned with singles who may practice deception on the Net—for example, a married man who claims in cyberspace that he's single, in order to initiate an affair. To be fair though, the dangers of online relationships are not very different from their offline counterparts, except that much of the physical-world complications have been removed. It's true that you, or anyone in your community, can be hurt emotionally when an online relationship goes bad, but we run these, and greater, risks when we engage in meatspace relationships. The advantages of screening potential mates, and getting to know a person intellectually before becoming involved physically, are tremendous arguments in favor of Internet-based singles mixers.

HELLO, I COLLECT LUNCH BOXES

Whatever your hobby is, whatever your interests are, you're likely to find a group online that shares your interest. You can pour over Usenet newsgroups to find alt.collections.lunchboxes, or you can hyperlink to Lunch Box World Online's Web site. If it isn't there, you can create it. Intellectual discourse may be the Net's big attraction, but even if your ego is relatively under control, you'll still enjoy the online companionship of folks who share your passions. Lunch box collectors, ham radio enthusiasts, classic car rebuilders, board game players, trivia buffs, and more meet online to share their pursuits and grow in their appreciation of whatever they have in common. This is a great idea for building your community, too. If lawn-mower drag racing is your bag, chances are you can find enough lawn jockeys out there to join you and build a thriving network of racers!

I AM PERSECUTED BY AN UNFEELING WORLD

In a world that often seems full of prejudice, racism, and bigotry, many folks in society come to feel disenfranchised, disillusioned, angry, or bitter. What they often lack (especially if they live far from heavy metropolitan population centers) is a support network. The Internet has the potential to make up for that lack. An obvious example is the gay community. These days, gay rights issues like military service and the right to marriage are debated in public forums and in the halls of government. By creating an online presence, gay activists, sympathetic supporters, and gay community members at large can interact to disseminate information, debate, and reach consensus about the issues that are important to them. This model of community, as an agent for social change and enlightenment, has been (and continues to be) adopted by a large variety of social and political groups. The ACLU, the NAACP, almost every major political party, most religions, women's groups like NOW, and many others use the Net to foster community and further their respective causes. The culture of the Internet places high value on the freedom of information and thought, so much so that tolerance of opposing opinions is perhaps the only cardinal rule.

Community Building From The Ground Up

Let's step back for a minute and ask a couple of questions: How does a community get to be a community, and how can our understanding of communities be applied to the Web? Communities start with an individual or a few individuals with a vision to fulfill. They gather more people and work together, constructing houses and schools and churches and shops until they've made the magic transformation from crowd to village…and *voila*, a community is born! From this point, the village continues to grow and form ties with other villages and soon, they're integrated into the larger civilization. As it turns out, the Internet works very much the same way: From the vision of one person a Web site is built, then others appear with similar values and aspirations, and soon a virtual community is born.

Dr. M. Scott Peck, author of *A Different Drum*, has developed a model and process for intentional communities to help businesses, nonprofit organizations, and other "designed" communities function more effectively. He describes community as the "actual experience of connectedness," and his paradigm extends to virtual communities quite nicely. He sees communities as being composed of individuals, and he identifies four fundamental stages of communities: pseudo-community, chaos, emptiness, and community. In addition, his model recognizes that for each individual at a given point in time, his or her stage in the community development process may be different from that of other individuals in the community.

- *Pseudo-community*—This stage is task-oriented. Groups in this phase are generally made up of equals striving toward the same goal, and members share the same values and outlooks. This is an essential phase in building anything, for this is when work is completed. The thing to be aware of in this phase is the underlying motivations of the individuals. Often, in an effort to belong and to achieve community goals, people are noncommunicative about their own ideas, feelings, and agendas. Later, as the community develops, and especially during rough times, resentments can grow. "This was Bill's idea, that's why we're failing!" or "You never listen to me, I could have fixed this!" To avoid future problems if you're spearheading a community, try to seek out and exploit the valuable contributions of all involved, and try to draw out their opinions, feelings, and ideas so that they will not only feel important, but actually *be* important to the process.

- *Chaos*—In this phase, creativity flourishes, but it's also this phase that leads to conflict, because the focus shifts from "we" to "you" as in, "You need to listen to me!" Egos are emerging, and power struggles ensue. Chaos is essential to a community, even though it can be destructive in many ways. From chaos, leadership arises, structure is improved, and overall catharsis can occur. It can be both exciting and nerve-wracking, but either way, or both, it's indispensable and unavoidable. It's okay that chaos is unavoidable, because normally, communities can't recognize that they're in chaos anyway. It's hard to see the forest for the trees.

- *Emptiness*—This isn't the lonely despair of a Bergman film we're talking about here, rather "emptiness" refers to the emptying of resentments, hostilities, and other roadblocks on the path to unity and deeper understanding. Welcome to the "I" phase. Introspection and reflection are characteristic of this stage. This can be a lonely time for many of the group's members. It's the time of epiphany—"I need to let go of power," or "I need to assert my feelings," are common realizations. As members or groups of members go through this phase, the road is cleared for community advancement.

- *Community*—This phase has a healing quality to it that's quite satisfying. Accomplishments have been made, and the essential damage of the "Chaos" and "Emptiness" phases has been patched up. Individuals finally feel connected.

The division and anger of chaos, under the guidance of emptiness, gives way to inclusion and a realization of the value of diversity. Now respect is forged, and happiness can be achieved. Birds sing, flowers bloom, and peace prospers throughout the land.

Birds, flowers, peace? If only it were true. While the final stage is rewarding, we all know that communities never stop evolving. As changes occur in the groups, or within individuals, communities often revert back to previous phases. It's important to remember that not every member of the community is in, or needs to be in, the same phase at the same time. In a group of 200 people, it isn't unusual for 10 to be in chaos, 15 to be in emptiness, and a few more to be still stuck in pseudo-community. This is not unhealthy. In fact, it's not unlike life. The miracle of childbirth, for example, is painful, traumatic, and brings about great change, but it's ultimately rewarding. As a baby grows, like a community, it discovers the world bit by bit and changes accordingly until it has reached a mature age (like the community phase), and even then, the new adult continues to grow internally, changing as it experiences its daily life. So it is also with a community.

Community, The "Killer Application" Of The Internet

Community isn't an application, like a spreadsheet or a database, but there are tools of both the hardware and the software varieties that foster virtual communities. A modem is an obvious one; a Web browser, a newsreader, even a graphics program like Paint Shop Pro, are all tools and applications that can be used to build a community. In Chapter 5, we'll look at applications for your community toolbox, but now let's look at some actual virtual communities and see what we can learn from them.

FROM THE DEPTHS OF THE WELL, A SUCCESSFUL COMMUNITY BUBBLES UP

The WELL is one of the most successful gathering places to be found online. With Internet access and state-of-the-art conferencing equipment, The WELL, launched in 1985, was transformed from a niche conversation space (a BBS in Sausalito, California) to the international, multi-faceted community known today. In the beginning, The WELL's core user group was baby-boomers who were highly educated, left-wing, and mostly male. Now it attracts people from all walks of life who participate in its infamous, heated, and often controversial discussions of subjects like free speech and privacy. Each conference room has a distinctly different sense of place and style, as shown in Figure 1.1.

What Makes The WELL Tick?

The WELL's first computer was a VAX 750. It was cooled by the largest air conditioner that could be bought at Sears. They then moved on to a Sequent multiprocessor in 1989, then to a Balance-8, and then to a Symmetry-27. From 1993 to the present, The WELL has employed a SUN SPARC Server 1000 together with a cluster of related servers.

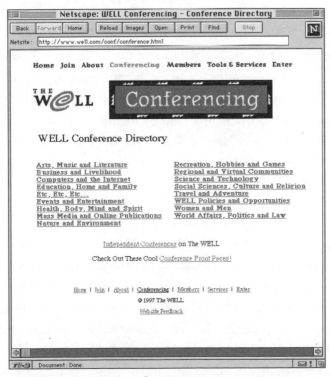

Figure 1.1 The multitude of conferences available on The WELL.

Management Philosophy

The WELL, possibly due to the influence of early participants and employees who came from intentional communities (as in communes), believed that user involvement should drive decisions. A democracy, so to speak. The WELL management also upholds free speech, but with a twist.

"You Own Your Own Words" is The WELL's signature tag line. Cofounder Stewart Brand's conviction was that people should take responsibility for what they say. No anonymity. As director of The WELL, Matthew McClure, (who had a vast background with "intentional communities"), together with Brand, created the "conference" concept: A conference would be devoted to a subject, then each conference would spawn "topics," which were more detailed in nature.

From A Legacy Of Print...

Interestingly enough, The WELL emerged from The Point Foundation (headed by Stewart Brand), publisher of the *Whole Earth Review* magazine (formerly *CoEvolution Quarterly*) and *Whole Earth Catalog*. Brand had been experimenting with conferencing equipment at The New Jersey Institute of Technology, testing the viability of such systems for scientific research communities. Larry Brilliant, a physician, owned NETI (Network Technologies International), which built computer conferencing systems. Brand was known for his character as a risk-taker and entrepreneur, and he was familiar with technology and computers, so Brilliant invited Brand to lunch to discuss an idea. Then...

Voila! A Community Is Born

Brand and Brilliant teamed up in 1984 to present their vision of an "online community." Brilliant, through NETI, would supply the computer and software. Brand, through his nonprofit organization, would supply the other half: people. They played around with a variety of acronyms, like WEAL, WEAVE, and WEB, but finally settled on WELL, "Whole Earth 'Lectronic Link." Brand envisioned reaching out to everyone, not just the Whole Earth crowd. He wanted hackers, intellectuals, even right-wingers to join. The most impressive strategy involved giving out free accounts to journalists, authors, and free thinkers, who invariably would generate interesting discourse. The WELL believes that its "product" is relationships, not software, hardware, and a bunch of wires that connect people. By the late 1980s, hoards of newspapers and magazines had written about The WELL, thrusting it into the public eye.

People were joining to take part in frank and open talk, unlike the fragmented and often redundant nature of Usenet newsgroups. The threaded discussions of The WELL Conferences are carried on in a conversational style, and the accumulated comments read like transcripts of engaging spoken discussions. From that rich soil, relationships blossomed—friendships, romantic interludes, and adversarial rivalries alike.

Beyond 'Lectronic

Although the online aspect is the driving force behind The WELL, Brand wanted to extend the online community into meatspace (although he'd never used this word before). He felt face-to-face experiences would strengthen the bonds of the members; he wanted the two worlds to overlap, not to exist separately. In the early days, parties and organized events were commonplace. Later, other communities would adopt the same idea (although perhaps the idea is rather obvious). Meatspace parties and gatherings of AOL groups, among others, are not uncommon.

Makin' A Buck

While The WELL had started as an experiment, Brilliant wanted it to operate as a business, so they charged users for connect time. The first business plan projected revenues of $1,000,000—a long shot by any measure, since the membership wavered at approximately 500 just a year later. At an $8 monthly fee and a $2 hourly surcharge, it would take lots of members spending lots of online time to reach this revenue goal. Throughout the 1980s and into the early 1990s, turning a profit proved difficult.

Today, The WELL attracts a global presence. It has long since moved from the BBS stage into a full-fledged Internet Web site, with roughly 10,000 members and more than 260 featured conferences. WELL members publish tens of thousands of posts each week, totaling more than 1 million words. The WELL now boasts a software arm that produces a Web conferencing application called Engaged, which is used by Minds.Com (a WELL spin-off founded by Howard Rheingold, a WELL core member) among others.

A Few Of The WELL's Milestones

In the late 1980s, John Perry Barlow took the term "cyberspace" from William Gibson's novel, *Neuromancer*, and applied it to the present.

In July 1990, two WELL members, Mitch Kapor and John Perry Barlow, started the influential Electronic Frontier Foundation after Barlow was visited by the FBI for his online activities. The EFF is currently instrumental in battling online censorship.

The Deadheads found a home on The WELL in 1986, and soon became responsible for anywhere from one-third to one-fifth of its activity. Subsequently, they've become the biggest revenue generator on The WELL.

In 1994, Engaged, a graphical, point-and-click Web-based system for threaded conferencing, replaced PicoSpan, a Unix-based conferencing system, on The WELL.

POISED TO CONQUER THE WORLD, IT'S GEOCITIES

Free home pages! You heard that right, we said free home pages. How can this be? Well, in a nutshell, GeoCities (**www.geocities.com**) "gets it" when it comes to Internet culture, which is why they decided to give away free space, rather than charge for it.

Actually, the strategic plan of GeoCities is quite ingenious. While offering up free Web pages and email accounts to its members, GeoCities sells advertising space on member pages, as well as on its corporate Web pages. The corporate pages sport some really cool content, like Best Of The Unsigned Bands (co-sponsored by *Spin* magazine), Restaurant Row (co-sponsored by VISA), and GeoCities Car Center (co-sponsored by Auto-By-Tel). Now, they do charge for some premium items, like extra disk space beyond the standard 2MB, customized URLs, and live news feeds from Reuters News. Later in this section, we'll look at the business plans.

So What Does This Have To Do With Community?

GeoCities has a core strategy that drives *every* component of their business: They believe that everybody has a right to their own personal home page on the Internet.

You can choose from a wide range of communities on GeoCities' pages, based on your interests. Are you a UFO buff? You can build a site in Area 51. If you fancy yourself a movie critic, perhaps Hollywood is for you. They have dozens of theme communities to choose from, named after famous cities or geographic regions, and each community has a theme based on that city. Tokyo, for example, is about the Far East. If you build your site in Tokyo, you'll have your own URL (Universal Resource Locator, or Web address) that will look like this: **http://www.geocities.com/Tokyo/xxxx**, where xxxx is your block number. Now you have a Web site! You can start building right away, just like we did.

Todd And Karla's Home On GeoCities

We staked a claim on some prime real estate on Capitol Hill. You can find us at **www.geocities.com/CapitolHill/9787/**. We are building a community Web site dedicated to linking folks together based on common ideas and interests. Stop by, meet us, send us some email, and see what we're all about.

GeoCities has more than 450,000 members, creating one of the most diverse, unique, and most-visited areas on the Web. And by focusing on their core belief, that every cybernaut has a *right* to a Web presence, GeoCities is destined to grow even larger.

TUNE IN, TURN ON, GET WIRED

There have been a few elite cyberpunk magazines like *2600* and *Mondo2000* that dealt with cyberculture, but with *Wired*, the "Digital Generation" has come of age. Self-appointed as the first truly new magazine of the 1990s, *Wired* is reinventing print journalism and has formed an almost perfect marriage of message and medium. It's irreverent, biting, and satirical, and it's always about an hour into the future! "*Wired* is the first magazine to understand that consumer lifestyle and technology are merging," Associate Publisher Kathleen Lyman said. "It's the only magazine that tracks not only how the leading edge of the Digital Generation— the Digital Vanguard—works, but also lives and plays with technology."

Wired is about culture, real business, information, people, and above all, community. Its innovative focus attracts advertisers from the computer industry, like U.S.

Robotics, Sony, and Intel, but *Wired* also attracts unlikely sponsors like Tommy Hilfiger (designer clothing), ORIS (really pricey Swiss watches), Deckers Outdoor Corporation's Simple Shoes, BMW, Absolut, Sunglass Hut, and PowerBar. What diversity! Shoes, sunglasses, clothing, liquor—these are not what you think of for a computer magazine, but *Wired*'s readership clearly isn't typical.

Wired, which hit newsstands on January 26, 1993, was produced independently of any other publishing concern, by venture capital brought together to fund Wired Ventures. From Wired Ventures, yet another radical magazine spewed forth. This one was digital. On October 27, 1994, HotWired (**www.hotwired.com**), shown in Figure 1.2, was born. Operating independently of the print magazine, but with close ties that include hosting *Wired*'s online presence, HotWired has evolved into more than just an online magazine. It's a thriving community of its own. But don't take our word for it, read it from HotWired's own manifesto, written by Louis Rossetto, editor-in-chief of HotWired:

> There are a lot of media companies shoveling their leftovers into the online world and calling them content. HotWired is not one of them.

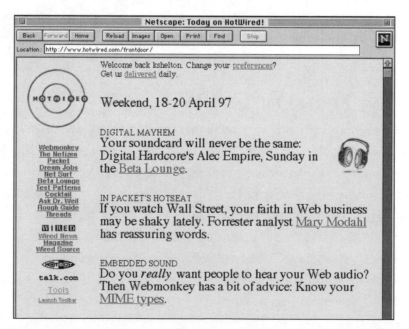

Figure 1.2 From here you can navigate through the whole community.

HotWired is new thinking for a new medium—context about the Digital Revolution and new art forms from the Second Renaissance, both tightly connected with an easy-to-use conferencing system that explores the concerns and controversies of the Digital Community.

Where *Wired* is a clear signpost to the next level, HotWired is operating from that next level. HotWired is a constantly evolving experiment in virtual community. It's Way New Journalism.

Why Is HotWired So Wired?

It's all about community. There's always some analyst out there, with maybe just a tad too much education, who wants to tell you that HotWired (or any other Web site) is successful because, "(insert your site here) recognized the information paradigm shift and leveraged this insight to adjust strategic marketing plans, which will increase brand awareness among its target market, and capture market share from more established competitors…" Now, concepts like branding and positioning are important, but what makes HotWired tick is something so simple that it's truly genius. Anyone can see that HotWired is a success because they built a place on the Web where people feel welcome to participate and feel connected to a community. As M. Scott Peck recognized, connectedness is very important to we humans. Now that's brilliant marketing.

In Chapter 12, by the way, we'll deal with marketing techniques you can use to get your community on the virtual map. Also, if commercial success is your goal (like HotWired's), we recommend you go out and get yourself some solid business education, and perhaps read *How To Grow Your Business On The Internet, 3rd Edition* (1997, Coriolis Group Books, ISBN: 1-57610-171-1) by Vince Emery.

Where Do Netizens Go To Fight Cyber Hall?

One feature of HotWired that's remarkably popular is The Netizen. Originally launched on HotWired to give daily coverage of the 1996 U.S. Presidential race, political authors like Brock Meeks and John Heilemann posted regular columns covering the race from a digital perspective, and readers were invited to create topics of discussion, post their ideas, and hash out the issues online. *Threads*, as these discussion forums are called, are designed with an easy-to-use interface, allowing anyone to submit articles for instant posting on the Web. Hundreds of issues were debated, with new ones added every day by the authors, the readers, and HotWired's editorial staff. The debate was always heated, dominant personalities arose, and a community formed, as people began to feel that they knew each other (and each other's egos). Wars raged and battle lines were drawn, but the one consensus was that, despite all the disagreement, freedom of expression was the paramount concern. No one would dare squelch another member's volume (but a member's statements were always fair game for attack). Now if you'll recall the four stages of community evolution that we discussed, we can see that The Neti-zen was in the "community" phase. Even though we're describing conflict and battles, this group was serving its purpose. Functional debate was the *raison d'etre* of The Netizen.

After the 1996 election, The Netizen stayed, but the community was rocky for a brief time, as Meeks left and Heilemann's reports became infrequent. The community had moved backward and members occupied two camps, the "pseudo-community" camp, and the "chaos" camp. Eventually, the HotWired staff asked Jon Katz (a contributing editor of *Wired*) to step up with Media Rant. Through Katz, and occasional guest columnists, The Netizen regained its strength by redefining itself, focusing on "cyberissues" like online censorship, intellectual property issues, and online journalistic integrity, to name a few. In the early months of 1997, Katz called for a boycott of Wal-Mart department stores, claiming quite accurately that Wal-Mart makes demands to music companies (like RCA, Warners, or Capitol) that they produce music CDs with potentially offensive lyrics edited out. He argued that in doing so, Wal-Mart was practicing a form of censorship because in many small communities, where Wal-Mart is the only CD outlet, unedited versions of these CDs would simply not be available. He also noted that Wal-Mart was stepping on the rights of the recording artists themselves to practice free expression. He expected that his "rant" would be popular because The Netizen is so heavily populated with champions of free speech; to his surprise, he received voluminous email attacking his point of view, some even accusing him of disregarding children's rights because he wanted them to hear dirty rap music!

He had said no such thing, so he fought back. For several weeks a war waged online, through threads and email, and at one point, Katz received over 200 emails a day. The great thing about communities like The Netizen is that, through the protective interface of the Web browser, people with passionate thoughts and ideas can really hash out their views. The same debate, raging at these levels in a bar, would ultimately result in a brawl. On HotWired, it's just another cathartic day—everyone learns something, everyone feels better, and ultimately most people manage to gain a respect for one another that must carry over into their offline lives.

Pointing At Finger Pointers

Another reason that HotWired gains so much respect is that they are as sharply critical of themselves as they are of anything else. The following excerpt is from one of Jon Katz's Media Rants (May 1996) on HotWired and it is about the older sibling, *Wired* magazine:

"But recently, the magazine has seemed to limit itself to a few consistent themes: existing structures suck, the Internet doesn't, and the future will transform everything anyway. It would be a particular shame if *Wired*, the embodiment of individualistic voices, were to become yet another despotic and top-directed editorial entity. *Wired*'s new futuristic tilt makes that possible, though not yet inevitable.

"One bad sign is that *Wired* is becoming humorless—a dangerous thing when combined with the magazine's enthusiastic, carefully crafted incoherence. It no longer laughs at itself or the geek culture it covers, which is desperately in need of poking, challenging, and prodding. Hilarious sendups like Douglas Coupland's *Microserfs* have vanished from its pages."

What Else Is There Besides All This Ranting And Raving?

Aside from Netizen, there's Packet, which covers the technology industry; Rough Guide, which deals with travel; Web Monkey (go check out this great feature), which deals with technical issues around Web publishing; Dream Jobs, which gives you the lowdown on…uh…well…dream jobs; and many more regular features and columns. HotWired also hosts Wired Ventures' proprietary search engine, HotBot, not to mention Talk.com, which allows any member to chat in realtime through a Java chat client about stuff on HotWired or anything else, for that matter. As you can tell, we're impressed, because this site has almost perfectly joined media and interactivity into a fully functioning virtual community. It's one of the Web's most exciting places, and a worthy model and source of inspiration for your own community.

COMMUNITY OF HEALING AND HOPE: THE PARKINSON'S DISEASE NETWORK

It's called the Parkinson's Digest: Worldwide Support Group Information Exchange (see Figure 1.3), and as intentional communities go, it's another model to strive for and a Web-based institution to be proud of. It's home to about 1,400 members; some are doctors and researchers. Most are afflicted with the deadly disease or have family members who are. This is a site where you can learn more about the condition; the medical information is in-depth, and the site is linked to The Parkinson's Web (affiliated with Massachusetts General Hospital), which

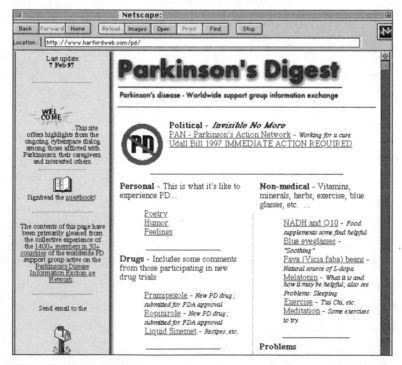

Figure 1.3   The Parkinson's Digest home page.

contains highly detailed technical information. The real strength of the Parkinson's Digest community, however, is not in its attention to science, but in its focus on the human factor: those afflicted with Parkinson's and their supporters. Although users do swap stories about medications and treatments, support, not medical advice, is the purpose of the Network.

What you'll find on this site has been assembled from the collective experience of the membership in over 30 countries. Sections include personal insight in the form of humor, poetry, and essays, including a wide range of writings by Parkinson's victims themselves. It can be somewhat numbing to read at first, but you can't help but be overwhelmed by the sense of hope and compassion that emanates from the site. Up-to-the-minute news about new drugs and research is available, as well as personal experiences of people who have tried (sometimes controversial) surgeries to "cure" the disease. There's also a section on vitamins, minerals, herbs, exercise, and other therapies. Of particular note is the advice to other sufferers on how to cope with depression, insomnia, pain, and other effects of the disease.

But it isn't all textual information, it's interactive. The Parkinson's Network runs an IRC (Internet Relay Chat) channel, a mailing list, and The Caregivers Network (see "A Closer Look"). These tools allow the Network to keep members highly involved, and the spirit of community and inclusion is certain to be an extremely valuable therapy to many members.

Karla And Todd Reflect On The Caregivers Network

Often overlooked, the role of Parkinson's Caregivers, or CGs, is vitally important. For the benefit of those not familiar with Parkinson's, the body does not properly produce the neurotransmitter dopamine, and the victim can often be in chronic and extreme pain, complicated by severe immobility. It's tragic, brutal, and still incurable, and death comes slowly, after as long as 30 years. The CG is charged with live-in care for Parkinson's patients, called Carepartners. Imagine: All day, every day, you care for a person who cannot get better, is constantly in pain, often feels bitter and hopeless, is sometimes suicidal, and can be down-right abusive. As a caregiver, you know the severity of the disease is the culprit, and cannot take the misery personally, but you're human. What do you do?

The Caregivers Network is strictly for CGs. It provides a safe place to sound off about the frustration, anger, sadness, and depression associated with this thoroughly noble pursuit. CGs offer one another support and guidance from their collective experience and understanding. In a profession where taking a break, walking away, or fighting back is impractical, potentially damaging, and largely unethical, The Caregivers Network is a vital Internet-based sub-community.

THE FAMILY THAT COMPUTES TOGETHER HAS A LOT OF COMPUTERS

Out there in the digital ether is a family called the Marshfields: a dad, a mom, and two boys ages 15 and 17. They're a typical family in many ways, except one: They're virtual. They live online. The patriarch of this family unit goes by the online handle of DataMaster, or DM for short. DM, a computer programmer of 19 years, started a unique experiment in December 1996. He networked the family's five PCs together, attached them to a proxy server, and then built a virtual home using a relatively new graphical-chat client called The Palace. (We'll talk at great length about The Palace software in several upcoming chapters.) He then took the whole family into cyberspace, establishing a dynamic Palace site that anyone can come and visit (usually by invitation), meet the family (shown in Figure 1.4), and tour the virtual rooms of their cyberhome.

We interviewed the Marshfield Family in their virtual home and came away with some interesting insights. DM's wife, known online as Jade, has a father who lives outside of the Marshfield's home state of Virginia. DM installed The Palace client software on his father-in-law's computer, and now they meet in the graphical world of cyberspace instead of using the phone. "We think this is better than a telephone," says Jade. She also notes that she likes her virtual home because she doesn't have to clean it.

DM adds, "I'd even set up the relatives with Palaces of their own!" (He's referring to the server software that allows users to create their own virtual worlds.) "They find it interesting," he quips optimistically, "but we'll see." He notes that the less computer-literate members of the extended family are slow to follow the Marshfield's virtual lead, but they're coming along.

Figure 1.4 DataMaster, Jade, Cyrano and Squirly are one big happy family in their cyberhome.

We asked the Marshfields if they'd like to hold virtual family reunions. The eldest son, Cyrano interjected, "that would be cool…and possibly cure dysfunctional families."

"And this [reunion] could be done, too," DM says, "this requires that the whole family be computer savvy, or at least know how to get online." As a computer programmer who was around when Unix was the cutting edge and DOS was a mere twinkle in Bill Gates' eye, DataMaster would be thrilled to help bring his whole family—aunts, uncles, cousins, everyone—into the twenty-first century. Since some of his work involves teaching, he sees this kind of computer interaction as a valuable teaching tool. "I want to use The Palace [model] as a medium for these classes," and he adds in reference to an upcoming auditorium feature of The Palace, "…it helps with crowd control."

We asked what the rest of the family's computer experience was, and were shocked to hear the 15-year-old son, code name Squirly, say, "I know nothing about computers…I'd rather be skating, or boxing." Clearly this teenager was more interested in the meatspace world and more physical pursuits, yet in spite of his self-proclaimed ignorance, we couldn't help but notice that he'd worked on a lot of the "room art" at the site, and that he spoke intelligently about the Internet.

Perhaps this is a testament to the ease with which any of us can get online and take part in virtual communities.

When asked how this project has helped the family, Jade commented that, "it's something to do together…family bonding time." Judging from the quick and seamless interaction between the family during the interview, and the technical complexity of the site, we'd have to surmise that this family has had plenty of bonding. (There's more talking online between them than between most folks we meet offline.) Then DM says, "The part you're not getting is the inter-room chatter in this house…it borders on silly!" Well, they must be having quite a ball, hosting their own virtual home, building a place for their extended family and friends, and even surfing the Internet, all together. Who says computer communities are cold and impersonal? The Marshfields would not agree.

As we left their home after the interview, Cyrano wished us a fond farewell with an archetypal digital musing, "…have a STRANGE DAY."

Moving On

We're all pioneers in this new world of online communities. What do we look for in these communities? Ideals like belonging, renewal, transformation, safety, spiritual discovery, education, opportunity, and peace are some of the goals of a healthy community, and they're also the long-term goals of most settlers in this brave new world of virtual communities.

In the coming chapters, we'll show you how online communities have evolved, and we'll talk about the benefits of creating an online community of your own for your family, your friends, or your business. We'll show you powerful new tools, and hopefully inspire you to use them, improve on them, and maybe create even greater tools for our noble and communal quest.

Chapter 2

So How Did Communities Get Online?

Chapter 2

- An Overview Of Internet History

- Communicating With Computers

So How Did Communities Get Online?

Chapter 2

A Brief History Online

Before we move on to the nitty-gritty of virtual communities, we think a brief history of the online world is in order. We'll look at how and why the Internet began, and follow its evolution up to the present. To get the whole picture, you'd need many volumes of information; fortunately, that's what the Internet is: many volumes of information. If you want to learn more about what we present here, you can fire up a search engine, enter some keywords, and dig up some really detailed data on any topic you like.

BIG MACHINES TO ADD AND SUBTRACT WITH

In the 1940s computers weighed thousands of pounds and took up whole floors in buildings. It took a team of scientists to use them. You definitely didn't want one of these things on your desktop. They had mechanical switches and vacuum tubes to make them work. In fact, the first "bug" (a word that has been commonly used to describe a glitch in computer hardware or software) really was an insect that got caught inside the machine.

Here's The Lowdown On The Bug

Grace Murray Hopper was working at Harvard University, on the Mark II computer, when she extracted the world's first computer bug. The insect had been beaten to a slushy pulp in the jaws of a relay. She glued it into the computer's logbook, and thereafter, when the machine stopped (which was far more often than not), she would tell Howard Aiken that she was "debugging" the computer.

That first "bug" still exists! If you want to see it, go to The National Museum of American History of the Smithsonian Institution. (They'll put anything in that place, won't they?) Now, to be fair to all you etymology buffs, the words bug and debugging had been used previously, but this was the first bona fide computer bug.

The first large-scale, automatic, general purpose, electromechanical calculator was the Harvard Mark I (IBM Automatic Sequence Control Calculator), conceived by Howard Aiken in the late 1930s to compute the elements of mathematical and navigational tables for the US Navy. The ENIAC, unveiled in Philadelphia in 1946, included the capacity for parallel computation; it was later modified into a stored-program machine. In 1947, the development of computers took a revolutionary turn. The "transfer resistance" device, or transistor, gave the computer the reliability that vacuum tubes never achieved.

COMPUTER, MEET COMMUNITY…COMMUNITY, MEET COMPUTER

In 1955, the first computer users group was formed. It was named SHARE, which was not an acronym for anything, but members eventually invented the words "Society to Help Alleviate Redundant Effort." SHARE was founded for IBM users. UNIVAC users also founded a group called USE; to the best of our knowledge, USE didn't stand for anything either. We can look at these groups as precursors to the virtual communities of today. There was clearly a desire to get online by the collective unconscious of these early computer users. As early as 1961, at the

Massachusetts Institute of Technology, the first time-sharing system was developed. MIT had created the first method of computer remote access. Soon afterwards, J. C. R. Licklider, at MIT, wrote a series of memos describing his vision of what he called the "Galactic Network." What made Licklider's network a real possibility was the work of Leonard Kleinrock, also at MIT, who was concurrently developing his theory of *packet switching*.

Packet Switching

Packet switching is a communications paradigm in which *packets* (messages or fragments of messages) are individually routed between hosts (servers on the Internet), with no previously established communication path. Packets take the fastest route. Not all packets traveling between the same two hosts, even those from a single message, take the same route. The receiving host reassembles the packets in the right order. Packet switching is used to optimize bandwidth on a network and minimize latency, or lag, which is the time it takes for packets to travel from where they are to where they need to be.

THE DAWN OF THE INTERNET

Then in 1965, it all happened. Thomas Merrill and Lawrence G. Roberts took a TX-2 (a really big, old computer) in Massachusetts and connected it over the telephone lines to a Q-32 (another big computer) in California, and BOOM! The first WAN (Wide Area Network) was born. Work soon began on the ARPAnet, which was launched in 1969 with a few computers connected to each other from a few major research universities, including UCLA, Stanford, and MIT.

From the ARPAnet came the Internet. It might be fair to say that January 1, 1983, was the day the Internet was born, for it was on that day (called "flag day" among network system administrators of the day) that all of the computers on the ARPAnet switched to a new communication standard called TCP/IP. TCP/IP is a hybrid of TCP (Transmission Control Protocol) and IP (Internet Protocol), and it has remained the dominant means of Internet networking to this day.

ARPAnet Communities: Not The Life Of The Party

For most folks, whose lives don't revolve around technical words like bit and byte, modulator and demodulator, throughput, packet switching, and so on, early life on the Internet would probably not have been too enthralling. Almost all usage of the Internet, and almost all the communities that bonded within the new medium, were centered around the medium itself. Researchers and engineers used the Internet to discuss, of all things, the Internet: How could they improve bandwidth? How could packet switching be made more effective? How could speed be increased? The military used the Internet heavily (and still does) as a tool to transfer data and coordinate operations, as well as for research of their own. In addition, it served as an access medium for databases on topics of specialized scientific concern.

There just wasn't a lot of call for garden clubs, motorcycle enthusiast forums, or pet care discussions at the time. The idea of online magazines, fan clubs, and such may have been in the minds of many pioneers of this technology, but it had no practical application until the average family had easy and economical access to the Internet.

Bring It On Home

Personal computing originated in 1971 when two products hit the scene: the first commercially available microprocessor, and the first floppy disk. The Intel Corporation produced the Intel 4004, birthing a family of "processors on a chip"; this first chip was developed for use in calculators, at the request of Busicom, a Japanese company. At the same time, IBM developed the first regular-usage, 8-inch floppy diskette. During the 1970s, the underground hobby of computing flourished. Usually, a hobbyist would have to build a computer from component parts, and then learn to write software to make it run. HeathKit was a major player in this arena. Then in 1979, Micropro International released Wordstar, setting the standard for word processing systems. More importantly, they created a product that would make home computers a truly viable commercial product, beyond the hobbyist realm.

For the next decade or so, until the commercialization of the Internet, home computers were championed for three "killer applications" (four, if you count games, and we certainly do): word processors, databases, and spreadsheets. Although modems were available, most people just didn't have a use for them, except for hobbyists who enjoyed using computer bulletin board systems or trading software with friends over the phone.

In 1980, hard drives made the scene, allowing for more powerful software, bigger files, and a more permanent method of data storage. IBM joined the home computer market in 1981 with the IBM PC, supported by Microsoft's DOS. With Charlie Chaplin as their icon, IBM created a machine that the average person could "use out of the box," and created a community of users interested in functionality instead of engineering. Other players rose to power, and then failed: Osbourne, Atari, Commodore, Tandy, Wang, and a long line of others. The only competitor in the home computer market that could really run with IBM was Apple. Using their different business models and marketing strategies, IBM and Apple managed to secure two seemingly permanent places in the home computer market, and there they rule to this day.

THE BULLETIN BOARD

To take part in the online world throughout the 1980s, you needed a modem, a computer, and a software package designed to talk to another computer. Popular packages included Telex and Qmodem, and there were many others, all with various strengths and weaknesses. After setting up your software, you entered a phone number to a BBS that you got from a newspaper ad or from a BBS listing that you might have got from a local computer vendor. The software dialed in, the remote computer answered, and on the off chance that everything was set up right the first time, you'd be connected to a BBS.

These BBSes were DOS-based, so they were navigated by text. First you entered a user name and a password, then you answered 20 questions (address, phone number, mother's maiden name, and so on), then you hung up and the BBS called your computer back to verify your phone number…and *then* you could use the BBS. It was a lot of work, but it was all necessary; to avoid damage to their systems by hackers, sysops (System Operators) needed to be sure you were who you said you were. They had a right to be careful and meticulous; after all, most BBSes were owned by hobbyists who provided the computer and a dedicated phone line, and who kept the system updated at all times, all at no cost to you, the user. If you donated a small amount of money, usually $10 to $20, they gave you bonuses like extra online time and unlimited file downloads. These BBSes had everything: message bases, thousands of shareware and freeware files to download, games, and in some cases, realtime chat capabilities.

Many small towns had a few BBSes, and in bigger cities there were dozens, even hundreds of BBSes. Through the registration process, which had to be completed for each BBS you visited, your name was added to a membership list, which was posted on the BBS. When you chose a message base to read and post to, you'd be reading messages from and posting responses to everyone else who used the system. This is the point at which online communities expanded out of the realm of the scientific and academic culture.

LOG ON AND ENTER YOUR PASSWORD

In 1977, Ward Christianson authored a *file transfer protocol* named Xmodem. (A file transfer protocol is a set of computer instructions that regulate the movement of data, be it in the form of a text file, a program, or a graphic image, from one computer to another over a modem connection or a network.) Xmodem was a protocol designed specifically for personal computers. Christianson is also credited with creating the first computer bulletin board; in 1978, he and a fellow named Randy Suess started a dial-in BBS called RCPM (for Remote CP/M, an operating system) in Chicago.

Tom Jennings, the sysop of FidoBBS (based in San Francisco), wrote his FidoBBS software in 1983; soon many BBSes were running the software. As if authoring a BBS wasn't enough, in June 1984, Jennings released the Fidonet software. It implemented a packet-based, store-and-forward networking system, which let FidoBBS users send a primitive form of email and take part in message-based discussions much like Usenet newsgroups. After collecting messages and mail all day, a PC running Fidonet would automatically call another predetermined PC at a set time (like 2:00 or 3:00 in the morning), and send all the messages it had collected that day to the next computer. All the computers did this, all night long, until eventually, all the messages and mail had been delivered. This system effectively extended the community structure of a BBS beyond its own locality. Unlike Usenet (which was based on the ARPAnet and the Internet), Fidonet ran on IBM PCs; this meant that anyone with a personal computer and a modem could be sysop of their own computer community.

We've written here about BBSes in the past tense, because they're no longer the focus of attention within the computer world. (They never really were.) The Internet has stolen the spotlight, supplanting the poor BBS in the average computer user's home. But we don't want you to get the impression that there are no BBSes left. The greatest surge in BBS popularity was in the late 1980s and early 1990s, and there are literally hundreds of thousands of BBSes still in operation today. Most of them are now connected to the Internet on dedicated lines, opening up their functionality and usability to anyone, anywhere, with a modem. BBSes are not part of a bygone era, even though they're no longer cutting-edge technology. If you're interested in setting up your community, *and* you enjoy the fussing and tinkering that goes along with being a hobbyist, a BBS-based system could be a good place to start. Mustang (**www.mustang.com**), the makers of Qmodem Pro, can provide you with good tools to use and their Web site will point you to other Web-based BBSes. *Sysop World* magazine (**www.sysopworld.com**) is a handy resource as well. On their site you'll find FAQs (text documents of Frequently Asked Questions) and more. Finally, *Boardwatch* magazine (**www.boardwatch.com**) is considered by many to be the premier BBS publication, so you might want to stop there first.

MONEY MAKES THE NET GO ROUND

For the most part, the major focus on the Internet was research- and military-based. BBS users were predominately hobbyists whose professions were connected to the computer industry in some way or another. The communities that were forming around all this technology were there largely because somehow, in some way, these people "touched the technology" and were eager to apply it. They were engineers, programmers, mathematicians, and so on. Then someone got the brilliant notion to try and make money with an online service. In 1985, America Online was founded by Steve Case. At the time, AOL was a content provider rather than an Internet service provider. Their online magazines, discussion forums, software libraries, and chat rooms were kept in-house. Today, AOL provides an Internet gateway to the World Wide Web, Usenet, FTP sites, and a host of other Internet services. With over 8 million members, AOL also provides proprietary news services, weather, electronic shopping, and chat, and handles approximately 6 million online sessions per day with as many as 140,000 simultaneous users. AOL delivers nearly 5 million email messages to roughly 9.4 million recipients, and processes over 50 million hits to the Web every day.

Perhaps AOL's greatest contribution to Internet virtual community building was the introduction of both an innovative chat function and dynamic email. An AOL subscriber can have up to five unique email addresses, one being permanent (the account address), and four that can change dynamically, for any number of reasons. You could have an address that you reserve for email with your friends, one for business, one for your spouse or kids, and maybe even one for an online alter ego. (We'll talk more about that later.) As for chat, AOL pioneered online chat by providing hundreds of AOL proprietary channels (they call them rooms) that hold up to 23 users each. If you just don't like the available rooms, you can create a member room to discuss almost any topic you'd like, or a private room where you can chat with a few close friends. AOL spawned a new generation of computer users who forged friendships, joined organizations, built business relationships, and even fell in love and got married, all by meeting initially in chat rooms.

Of course, all communities have their problems. Soon after AOL was launched, other content providers and Internet service providers (ISPs) emerged. A *content provider* is like a huge bulletin board with access to information, message bases, chat, and more, whereas an *Internet service provider* is an Internet gateway that connects a user to the Internet, but provides no actual content. As computers became more prevalent in the home throughout the 1980s and 1990s, users tried other services (like CompuServe, Prodigy, or the ill-fated GEnie) and ISPs, and began to compare notes. Many liked AOL, with its focus on entertainment and mainstream middle-American living. Others migrated to CompuServe, preferring its focus on more serious business. Still others, the savvy and more computer-literate element, preferred the total freedom of a good local ISP. Separate communities were forming more rapidly than ever before, and a few of them were (and still are) extremely hostile toward AOL. Complaining bitterly about AOL's Terms of Service agreement and billing policies, two new Internet-based communities emerged: AOLHell and AOLSucks were informally founded as havens for AOL survivors who held bitter feelings for the online service. In spite of lawsuits and shrewd marketing, AOL could not squash these groups, which have evolved into fully functioning communities of their own on the Internet.

The Eye Of The Beholder: AOL

Does AOL deserve the abuse it takes? Well, yes and no. AOL did pioneer many of the Internet functions we take for granted today. They did play a major role in drawing millions of people toward rewarding Internet experiences. They do offer a very easy-to-use service, as well as great email benefits. On the other hand, until 1997 they billed users by the minute, at what many considered ridiculous prices. It was not hard to have a $200 AOL bill for a month's service. To many adult users without children (and even to some with them) AOL's user policy, called Terms of Service, seemed Draconian and without merit. And finally, many Internet functions readily available on standard ISPs were difficult to access through AOL's software, or at best were late in coming. To this day, AOL is notorious for its lackluster Web browser.

It all boils down to this: AOL is great as Internet training wheels for almost any new computer user; and for many experienced end users who want easy email and access to the types of services AOL offers, it's a great service (and finally at a reasonable price). To advanced users who don't care for AOL's in-house content, and who want to use a slew of software and Internet resources, a local ISP is likely to be far more desirable. AOL is simply a tool, and we choose tools based on how well they serve our personal needs.

THE WORLD WIDE WEB

Tim Berners-Lee is the one-man brain trust credited with the creation of the World Wide Web, and the originator of HTTP (Hypertext Transfer Protocol) and HTML (Hypertext Markup Language). Before the Web and HTML, actual navigation on the Internet was achieved with complex and archaic text, and codes based on languages like Unix. Hypertext simply means that anything on the Internet, or an intranet, or even a standalone computer, can be linked to anything else on that system, and that hypertext links allow you to move easily from document to document without actually needing to know the IP address (or location) of the document you're trying to access. When you click on an icon on a Web page to call up another page, you're using hypertext. HTML is the code (and an easy code to learn, too) that allows you to create and move between documents on the Web.

Unix Do Not Have High Singing Voices

Unix (pronounced "yoo'niks") was authored by Ken Thompson in 1969 because Thompson wanted to play computer games on a homemade PDP-7 computer. Unix was the first source-portable computer operating system. It's flexible and friendly if you're an application developer, and because Internet technology is Unix-based, it's quite handy for ISPs that control the computer networks that serve as Internet gateways.

The Webs We Weave

Technically, the World Wide Web is the collection of all the servers linked together on the Internet. Specifically, though, it's all of the HTML documents residing on all of these servers. The Web is most likely the best place to start your virtual community, for several reasons:

- First, it's a popular and proven technology—there are at least 80 million pages on the Web. Plus, it doesn't hurt that millions of people use the Web every day, so you're guaranteed a large potential audience. If you're worried about not getting enough traffic to your site, fret not, friends; in Chapter 13 we'll show you several ways to market your Web site. You *can* attract attention in a crowd.

- Second, it's easy to use, for both the user and the producer.

- Third, most Web browsers are *modular*—helper applications and plug-ins may be added to extend functionality. This means that you can use RealAudio, Java scripts, and more in your site.

- Fourth, Web sites are *scalable*, enabling a community to grow and contract as required. Not only that, but the actual parcel of Web real estate you'll need to get started is small, and often you can even start for free.

All Of History Leads To Today...

And today we begin our journey into the future. In spite of all the talk we hear in the media about how big business is shaping the Net, the fact is that the Net is a powerful tool for all of us. It's people just like you, people with families, small business owners, social activists, artists, students, people from every walk of life with varied and complex opinions and visions, who make the Web thrive. Without you, the Web is empty. We don't go there just to buy products, to look at graphic files, or to research term papers. We go there to connect, to communicate, to learn, to grow...and we go there to plant our flags in a rapidly changing world.

In the coming chapters, we'll look at some of the tools we have available to us and how to use them. We'll see more technical and social innovations that are shaping the future. We'll look at laws that help (or sometimes hinder) what we do in cyberspace. We'll examine management techniques that you'll want to use when running your new online worlds. And we'll even look into the future of Internet-based communication and virtual communities.

Just turn the page...

Part 2

Creating A Virtual Community

Chapter 3

Planning A Successful Community

Chapter 3

- COMMUNITY PLANNING STRATEGIES

- INCORPORATING INTERACTIVE TOOLS

- USING PUSH TECHNOLOGY

- CHOOSING AN ISP

PLANNING A SUCCESSFUL COMMUNITY

Chapter 3

In the film *Field Of Dreams*, a mysterious voice in the cornfield told Ray Kinsella (Kevin Costner), "If you build it, they will come." It was a great line for a movie, but the voice obviously wasn't talking about a Web site. In *virtual* life, if you build it, they won't necessarily come, and you probably won't have people lined up for miles waiting to see this magnificent thing you've built, unless you build a plan, provide something of interest, and advertise, advertise, advertise. Cyberspace communities need planning, just like meatspace communities. So if you want your *virtual* community to flourish, preparation is the key.

Writing Your Community Plan

Building a community is like manufacturing a product. If you were opening a business, you'd probably write a marketing and business plan to obtain operating capital from a lending institution, develop advertising plans with an agency, and determine distribution channels for a product or service. You can apply similar ideas to your virtual community: create a community marketing plan.

THE SIX PS

Always remember the Six "Ps:" Proper Planning Prevents Poor Performance, Pal! And it all starts with a *mission statement*. This is probably the most crucial step in your planning process. It defines what your community *is*. It shapes the rest of your plan. And it will help give you a sense of purpose. Give good hard thought to this statement. Many a dream has crumbled into dust due to a lack of direction.

Electric Minds

When you click into Minds.com (**www.minds.com**), you are welcomed by Howard Rheingold, creator of the site. You'll recognize him, he's always adorned in subtle attire (most notably his signature Hawaiian luau shirt). His message to the visitor enthusiastically states the objective of Electric Minds.

Welcome To Electric Minds

We want to invite you to help us create something new, useful, and fun. Electric Minds brings together information and conversation about technology and its effects on our lives, community, and the future.

We've found the best writers and thinkers around. They're gathering breaking news, doing deep analysis, and writing thoughtful and passionate rants on things that matter. What the future will look like. Where technology is taking us. How people are living together online right now. How new tools are shaping virtual communities and the World Wide Web.

We are creating something that is more like a jam session than a magazine, more like a community than a reference tool, more like a place than a publication. We will count on you to help us do that.

Electric Minds is for you because:

You're a smart person who wants to get the first word about what tomorrow's going to look like.

You have ideas of your own: you want to jump on stage with our troupe of futurists, journalists, and artists, and help us create something that has never existed before.

Electric Minds is a marriage of community and content. We intend to be exploratory, critical, and experimental. And we invite you to come explore, criticize, and experiment with us. We are going to discuss what is right and what is wrong about the ways technologies change the way we live, work, and think.

We invite you to come in, read our contributors, respond to them and each other, and build something new and exciting with us.

What it is—is up to us.

—Howard Rheingold

When developing your mission statement, keep in mind that your community will be more successful if your vision is unique: What are you offering that's compelling or different? Can you exploit a niche that larger communities have overlooked? Do other communities exist that are similar to yours? Will your community stand alone, or should you network or partner with other communities? Also remember, you do not have to compete with the previous statement. Your statement can be long or short, inspirational or clinical, simple or magniloquent, but it must be one that your target audience will be interested in and feel welcomed by.

Karla And Todd Talk About Planning

Where do you see yourself in five years? If you want to be a community for the long haul, you need to envision where you'll be in one, three, five years. This is called *strategic planning*. For example, you want to be the premiere site on the Web for collectors and enthusiasts of little porcelain trolls. To achieve your strategic troll goal plan, you need to create tactical plans. If strategy is where you want to go, then tactical is how you will get there. Try to anticipate the resources you'll need as your troll community grows and make provisions for acquiring them. Troll graphics? Troll mailing lists? Troll chat? Maybe a troll bridge? You get the idea.

COME ONE, COME ALL—OR INVITATION ONLY?

Do you really want all 40 million people (so far) on the Internet knocking on your front door? Maybe you do. If so, good luck. If not, you'll want to specify who you want to attract to your community. This can be achieved through *segmentation*. It means looking at all 40 million people on the Internet and placing them into "groups" according to common characteristics, such as geography, demographics, or lifestyles. Then, it's easy. Pick the segment or segments you want to join your community.

Geography

Some communities are based on geography. The early years of The WELL, mentioned in Chapter 1, are a prime example. Here are some possible ideas for you to consider in planning your community:

- You could replicate your real city, virtually.

- How about creating an educational chat forum for parents, teachers, and students in your school district?

- You could link your sales force and vendors in a territory or state.

Demographics

Demographics refer to "states-of-being" such as age, gender, income, occupation, race, or nationality. Many online communities have successfully used demographic segmentation to build successful sites. Kids Nation (**www.kidsnations.com**) and Kyleen's Kids World (**www.comet.net/personal/landru/kids**) attract 8 through 14 year olds. Webgrrls (**www.webgrrls.com**) targets women. Net Noir (**www.netnoir.com**) attracts African Americans. Other ideas for you to consider:

- What about targeting the growing number of seniors getting online? (Seniors are currently the fastest growing online demographic.)

- Try building a social space for your professional trade association. After all, in business, networking is everything.

- You might create a site to discuss contemporary men's issues.

Lifestyle Or Attitudes

Lifestyle is a pattern of living that reflects a person's activities, interests, and opinions. The definition of *attitude* is similar, but takes into account an individual's feelings and belief systems. Here are a few examples of segmentation based on lifestyle or attitude considerations. The House of Blues (**www.hob.com**) targets music lovers. TEN (**www.ten.net**), an online gaming service, fosters community among multi-player gaming fans. Generation.net (**www.generation.net**) highlights French culture. Your imagination can literally run wild with ideas. Here are a few possibilities to consider:

- Think about mountain biking, sailing, rock climbing, or other sports and recreational activities.

- How about hobbies? Arts and crafts, stamp collecting, or people who like to play in quicksand. Really! (**www.xnet.com/~cmd/qs/qs.htm**)

- Always a hot topic, politics or special interest groups can inspire a lively community.

YOUR VIRTUAL VISITOR'S BUREAU

Every community needs a visitor's bureau to encourage guests to visit, and a chamber of commerce to attract businesses to set up operations. The same holds true for virtual communities. For your community to flourish, you need a steady influx of members to build continuity. Continuity is fostered when people join and participate in community activities on a regular basis. However, a community can get stale if new members don't continually join to add fresh ideas and contributions to the mix. Also, it's natural to experience attrition as some established members move on in their virtual lives and leave the community. Just like a town, some people move in, some move out, and the community evolves. In Chapter 12 we'll show you how to publicize and grow your community effectively, and how to keep people coming back. And in Chapter 13, you'll learn some important steps to take to attract businesses to sponsor your community.

Chapter 3

Assembling Your Community Toolbox

At this point, you've decided what you want to do. Now you need to figure out how you're going to get there. You have three aspects to consider: technical issues, design (or style), and content. We'll look at the latter issues in Chapter 4. Right now, let's look at technical issues and tools. The first technical issue you'll face is planning the contents of your community toolbox. This toolbox will consist of many interactive gadgets that you'll use to construct your Web-based virtual community. Karen Wickre, who contributed to the November 1996 issue of *Computer Life* magazine, observes that "interactivity" can mean anything from clicking through a Web site to gabbing in realtime chats.

Karen Wickre, Author

[Being interactive gives] the opportunity to discuss, share information, and formulate new ideas and relationships based on what brought you together in the first place.

Interactivity allows users on your Web site to participate in at least a threaded message board or some other method of collaborative information-sharing, as well as some amount of aggregated information meant to draw a specific audience.

Interactivity in meatspace uses a variety of tools like snail mail (letters), telephones, and our own voices. In cyberspace, the tools are analogous, but they are also new, and new tools are constantly being introduced. Let's look at a number of these tools. There are far too many to look at all of them, so we'll focus on what we think are the best tools available, and in subsequent chapters, we'll look at integrating these tools into your community. Not every tool is usable with every ISP, so we'll try to narrow our scope to the tools that are available over the broadest platform so that your community doesn't exclude anyone due to technical limitations.

Chattin' About Stuff

Chat is something like having a telephone party line, except you type in text instead of talk. Chat is one of the most important tools, because it gives you and the members of your community instant access to each other—to cry, laugh, argue, cajole, or whatever. It's in realtime, like speech. Hundreds of thousands of online citizens use chat because it feels personal and forges real relationships. Web surfing can be enjoyable and informative, but chat puts you directly into the content. Simply put, chat makes people come back. It's been said that AOL only provides content to give people stuff to chat about. Anyone who's ever logged on to AOL knows that hundreds of rooms are operating simultaneously, with a cacophony of voices ringing out. By the year 2000, chat is expected to generate about 7.9 billion hours of online use per year, according to *Advertising Age*. And many companies are looking ahead (remember that word, strategic?) to figure out how to capitalize on this by developing revenue-generating models to create a profit center.

Bob6723> Hi, How Are You All Tonight?

There is a line of text chat for you. Vanilla. Plain. Unpretentious. A user name, Bob6723, an arrow, >, and what the user says, "Hi, how are you all tonight?" If you use commercial online services, it's ubiquitous. Until recently, however, chat on the Web has been the ugly little stepchild, shadowed by its mammoth siblings at AOL and CompuServe. Notably, Web chat has been awkward, primitive, and slow, but it is maturing. Even online services are taking notice of Web chat. AOL is reported to be spending millions to develop a chat presence on their Web site (which is separate from their online service).

The roots of Web chat can be traced back to its cousin IRC, Internet Relay Chat, developed by Jarkko Oikarinen of Finland in 1988. In use in over 60 countries, IRC is a multi-user chat system where people congregate in channels, or rooms, to form specific communities based on subject matter, as shown in the following text;

```
<TrixR4Kids> Thanks for the tips on logging :) Do
  you know where there is a good FAQ that lists all
  of mIRC or IRCs commands?
```

```
<KnightinWhite> TrixR4Kids - if you want to know more
    about mIRC v5.0 go to: http://www.lynx.bc.ca/~despayre/
    (or) http://www.mirc.co.uk. You can also read the
    version.txt in your mirc directory.
<TrixR4Kids> Outstanding, thanks.
```

IRC operates through a client/server network in which all servers are interconnected and pass messages from user to user over the IRC network. One server can be connected to several other servers. Currently, there are several IRC server networks, the largest being EFnet (Eris Free Network), which serves over 15,000 users at any given time. There is also IRCNet and Undernet serving about 10,000 each, and the baby of the bunch, Dalnet, serves about 8,000 at any time. These nets host many channels, one of which you may create at will with simple commands.

Why is this good for you? Many online communities use IRC as their meeting place, and you can too. Say you want your online group of salted pretzel enthusiasts to meet online on Wednesdays at 7:00 p.m. EST. Email all the group members telling them when to meet, where to meet, and the channel name, let's say #TwistedPretzel. You log onto IRC with a client (see next section) and create your channel with that name—the others simply join that channel using their client. IRC is a cross-platform network, so users with Windows clients can chat with users on Macintosh clients. In Chapter 5, we'll learn just how to make all this stuff go, with a close look at the commands and features of IRC, and we'll show you how to get Web traffic into your IRC channel.

Cool Chat Clients

There are plenty of big companies out there with chat clients for you to use. Let's look at some high-powered, low-cost clients that are capable of great flexibility for advanced computer users, yet very easy to learn and operate if you are a newbie. We'll look at mIRC for the Windows platform and Homer for Macintosh.

- *mIRC*—As of this printing, mIRC (authored by Khaled Mardem-Bey) is up to version 5.02 and is one of the most powerful IRC-based chat clients available. You can download the program from hundreds of Web sites and FTP (file transfer protocol) sites on the Internet. It is easy to install, and comes with a ready made list of many popular IRC servers that you can immediately connect to. Its power comes from an easy-to-learn scripting language that allows you to modify the functions of mIRC and to create many automated actions, like automatically saying "hello" to anyone who enters your IRC channel. mIRC is shareware, so it's free to download and use, but it would be nice if you paid the reasonable $20 fee if you decide to keep the program.

- *Homer*—Similar to mIRC but designed for the Mac platform, Homer offers many comparable features. Written by Toby Smith, it is also shareware and is available from hundreds of sites. This client has a modest $25 registration fee, and Toby will smile and think of you lovingly if you register Homer.

Perhaps the best feature of using a channel on IRC to host meetings for your community is that you do not need server software. The networks are free to use, very flexible, always running, and allow you to register channel names and online nicknames through simple keyboard commands so that they cannot be used by other users, thus establishing your own identity on the Web. Of course, if you like more control, and want to use server-side software packages, then perhaps Java chat applications that integrate with your Web site are what you need.

Cool Chat Servers

As Java technology emerges, commercial products such as Eshare's Reunion (**www.eshare.com**) contain Java-based chat solutions that you can even run from your personal server. Trolling through the Java libraries at Gamelan (**www.gamelan.com**), we've found other free or shareware Java scripts that you can easily integrate into your Web community.

In Chapter 5, we'll see how to incorporate these technologies into your community. Now let's move on to two-dimensional chat, which is quite different from text chat.

PALACE CHAT

The Palace is a multimedia digital world that uses a GUI (graphical user interface, pronounced goo-ee). It offers a two-dimensional environment for chat. The Palace is perhaps one of the most exciting new Web-based applications to arrive in a long time. It was created by Mark Jeffrey and Jim Bumgardner and it is the only 2D chat client currently available on the Web. There are proprietary 2D chat services available on commercial services such as CompuServe, but the Palace offers something very special. Like most Internet applications, the Palace is networked through a client/server system. Let's take a closer look.

The Palace Is Chat

The Palace chat interface was designed using the comic book metaphor. Graphic panels, which are easy to design and customize, represent place. You are represented by an *avatar*, which is a visual representation of the physical "you." (We'll talk about how you can create your own avatar in Chapter 7.) To further distinguish yourself, you may create a nickname for your avatar. Avatars talk with balloons suspended over the their heads. These balloons may be customized to reflect your mood or state of mind, as shown in Figure 3.1. There is a big spiky balloon for exclamations, a standard balloon for conversation, and a thought bubble well-suited to sharing quiet introspection. You can also follow the conversation in a text window and archive the conversations for later reminiscing.

The Palace Is Graphical

Look at the room in Figure 3.2. This looks like a conference room, complete with chairs, a table, carpeting, draperies, and what looks to be a whiteboard. All of these items make up the "room art," or background image, which consists of a GIF (one of the graphic formats used on the Web). It looks as if the room is occupied. See those funny little figures with black name tags? Those are the avatars.

We also see movable objects, commonly known as "props," in the room. Props can be hats, cans of soda, or bags of chips; in this case, the trophy sitting in the middle of the conference table is a prop. As a visitor to this chat room, I might say, "Excuse me, McAdam, could you please move over so the kind folks reading this could see this wondrous object?" Now, if McAdam chose to, he could move his avatar within this graphical environment—perhaps to one of the chairs. Or he could point and click his mouse to transport his avatar to the next room, or even to another Palace site.

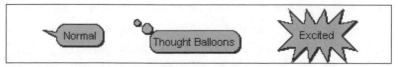

Figure 3.1 Types of chat balloons.

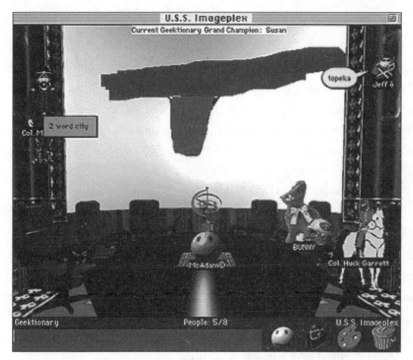

Figure 3.2 Playing Geektionary at the U.S.S. Imageplex.

When you participate in a graphical world, you may feel something really weird happen: the human interaction feels "physical." Users have at their disposal not only words to communicate, but also nonverbal behavior that can create almost tangible sensations. Users in a text-based chat environment may imitate nonverbal behaviors with action command descriptions ("Sally gives Bob a push"), but the effect is not the same. Actually seeing the behavior has a much greater psychological impact.

Jim Bumgardner, Co-Creator Of The Palace

There is no attempt to mimic real world physics in the Palace. There is no gravity, nor is there a real sense of location. Early attempts by myself to create "real world constraints," such as limiting a person's movement to the "floor" area of the room, were quickly removed, because they were perceived by myself and the other users as unnecessary obstacles.

Chapter 3

According to the Palace folks, there are several reasons they took the 2D approach rather than 3D, or VRML—primarily, their aim was to design a space that is inherently social. The Palace is not meant to be an imitation of reality. In a 3D space, you can't always see the people that are in a room with you; in addition, you need to walk between spaces that are far away from one another, and the programming necessary to make interaction possible in a 3D environment is extremely complicated.

The Palace Is Multimedia

Props, room art, and avatars can all be animated—your eyes may blink flirtatiously at the cute avatar across the room; your T-shirt may flash like a bright neon sign; a fire may blaze brightly in a fireplace. In addition to images, the basic Palace software includes 16 standard sounds and allows users to add more. These sounds allow you to extend your communication from textual to "verbal:" You can blow your boyfriend a kiss, or giggle at a joke, or applaud a great idea.

Todd Calls For Gamers To Unite

I love playing interactive video games over the Internet. Palace is planning to implement Direct Play technology to allow PC gamers to use Palace as a meeting place to organize games, talk about strategy, and trade tips. When they are ready to play, the gamer can activate his or her game from within PalaceLobby (an updated version of The Palace client designed just for gamers). After a rousing game, players can return to The Palace directly from battle to debrief (or whatever we gamers do after we play). With the Palace's customizable graphics, avatars, and props, the phrase, "pass the ammo" will take on a new meaning for players of Quake (id Software) or DukeNukem3D (3DRealms).

The Palace Is Interactive

The Palace supports interaction in a number of ways:

- You can interact with each other. The members in Figure 3.2, (including Karla, AKA Bunny) are playing a game of Geektionary, which is similar to Pictionary. It's Captain Mitchell's turn, and he's using the whiteboard to draw. His subject is a "two-word city."

- You can interact with props. Props may be worn, taken, stored, or traded. For example, the trophy sitting in the middle of the table will be given to the Grand Champion of the Geektionary tournament. Looks like Susan is the current Champion; she probably has her trophy prominently displayed somewhere, maybe even on her own Palace site.

- You can interact with your environment. Much power has been granted to the creators of Palace sites in the form of "scripts." This programming language, called Iptscrae (pig latin for the word script), allows you to build functionality into your Palace site. In Figure 3.3, you'll see that I'm playing a game of backgammon, and the script says that I've just rolled a 4 and a 3 with the dice. Other cool scripts allow you to turn lights off and on in a room, randomly teleport from room to room in a site, have your fortune read by a genie, or trigger a laser beam that dissolves your avatar into electrons. The interactive possibilities using Iptscrae are endless and the Palace bundles entertaining, but extremely powerful, scripts with their software that's included on the companion CD-ROM. But we'll get to programming a little bit later, in Chapter 8.

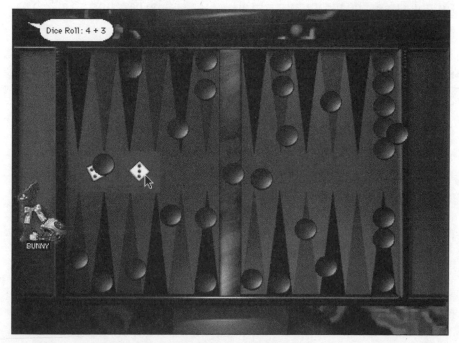

Figure 3.3 Interacting with a Palace environment.

Karla Is Shocked

Palace headquarters is promising Macromedia Shockwave support by the time you read this book. Macromedia Director, the underlying engine of Shockwave, is a tool for creating interactive business presentations, games, and graphics. It is object-oriented and uses predesigned scripts to carry out visual and auditory tasks through the Shockwave application plug-in. It will allow for complex animated avatars and highly interactive games within The Palace walls themselves, and will make for a very kinetic experience.

The Palace Uses Client/Server Technology

The Web is a perfect example of client/server technology. When you surf the Web with Netscape Navigator, Microsoft Internet Explorer, or any other browser, you are using a *client*. Each time you click on a link or type in a Web address (URL), you're accessing pages from a *server*, which is usually a high-end computer system connected to the Internet through a high-speed phone line. The Palace uses similar technology. With this system, you may roam seamlessly from room to room, or from site to site on the Internet. A Palace site may also have links to a Web page or an email form.

Palace Design Reduces Lag

Palace servers perform very little work. Scripts are executed by the client— not the server! Actually, the server does little more than act as a traffic cop, thus the ability to run a server on a relatively low-end PC or Macintosh computer. The design of the server software is similar to the design of many new Internet-playable PC games. By reducing server tasks in favor of client tasks, latency (or lag) is significantly reduced. Now you know what to do with that old 486 you put in the closet; set up a server!

The Palace is exciting new technology, and it's easy to use and design for. Its a frontrunner in the community-building arena. Because the Palace integrates so easily into your Web site, we will place a lot of emphasis in this book on adding Palace functionality to your community. Chapter 6 provides an introduction to Palace culture, while Chapter 7 instructs you in avatar building, and Chapter 8 teaches basic client/server mechanics.

Next is three-dimensional chat—another leap in the evolution of chat technologies. This stuff is still very young and the subject of a lot of experimentation, but its potential is exciting and there are plenty of VRML applications available from the Web and commercially.

3D Chat: Black Sun Interactive

Black Sun takes the concept of graphical chat to another dimension, literally. Using a technology called VRML (Virtual Reality Modeling Language), Black Sun brings the user into a world with width, height, and depth. The concept of 3D chat is similar to the Palace, except that now the user has a first-person perspective. You won't "see" your own avatar, unless you specifically "look" at a body part like a hand or foot. It's just like moving through meatspace, only it is cyberspace, as shown in Figure 3.4.

Black Sun offers several benefits as a community-building tool:

• Seamless integration with existing Web sites on both the client and server sides. Users may reach this virtual world from a Web site by clicking on hyperlinks, in turn launching the Black Sun plug-in.

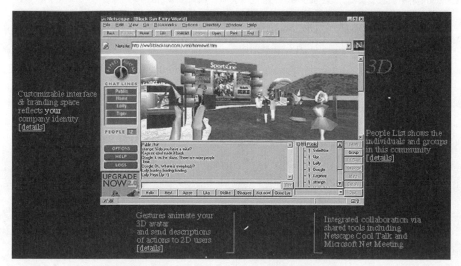

Figure 3.4 Walking through a Black Sun party with a 3D avatar.

- You get unlimited community growth. The chat server, CyberHub, is highly scalable, which allows you to build communities with thousands of users in each virtual world.

- VRML offers easy interaction and the ability to locate and communicate with others. CyberHub includes a directory of all the members in a particular world, and users can easily communicate with each other in public or private areas.

In order to operate a Black Sun CyberHub server, you'll need considerable processing power: a Sun Sparc or Windows NT machine with at least 32MB of RAM. A co-located server (a dedicated computer at your ISP) is your best option if you don't have high bandwidth connections to your home or office.

3D chat does have its critics. The processing power and bandwidth necessary to host and participate in a 3D world is high-end. However, eventually these stumbling blocks will disintegrate, as they always do, and VRML, no doubt, will become extremely prevalent in the future. If you'd like to implement a 3D world within your community, we'll show you how in Chapter 9.

Following The Threads

Today's Web-based discussion boards allow you to add online conferencing capability to your community quite easily. You can set up and maintain ongoing Web discussions, or threads, about any number of subjects simultaneously. Members of your community can access any of the multiple threads via the Web. Messages are stored in a structured database. Your message is viewed and commented on over time by others. This allows conversations over a long period of time.

Web-based threaded messaging applications have evolved. They're interactive and dynamically generated, and some even support user profiles, message searching, and forum moderation. Plus discussion forums can be used to supplement chat, or they can stand on their own merit. Ideas for incorporating this technology into a virtual community include:

- Supplementing chat activity

- Archiving important topics that may be searched by members at a later date

- Allowing interactivity that is not tied to realtime

- Creating content important to business, education, or nonprofit organizations

In Chapter 5, you'll see how to set up a discussion forum using easy-to-install, low-cost commercial applications, such as O'Reilly & Associate's WebBoard and eShare Technology's net.Thread.

Get The Word Out And Get People Talking

If you want to keep your community together, your citizens need to be kept informed. Announcing community events and late-breaking news with community updates, bulletins, press releases, special-event notices, and product offerings will help build continuity and encourage traffic to your Web site. Using old-fashioned (in Web terms, anyway) mailing lists or sexy new push technology are two handy ways of achieving these ends.

Good Old Reliable Email

Email—it's the fundamental form of computer-mediated communication. Mailing lists are one of the Net's most effective, yet least understood, methods of communication. A mailing list is like a discussion thread, but it shows up in your mailbox.

Asha Dornfest, Clnet Guru

Mailing lists go by different names—listservs, mail reflectors, discussion lists—but they all do basically the same thing: people subscribe to the list, and email messages sent to a central address are redistributed to everyone on the list.

…whatever your objective, the town-hall atmosphere of mailing lists makes them a great way to communicate with a group.

The Marathon Palace (**palace://marathon.lag.com**) is created and operated by a Macintosh evangelist, Curt Lewis. Much public discussion took place at the Marathon site when The Palace, Inc. did not release an updated version of the Macintosh Palace client in March in conjunction with the release of the 32-bit Windows client. Curt decided to enhance this discussion by creating a mailing list, the Mac Palace Mailing list (**mac@palace.lag.com**).

WHEN PUSH COMES TO PULL

Push technology is exciting new stuff. Essentially, a *push* program will scour the Web and bring back news and information that you've specifically requested. That makes it *pull*, doesn't it? Well, not really. Let's look at the cable TV model to illustrate: as a coach potato, you subscribe to various channels, like HBO or the Disney Channel. Then, the cable operator "pushes" the programming to your television through the coaxial line. This is almost identical to how push technology works on the Web. People subscribe to your "channel." Then, your content is broadcast directly to them. This technology can benefit your community because members can request information that will be sent to them as it becomes available.

BackWeb

BackWeb (**www.backweb.com**) is one program that does this. It allows you to create different packages such as "info" and "soft" flashes and more that are sent automatically to your channel's subscribers. Let's say that your community is made up of inline skating enthusiasts. Your Web site, Inline Online, has a skating forum. World Inline skating champion, Bjorn, is going to be leading a discussion on Inline Online's Palace site. In order to let everyone know, you'll want to push information to them. This information is your *infoflash*. It can be more than just "Bjorn is coming on Friday." It can include a photograph, a biography, a RealAudio clip, or a movie file of Bjorn wiping out at the World Inline Championship last year. This is in addition to any regular supplements that you may already publish periodically. A soft flash is similar, but an executable file is sent, such as a software update or demo.

BackWeb is free to your clients and works with their Web browsers, which makes it accessible and easy to use. On the server side, the technology is scalable, meaning that you have control over how much data you send to your community members. However, the costs involved are variable—the more data you send, the more it costs.

PointCast

PointCast, the leader in push technology, has traditionally only allowed big media outlets to use their push server. With PointCast, you can now choose to have news from CNN, *The New York Times*, and more automatically updated and pushed to your desktop. However, PointCast has announced that they are opening up the technology for use by anyone and everyone who has a Web site, and very soon, that will be you! Best of all, PointCast has said that their service will be free! This is most likely a response to BackWeb, proving once again that competition is good for the Internet.

We'll talk more about push technology in Chapter 5.

Give Them A Way To Say I Love You

To keep up with your members and improve your community, you'll want to implement a virtual suggestion box, otherwise known as feedback forms or guestbooks. While you don't have to implement everything that your members suggest, you should let people know that you care about their opinions and ideas. In Chapter 5, you'll learn two easy ways to create an interactive form on your site.

Ten Strategies For Planning Your Community

Amy Jo Kim has helped large Web sites such as MTV Online, Net Noir, Talk City, and ImagiNation Network's Cyberpark launch thriving digital hangouts. Amy, founder of Naima, a strategic design company specializing in online environments, compiled a laundry list for *New Media* magazine (March 3, 1997) for community builders to follow when planning new environments. As we go through the list, we'll illustrate each of Amy's points with examples drawn from communities that exist on the Web.

Create A Mission Statement

As mentioned previously, and illustrated with the Electric Minds site, your mission statement should be compelling and persuasive. Tell new users why they would want to join your community. In addition, identify the founders, and explain why they started the community and how they'll be participating.

Provide A Meaningful Membership Form

This form should do more than just ask questions that benefit you, the site host. The content of your membership form will help to establish the tone of your community.

Talk City

Talk City, an Internet community, believes in people and in the power of conversation. The builders of Talk City designed their membership form, shown in Figure 3.5, to extract information pertinent to other Talk City users, such as a member's name and email address.

The Talk City architects also placed photographs and facts about Talk City users on the registration page. By inviting the visitor to explore the "parade of friendly faces belonging to folks who hang out at Talk City," the Talk City builders have set a tone of camaraderie and warmth. Instead of just filling out a form, the reader feels a sense of connectivity within the community. And we'd expect the registration rate to be much higher than it would be if the visitor encountered nothing but an impersonal registration.

Provide A Member Directory

"Let members learn about the other people who hang out on the site," Amy Jo Kim advises. Friendships are the social glue of your community. By providing a way for people to meet, you encourage relationships among your members.

Kyleen's Kids World

Created by a 9-year-old girl in Charlottesville, Virginia, Kyleen's Kids World (**www.comet.net/personal/landru/kids/guestbk/penpal1.htm**) draws an international crowd. Kyleen's Kids World allows children all over the world to communicate with each other through a pen pal directory (see Figure 3.6). In addition to including pen pal information, Kids World features game, story, and art content.

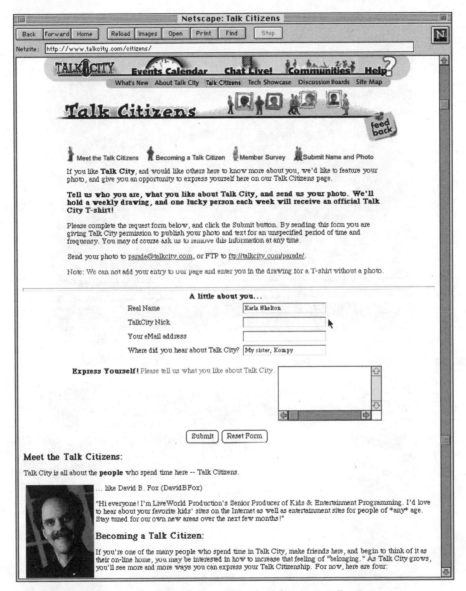

Figure 3.5 Filling out the friendly membership form at Talk City.

GeoCities

GeoCities organizes members by interest. The architects at GeoCities accomplished this by designing "neighborhoods." Residents build Web pages, which are placed in one of thirty themed communities based on the content of their home page. A membership directory, shown in Figure 3.7, allows visitors to browse pages by neighborhood.

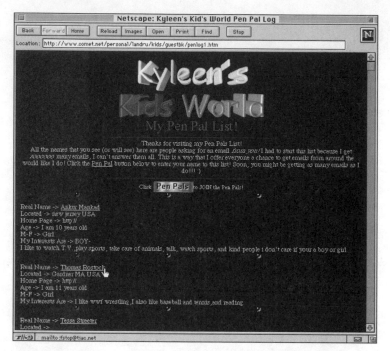

Figure 3.6 Scanning the pen pal directory at Kyleen's Kids World.

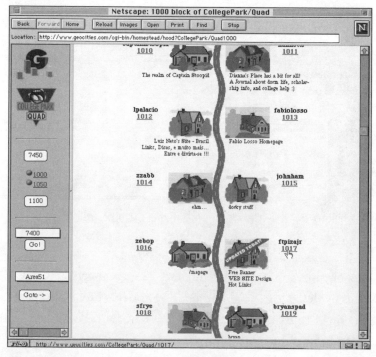

Figure 3.7 Browsing a GeoCities neighborhood.

The WELL

The WELL went a step further by including member profiles in its directory (see Figure 3.8). The profiles contain such pertinent information as age, geographical location, interests, likes and dislikes, favorite conferences, favorite URLs, and contact information. If you specify the URL for a personal Web page, the page will appear in a frame at the bottom of the browser.

ESTABLISH A WAY TO DEAL WITH CONFLICT

The best way to encourage camaraderie and friendship is to "manage gently." People won't appreciate a heavy-handed approach, but processes do need to be in place so members can learn to deal with uncomfortable or hostile situations. Chapter 14 will provide more information about handling troublesome citizens.

PROVIDE HOSTED OR FOCUSED CHAT

Guided conversations are less likely to degenerate into "Who are you? What do you look like?"

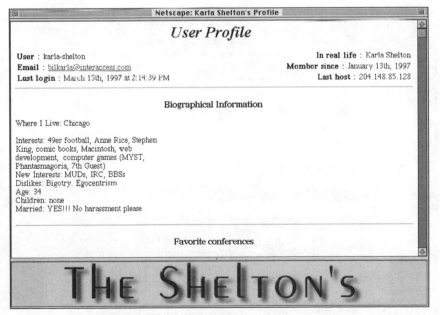

Figure 3.8 Karla's user profile at The Well.

Talk.com

Talk.com (**www.talk.com**), created by Wired Ventures, is a Java-based Internet chat system available to HotWired community members only. Becoming a member is free. Talk.com boasts several focused areas, such as Head Space, Electronic Frontiers, and Doc Talk, each hosted by a regular moderator. Moderators facilitate the conversation between special guests and the general audience.

CREATE INTEREST SPACES

Develop different rooms for different areas of concern. This tactic combines information with socialization.

Talk City

Talk City offers forums based on interests. Take a look at Figure 3.9. Talk City's experience has shown that when groups of people with like interests find each other through realtime communication, they often want to create communities with more permanence and room for growth than you find in a typical chat room. Within Talk City, you'll find a number of such communities.

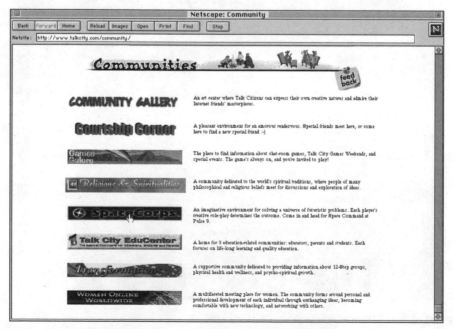

Figure 3.9 The community forums available on Talk City.

WBS

In addition to providing interest spaces based on subject matter, or *chat hubs*, WBS allows members to create private spaces, as shown in Figure 3.10. These spaces can be used for one-on-one conversations with a friends, for business meetings, or even for romantic interludes. The "private rooms" icon on just about any WBS page makes it easy to create such a space, and you can use the Private Message system to tell your friends about your private room.

GUIDE NEW MEMBERS AND FIRST-TIME VISITORS

Kim highly recommends making your guests feel comfortable in their new environment. This can be achieved through three primary methods: posting standards of behavior, creating a tour of your site, and developing a buddy system. Since standards vary from community to community, you can post a visitor's guideline about acceptable behavior for your community. Talk City for example, posts extensive guidelines.

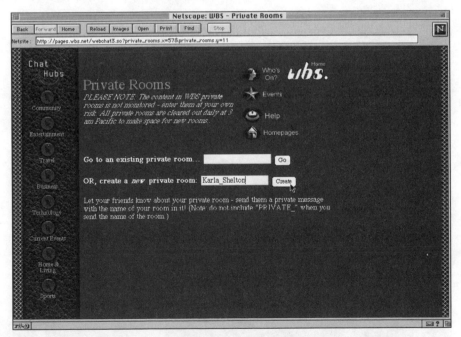

Figure 3.10 Creating a private room on the WBS site.

Finch Nest

A tour is a friendly way to "hold the hand" of a new visitor while explaining your community's mission, navigation method, features, and benefits. At the Finch Nest Palace site, Finchy, the creator of this virtual world, developed an automatic tour (shown in Figure 3.11) that guides users through the site. This tour was generated through an advanced script; see Chapter 8 for details on how to implement this feature on your Palace site.

For Web sites, try placing a "Click here for a tour of our site" statement on your home page. This feature can be easily generated through hyperlinks on your Web pages and will be discussed in Chapter 4.

CREATE MULTIPLE JOB ROLES

You can build strong community ties with your members by giving responsibility to individuals who want to get more involved. They can host a chat, maintain an area, or greet new members.

Figure 3.11 Taking an automated tour at the Finch Nest.

IRC Ops

When you create and register an IRC chat channel, you are automatically granted SOP, or Super Operator, status. That's a fancy way of saying that you control every aspect of the channel, from content to conduct. You can change channel topics, kick out and ban unruly guests, invite others in, and give and take voice from users, among other things. Unfortunately, you can be there all day and all night to run the show. That's why IRC gives SOPs a very cool power. You can grant your power to any other community member who you think deserves it. They become AOP or Automatic Operators. Being granted "Ops" is an honor on IRC, and your Ops can help maintain the community.

Palace Wizards

The Palace software's Wizard feature allows people to become active in Palace-based communities. As Chapter 6 will show, Wizards (see Figure 3.12) are power-users

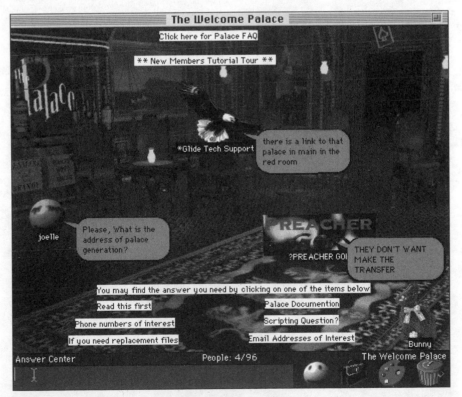

Figure 3.12 A Wizard at the Welcome Palace (**palace://welcome .palace.com**) assisting a new user.

who've been entrusted with additional responsibilities. They have the ability to create and destroy rooms, and to ban unruly users. Some Wizards are interested in helping to design the site, while others prefer to manage the socialization within a site by greeting and helping new visitors, developing special events, and hosting forums.

HOLD REGULARLY SCHEDULED EVENTS

Scheduled events encourage continuity, which adds stability to your community. Make it easy for your guests to find your events: Schedule them, and stick to the schedule.

Electric Minds

The Electric Minds calendar in Figure 3.13 shows that this site not only hosts many events throughout the month, but the events are scheduled consistently.

Talk.com

Talk.com hosts regular chat events, such as Electronic Frontiers, a forum for discussion of techno-culture and digital activism, and a gathering place for netizens

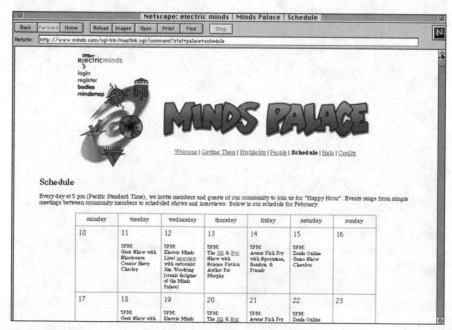

Figure 3.13 A schedule of events from Electric Minds.

Figure 3.14 Cyberrights expert Mike Godwin keeps online users up-to-date about legal issues at Talk.com.

to discuss social, political, theoretical, and practical issues of frontiers in cyberspace. (See Figure 3.14.) Electronic Frontiers is hosted by journalist/activist Jon Lebkowsky (jonl@hotwired.com), formerly of FringeWare Inc. and a founding member of the Texas chapter of the Electronic Frontier Foundation. The forum is hosted every Thursday at 6 P.M. PST.

CHANGE VISUALS SEASONALLY

It's important to establish cyclical rhythms that tie into the rhythms of people's lives. Ongoing communities mark the passage of time and give members the feeling of sharing that time.

Firebird's Forest

Special rooms were created during the month of December to encourage members to spread holiday cheer. Look at the happy Bunny sharing Christmas cheer with Santa in Figure 3.15. Members shared season's greetings with one another, and traded shopping tips.

Figure 3.15 Exchanging season's greetings at Firebird's Forest.

A Few More Tips To Consider

Here are some lessons we've learned from our past journeys in cyberspace.

DIVERSITY IS THE KEY TO SUCCESSFUL COMMUNITIES

Don't be too limiting in the scope of your community topics. Snowboarding or skiing, for example, are very precise topics that will not attract a diverse group, but rather a narrow group. However, outdoor recreation will open your community up to a nice broad mixture of potential citizens.

AVOID THE WALLFLOWER SYNDROME

When you start your community, handpick some folks from other communities you've been involved with to spearhead conversation and discussion. No one dances at the prom until someone dances first. It's up to you to get the ball rolling.

DON'T LIMIT LENGTH

If you choose to include discussion boards or threads in your community, don't limit the length of members' posts. Sometimes a post will get windy, but that's part of communicating. It's better to let a member be satisfied that they got their point across, than to have them feel stifled by an arbitrary length restriction. You'll discover that most postings will be brief anyway—the occasional verbose diatribe will not adversely affect your discussion group.

THE ANNALS OF TIME

When a new member arrives in your community, they will get a better idea of what your group is all about if they can look at your history. Also, established members will enjoy looking up past archived debates in order to reflect on their participation there, or maybe to blast an opponent in a heated debate (and heated debate is a good thing: it's cathartic and fun).

KEEP CITIZENS HAPPY AND INTERESTED

The WELL is a great example here. Their core membership of about 200 have been online since the beginning. This gives The WELL a real community feeling and has fostered many long-lasting relationships. Keeping content and discussion fresh and calling on your resources (other people) to help keep activities going will make members want to stay. Palace site owners use their Wizards for this.

By now, you should be well on the way to fleshing out your initial ideas into a full-fledged community plan. Now let's start looking at where you will host your community.

Home Is Where The HTML Is

Most of you reading this don't have the luxury of high-powered, dedicated servers and/or high bandwidth connectivity to your home or office, as these require much expense and many resources.

Taking the path of least resistance, you'll want to investigate your current Internet service provider (ISP), since most ISPs provide a minimum amount of disk space for free. Typically, this is the easiest and most cost-effective solution for housing a community. First, we'll show you how to find an ISP, and what you should look for in a host. Next, we'll introduce you to alternative ways to house your community.

SHOPPING FOR YOUR ISP

The ISP you're using to connect to the Internet may not be the ideal place to host your dynamic Web community. Obtain at least three quotes from ISPs before making a hosting decision. If you're having problems locating ISPs, these resources should help.

Internet Directories

A plethora of ISP directories exist on the Web. Some of them are searchable by area code; others are listed alphabetically by state. These indexes are a good place to begin your hunt:

- Mecklermedia's The List—**www.thelist.com**

- Yahoo—**www.yahoo.com/Business_and_Economy/Companies/Internet_Services/Internet_Access_Providers**

- Celestin Company's POCIA (Providers of Commercial Internet Access)—**www.celestin.com/pocia**

If your community is established as a nonprofit organization, you may want to look at the PDIAL Web site (**www.pdial.com/public-access/PDIAL-By-Section**).

Internet Reviews

Cnet (**www.cnet.com/Content/Reviews/Compare/ISP**) has compiled a great handbook for selecting and comparing ISPs. They've provided vital statistics on national and local ISPs, and they let you read what other users think of their current provider in the Rate Your ISP section.

Local User Groups

There's a good chance that organized computer/Internet user groups have formed in your area. These groups are a literal gold mine of information. Check your local phone book or newspaper for information, or check out Yahoo (**www.yahoo.com/**

Computers_and_Internet/Internet/User_Groups and www.yahoo.com/ Computers_and_Internet/Personal_Computers/User_Groups).

Magazines And Resource Guides

Boardwatch magazine is an excellent resource. *Boardwatch* publishes, in print and on the Web, an Internet Service Providers guide. Call 1-800-933-6038 to order, or visit **www.boardwatch.com**.

GROCERY LIST OF CONSIDERATIONS

Now that you have a list of three or more ISPs to interview, run through the list below and answer the questions for each ISP on your list:

- *Points of Presence*—Since you'll be spending much of your time managing and governing your community, you'll want to find an ISP that has a Point of Presence (POP) geographically near you to minimize any access charges. How many POPs does your ISP offer, and where are they located?

- *Size of pipeline*—Your ISP is typically connected to the Internet backbone by T1 and/or T3 lines. What bandwidth does your provider have?

A Warning From Todd And Karla

Listen up, this is important. Some ISPs brag about having two, three, five, or more T1 or T3 connections, but this can be deceptive. If a client of the ISP has a dedicated T1 or T3 to their business, the ISP may include that line in the line count, but can you use it? Of course not! Demand a straight answer, "How many lines to the Internet backbone do you have?" Also remember, more lines may not be better. An ISP with one line and few users might be able to offer better service than an ISP with three lines, but thousands of users.

- *Space*—ISPs usually bundle approximately 5MB of space for Web content. Are mail, log files, and system programs counted in the allotted disk space? For a growing community, you'll want more than 5MB, so shop around for the best deal.

- *CGI-bin access*—Do you have access to programs in a CGI-bin directory to run various community operations, such as guestbooks, forms, and database queries?

Get The Edge

One of the larger and more aggressive ISPs, Netcom, has announced support for and integration of Lotus's family of Domino Applications. This suite provides you with tools for modifying ready-to-use applications so you can build an interactive home page and create a virtual private community. Although this is not an endorsement, we do want to emphasize that some ISPs will offer advanced, cutting-edge services and programs, and others will not. Again, it pays to shop around.

- *Virtual hosting*—Can you have your own domain name? Nearly every ISP offers "virtual hosting"—rather than use your ISP's domain name with a subdirectory designating your site, such as **http://www.isp.com/mycommunity**, your address would be **http://www.mycommunity.com**. You definitely want to take advantage of virtual hosting, so pay the $100, if you can afford it, to obtain a domain name. Consider it an investment in growing your community and building continuity.

- *Email aliases*—How many email mailboxes may you set up? Many ISPs allow you to set up multiple "aliases" such as **mayor@mycommunity.com** or **support@mycommunity.com**. Also ask if different aliases can be forwarded to more than one email address.

- *Quality of service*—The Internet never shuts down. Does your ISP offer 24/7 support—24 hours a day, 7 days a week? Does your ISP guarantee turnaround times for support? How many support technicians does your ISP employ? Are backup services available? Also, some smaller ISPs may not be able to provide 24/7 live support, but by trading that off you might find more personal one-to-one service. Is being on a first name basis with your ISP important to you? Don't discount an ISP only because it's small.

Check Your ISP's Pedigree

We recommend that you check references. You can ask for a list, but you'll probably get names that have been screened by the ISP. Instead, check out user pages. Typically, an ISP will publish an index of businesses, organizations, and individuals using their service; select a random number of sites, obtain contact information, and start asking questions.

- *Costs*—How does your ISP calculate costs? Vince Emery, in his book *How To Grow Your Business On The Internet, Third Edition* (ISBN 1-57610-171-1, Coriolis Group Books) offers advice that's applicable to community builders:

"The costs to watch out for are transaction-based. If you put your home page on a provider's computer, it is reasonable to pay for the disk real estate you use, and an amount for maintenance. But your provider pays a flat monthly rate for its Internet access, and it is unreasonable for you to be charged each time someone visits your page. You should smile when someone reads your Web page, not cringe at the additional expense. When you budget for a Web site, watch out for charges that are per hit, per access, or per mega-byte transferred."

- *Stability of host*—Many ISPs have come and gone during the Web boom. How long has your ISP been in business? Has it been the subject of complaints to the Better Business Bureau or your state's Attorney General's office? How long have other individuals or businesses used this provider? This last one can be a tough question. If an ISP has been around for five years, in Web life, that's a long time.

DO YOU WANT A T1 TO YOUR HOUSE?

A dedicated line is a great idea for a well-established company (or a millionaire hobbyist), but they are very expensive. A dedicated ISDN line is considerably more manageable, but still not a good idea for someone who isn't planning to use their Web presence as a money-making tool. Don't jump into dedicated lines without thoroughly researching the costs, the requirements, the technical knowledge you'll need, and definitely not without having a plan to pay for it all.

A GOOD COMPROMISE

With a co-located Web server, you install your own computer at your ISP's facility, which is then connected to the Internet using a high-speed line such as a T1 or T3. You gain all the benefits of a high-speed connection, without the high costs of a leased line to your home or office. This avenue may be appealing if you plan to evolve your community into a profit-making business model or if you want to involve a high degree of complexity with tools from your community toolbox (like specialized CGI scripts or VRML server applications). With your own server at your ISP's physical location, you can set up electronic commerce and other advanced operations. Remember, you can still do most maintenance to your co-located server through a dial-up account from your home.

System Requirements

The box that you purchase obviously needs to be better than your garden-variety PC. Here are four general recommendation for a high-end Web server solution:

- *Sun SPARC*—Considered the *de facto* standard by many Information Technology experts.

- *Intel-based Unix workstation*—Minimum of 16MB of RAM, Pentium P-60, or P-90 processor and at least 1GB of hard disk space.

- *Windows NT Server*—Minimum of 24MB of RAM, a P-90, and at least 1GB of hard disk space.

- *Others*—SGI, Apple, and HP-UX are other possible configurations.

Check with your ISP for their exact system requirements, since they may vary from the previous list. In addition, they will probably require a 10BaseT Ethernet port and TCP/IP networking.

Costs

Besides the cost of the computer, your ISP will assess charges for connectivity to your server. There will also be a one-time installation charge of about $350 or more, depending on the ISP. Other charges to consider:

- Monthly rent

- Usage charge on all data moving to and from your server. This may include all forms of data, including Web, FTP, and mailing lists.

- Additional IP addresses

YOUR PERSONAL COMPUTER AS A HOST

The age of personal empowerment is here—some of the applications in your community toolbox, such as Palace, allow you to turn your personal computer into a server or host. If the purpose of your community is to invite personal friends or family over for a reunion or party, this may be the simplest solution for you.

The benefits are many. You have:

- *Administrative control*—Allows you to extend remote access privileges to your community leaders or assistants, or to change passwords if there is a security hazard.

- *Content control*—Allows you to make changes to your community when you want and how you want.

- *Server control*—Allows you to add memory to your computer, update your operating system, or upgrade your processing power, whenever you feel the need.

Drawbacks exist, however. Your community may experience slow connect and/or throughput speeds, or you may not have the resources required to maintain the server. Smaller, more intimate communities have found a compromise—house part of the community on an ISP and part of it on a personal computer. Web pages are suited for ISP hosting, but many ISPs will not allow you to set up chat servers or other interactive applications. Some chat and conferencing software may run well on your PC instead. Our advice? Start slow and begin building your community. Then reassess your situation. If you need higher-end solutions such as co-location, you'll have acquired the experience to make that decision.

We Have Our Tools, Let's Start Building

Okay, we've looked over a variety of nifty tools, gotten a head full of ideas about our communities, and taken a hard look at ISPs. In the next chapter, we'll look at design and content and we'll get you started on your Web site. We'll also show you some places to get free (yes, free) Web pages. We'll look at how to marry style and content to best suit your community. So, turn a few pages, and we'll see you there.

Chapter 4

Creating The Foundation
Of Your Community

Chapter 4

- Brainstorming

- Creating And Acquiring Content

- Implementing Smart Web Site Design

- Managing A Growing Site

- Avoiding Crisis

CREATING THE FOUNDATION OF YOUR COMMUNITY

Chapter 4

Content: The Foundation Of A Strong Community

Every structure needs a solid foundation. Providing the initial content to your community members is like pouring the concrete that your community will rest on. You need to have something for people to talk about; to bind them together in a cohesive environment. Apple learned this the hard way with eWorld, Apple's entry into the proprietary online service provider market. Not only did the service have lots of management problems, which we'll address in Chapter 14, but eWorld also suffered because it didn't attract enough publishers to provide interesting or compelling information to its member base. In a manner of speaking, eWorld was too thin. And the situation worsened: Paradoxically, Apple needed content, but potential content providers weren't interested in a community with so few members. So Apple needed members, but people weren't interested in a community with so little content. It was a classic catch-22.

In this chapter, we'll look at brainstorming, presenting, organizing, and generating content—and finally, how to manage all the content your community will generate.

Coming Up With Ideas

Because Web site design is dictated by content, you'll need to start things off by defining what your content will be. It would be a shame to invest valuable time and energy in Web and navigational system design, only to discover in the end that your concept fails to do anything for your content.

But developing content can be difficult, especially when you're staring at a blank computer screen with an equally blank mind. Try a brainstorming session to get you over those pesky brain freezes. While you're brainstorming, don't throw away any ideas just because they seem silly, or perhaps too technically complicated. Remember pet rocks? How many people have discarded ideas like that because they were just too crazy? Try to think of everything that could possibly be unique to your community. You may end up throwing out a lot of ideas in the long run, but what you have left at the end of the process could be the basis for that strong foundation. Take a look at the following list, in which we've sketched out some ideas for a kitchen remodeling community, hosted by a theoretical design firm, The Kitchen Place:

- Cabinetry and Countertops

- Design Services

- Recipes

- Contests/Promotions

- Appliances and Fixtures

- Designer Biographies

- 3D Design Gallery

- Design Portfolio

- Buying Tips

- Ask the Designer/Installer

- Showroom Virtual Tour

- Trade Show Calendar

- Schedule an Appointment

- Driving Instructions/Interactive Map to the Studio

- Client Testimonials

- Java-Based "Put Away The Dishes" Game

- Kitchen Planning Guide

- "Advice from Previous Customers" Discussion Board

- Kitchen Planning Theory

- Links to Other Sites of Interest

- The Installation Process

- How to Survive Kitchen Remodeling Guidebook

- Kitchen Design Software

- What Style Is Perfect For You? Quiz

- Company Information

- Customer Surveys

- RealAudio Infotainment Broadcast

- Java-Based Design Your Own Kitchen Online

- Do-It-Yourself Tips

- Refrigerator Art (artwork of customer's children)

- Payment Plans/Financing

- Kitchens of the Artists (Dali, Rembrandt, Picasso)

This list took less than 10 minutes to generate. It was relatively easy, since the community had a theme. As stated in the previous chapter, your theme is derived from your mission statement, which describes what your community *is*.

BUT I'M STILL HAVING A BRAIN FREEZE

You might want to consider investing in a brilliant tool called the *Creative Whack Pack* (U.S. Games Systems, Inc., 1988, ISBN 0-88079-358-9), a deck of cards created by Roger von Oech. The idea behind the cards is simple: Whenever you're stuck, you deal a card, which provides you with direction, advice, or inspiration of some sort to spur your brain into bypassing the freeze-up. Each card isolates a single principle of creative thinking. By the way, Roger is president and founder of Creative Think, a consulting company whose mission is to stimulate creativity and innovation in business. His clients have included Apple, Coca-Cola, Disney, Intel, MTV, Microsoft, PepsiCo, Procter & Gamble, Sony, and the U.S. Air War College.

An Online Head Whacker

*If you point your browser to **www.kinecomm.com**, you'll discover an online, Java-based tool to whack your head with. (See Figure 4.1.) We shamelessly nabbed one example; hiding behind the shield of "fair use," we present it here. This Creative Whack Pack parable is called "Get Out Of Your Box:"*

"Each culture has its own way of looking at the world. Often the best ideas come from looking across disciplinary boundaries and looking into other fields. As Robert Wieder put it, 'Anyone can look for fashion in a boutique or history in a museum. The creative explorer looks for history in a hardware store and fashion in an airport.' Example: World War I military designers borrowed from the cubist art of Picasso to create more efficient camouflage patterns for tanks."

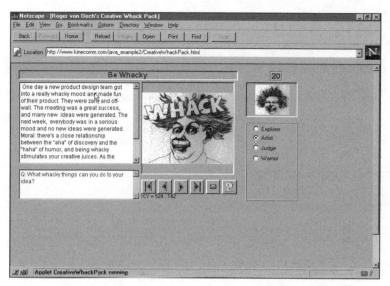

Figure 4.1 Thawing out a brain freeze with the Creative Whack Pack online applet.

Dividing And Conquering Content

After you've finished brainstorming, you can begin the process of "weeding out" and organizing. From our list, we can generate a few primary content categories, such as "About The Kitchen Studio," "Products And Services," "How To Buy A Kitchen," and "Mother Hubbard's Cupboard." A general rule of thumb is to divide your community into no more than seven main sections, to avoid overwhelming your visitors with too many decisions. Some designers don't understand that sometimes less is better than more, so they'll cram as much content on the home page as possible. It's preferable to build a pyramid-like hierarchy, presenting just the top level on your home page. Many community builders create flowcharts that depict this structure.

Next, you'll want to organize your list into subcategories. For instance, you could collate all the "cool" stuff like Refrigerator Art and Design Your Own Kitchen Online within Mother Hubbard's Cupboard.

We're not saying this process is the only way to tackle the organizational process of your site, but it's wise to establish the structure of your community before you begin. Once the skeleton is in place, you'll need to decide how the actual content will be generated.

Keeping The Virtual Shelves Well Stocked

Content is everything on the Internet, and it needs to stay fresh. That means making new content available all the time. In speaking with various builders of virtual communities, we found five basic ways of generating content:

- Inviting member-generated content

- Hiring in-house editorial staff

- Obtaining content through partners

- Soliciting content from guest columnists

- Reprinting/licensing existing material

In the following sections, we'll illustrate each method with examples from About Work (**www.aboutwork.com**), a community developed by iVillage. iVillage describes About Work as an "office away from the office—a place to scream, laugh, get good advice, or meet others who are equally obsessed, thrilled, frustrated, or completely gaga about work."

MEMBERS: YOUR BUILT-IN EDITORIAL STAFF

Content generated by your members is not only the most valuable and informative content, but also probably the easiest to collect and archive. Unlike features or editorial pieces written by "experts," the "collective expertise" of your members forms a knowledge base that no individual could ever hope to acquire. The authors of *net.gain* agree.

John Hagel III And Arthur G. Armstrong, Authors Of *net.gain*

"In many cases, the value may not be so much in the experience and knowledge of any one individual, but in the comparative experiences and perspectives of many individuals. A good example of this concept

are the Zagat's guides that have become a staple for restaurant-goers across the United States. The value of these guides is not that they present the perspective of one expert but that they provide us with a broad cross-section of perspectives and experiences of people who share a passion for food.

"It is precisely this kind of expertise and experience that virtual communities do such a good job of marshaling. No combination of 'published' experts could match the collective insight and experience of a community of people who share a passionate interest."

So how can you accumulate and deliver the "collective insight and experience" of your community members? To illustrate a few possibilities, let's turn our attention to iVillage's community, About Work.

Discussion Forums

Discussion forums are a great thing. Messages are stored in a database, ready for the next user to read or reply to, and as we saw in Chapter 3, discussion threads allow conversations to be tracked over a long period of time. About Work has used this model extensively. Figure 4.2 shows the section Across The Board, offering places to talk with other visitors about Jobs, Work from Home, Start-Up Dreams, Career Planning, and Office Stuff. Across The Board also provides a Tax Center and a place to Gripe & Groan.

Voting

Whether participating in a David Letterman-esque man-on-the-street poll, or an exit poll from a voting booth, people love to voice their opinion. And they also like to see what other people think. About Work presents "Today's Poll" every weekday, as shown in Figure 4.3.

After readers vote on the topic of the day, they can see how other people voted (Figure 4.4), or they can comment on the topic in the Share Your Thoughts section. And if all this current content isn't enough, members can rifle through the Poll archives.

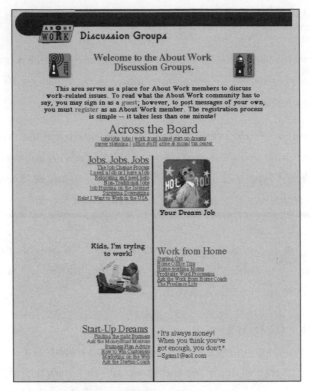

Figure 4.2 About Work's Across the Board discussion-group areas provide much member-generated content.

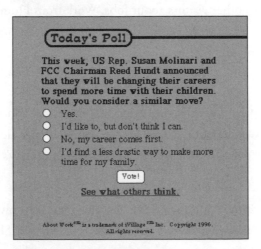

Figure 4.3 Today's Poll generates a plethora of member-generated content about controversial issues.

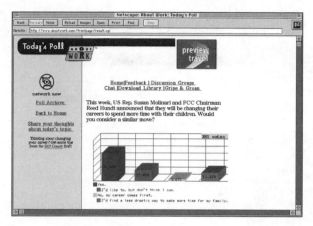

Figure 4.4 Members can see how other people voted.

Surveys

More in-depth than voting, surveys can glean a rich trove of information from your community members. These surveys can be designed for a number of purposes, including entertainment, market research, cerebral efforts such as academic research, or financial rewards, as we'll discuss later in Chapter 14.

In a survey conducted by About Work (Figure 4.5), the project was clearly geared toward market research—would community members be interested in taking classes in a new online school? If there's enough interest, the survey will also provide pertinent information that will help iVillage create the courses, and by extension the content, that its members really want and need.

Sound-Offs

People love to complain. This phenomenon has been greatly leveraged by local newspapers with "sound-off" columns, where readers may mail or phone in their opinions. These statements can be anonymous, which is a radical departure from the policies of traditional op/ed sections, where each letter must be signed before it will be considered for publication. The cloud of anonymity in a sound-off column allows participants to express their true feelings. About Work realizes this and offers a fun (and revealing) section called Gripe & Groan, shown in Figure 4.6, where members can grumble about coworkers from hell, the never-ending work day, ridiculous company policies, and more.

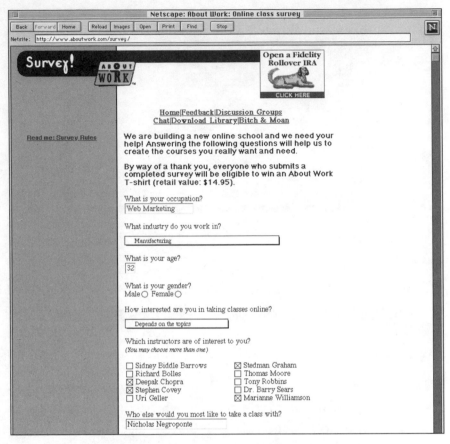

Figure 4.5   iVillage conducts market research online.

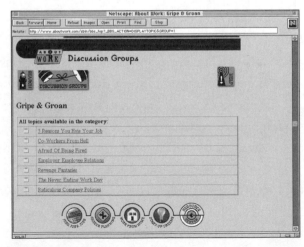

Figure 4.6   About Work members really let off steam in the Gripe & Groan section.

Quizzes

Ubiquitous in the pages of self-improvement magazines, quizzes allow people a glimpse into their own psyche. For some reason, Americans find this tantalizing. As a community builder, you can take advantage of this by giving a short test that provides the participant with a helpful nugget of information. In Figure 4.7, About Work dishes out a quiz that lets members discover whether they have what it takes to start their own business.

Q&A

Well, About Work decided to include the "experts" in its virtual community after all. But rather than writing long editorials, the experts offer their opinions in an interactive question-and-answer format, as shown in Figure 4.8. As John Katz stated so eloquently in the Foreword to this book, columnists, academics, and politicians rarely get the last word online—your community members do.

IN-HOUSE WRITERS

In addition to integrating member-generated content, you'll also want to include original editorial material. If you're working with a small group of writers, divide

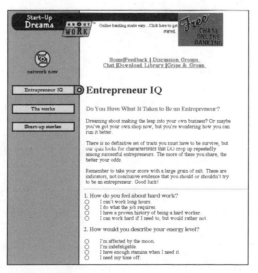

Figure 4.7 Entrepreneurial wannabes take a short test in About Work to see if they have the savvy to start their own business.

Figure 4.8 Members pose questions to the expert panel of About Work.

the tasks of writing copy among the group, beginning with the basics: your mission statement, the community tour, and your community's standards of behavior.

Of course, not just anybody can be a writer. If you aren't starting out with professional writers, make sure the in-house writers you recruit meet certain requirements: a strong command of language, the ability to meet deadlines, a willingness to research their topics, and above all, the ability to express ideas clearly and succinctly.

Tips On Writing Style

Although this advice may seem straightforward, it's often overlooked. Your writers will need to slant their writing styles to speak to your audience. If your site is devoted to a very specific theme or topic, there's nothing wrong with using industry-specific jargon and acronyms, especially if that's the normal lingo. But you may also want to consider including a definitions page, so that casual visitors who stumble across your community can learn something, too.

Don't Write Too Much

Web surfers don't want to read. Reading speeds are 25 percent slower on computer screens than on paper. That's understandable, of course, staring at a computer screen can be quite a strain on the eyes. But that doesn't mean you should write 25 percent less than you'd write on paper—it means you should write 50 percent less! Surfers tend to skip over any text that they perceive as fluff.

Having And Using A Consistent Voice

It's vital to write with a consistent "voice." References like *The Webster's Unabridged Dictionary* and *The Chicago Manual of Style* define standards for style and usage issues like capitalization, spelling, and hyphenation. These standards exist because language, and in particular written language, is the primary form of communication, and your written material is the primary means of communicating what your site is about.

Slang and colloquial expressions are fine in non-formal writing, as long as you're certain that your audience will understand them. You are likely to be the best judge of that, as you probably know your audience. Still, it's a good idea to have your copy proofread by two people who know nothing about your virtual community project, and whom you trust will be honest in their critique. Listen to what they have to say, and don't be defensive about your writing. If they don't understand it, neither will others, and you should adjust it as necessary.

Another Reason To Avoid Slang And Colloquialism

Did you know that engines exist on the Web that instantly translate sites into different languages? With this in mind, be sparing with your use of colloquialisms and nonstandard language and syntax. Translating text into a foreign language is a difficult process at best, and your site may be translated without your knowledge. If you use standard language, the engines can generate better translations. Also, translated text can grow to be 50 percent larger than typical English text, and the direction of reading (right to left, left to right, up to down, or down to up) can change during the translation process as well. Keep these points in mind when you design your layout.

The "About" Section

It's a nice idea to credit the people who devote time and resources to your community project. In Figure 4.9, the leaders at About Work highlight the efforts of their core team. This is an especially good idea if you have lots of volunteer community leaders, where a pat on the back is a substitute for cash payment. This is also the place for information about your community, organization, or company that goes beyond the mission statement. Other ideas to consider include:

• A press room, complete with press releases, downloadable logos and collateral materials, fact sheets, and press registration forms

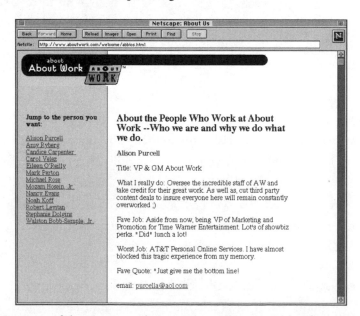

Figure 4.9 One of the many credits given to a community leader at About Work.

- Legal and copyright information

- Advertiser and sponsor information

Keeping In Touch

It's a great idea to create an email link just for your community's site, so that members can contact you directly. However, it's a bad idea to have just one email address. Suppose your email address is me@mysite.com, and that's the only address you have. Everyone will write to you there: Folks with complaints, folks with questions, folks with business to transact, mailing lists you subscribe to, your personal friends and family... they'll all be sending mail to that one box. It'll be unwieldy, to say the least! Even if there's nobody there but you, have an email address for comments, one for business, one for the editor, and whatever others you need—and one that is your personal address, not published on your site, so that when your father emails you about the fishing trip next week, it won't be lost among 500 other assorted messages.

References And Resources

Considered a staple on just about every Web site, launch pads to other resources on the Net can provide your community members with more information about a particular subject. In Figure 4.10, About Work furnishes its members with a comprehensive hot-link list to career-related sites, ranging from job hunters to career builders to entrepreneurs. Each week, the editorial staff swaps out the "hottest site" with fresh material to encourage repeat visits to the site.

Special Interest Material

Here's where your staff can show off their writing skills, and where you'll be able to make the biggest impact in your field of interest. About Work has done this by developing the Jobs, Jobs, Jobs section, where they've written about important topics like resumes and cover letters, networking and interviewing, and hot jobs.

PARTNERING UP FOR CONTENT

Partners can be an asset not only financially (see Chapter 13) or promotionally (see Chapter 12), but they can be a great source of content as well. Let's take a look at

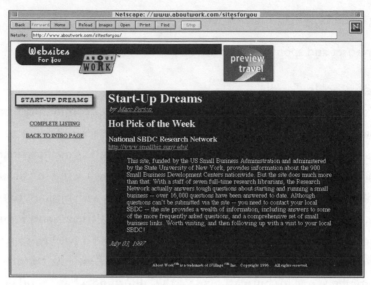

Figure 4.10   About Work assembled a launch pad of useful links to places like job-bank databases and other career-building sites.

the About Work site again, shown in Figure 4.11. In a partnership with Hoover's Online, a database consisting of contact information for businesses, About Work delivers a significant chunk of value-added content to its community members. Users can not only search for the address, phone, fax, Web site, and names of major company officers—including the Human Resources Director—but they can read Company Capsules, which give job seekers a "leg up" with timely information about a company, such as financial information and news stories.

If you scour the Web, you're likely to find your own opportunities as well. One of them might be the partner program offered by InfoSpace, an Internet directory service that offers co-branding opportunities to small and large sites alike. Your community members may find it helpful to have extensive international databases, ranging from email address and business directories to city guides, easily accessible from your Web site. With it's co-branding program, InfoSpace incorporates your look and feel into the "return" information, so that users feel as if they'd never left your site. For more information, take a look at **in-151.infospace.com/ _1_112270549__info/pbi/cobrand.htm**.

Opportunities for smaller communities exist as well. Look toward trade associations, local government, civic groups, clubs, and other groups for content. We've

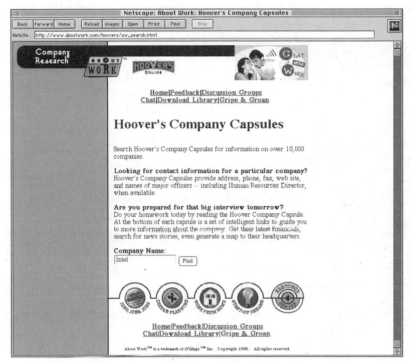

Figure 4.11 By partnering with Hoover's Online, About Work offers its members crucial value-added content.

observed collegiate communities partnering with local Chambers of Commerce to make hotel, restaurant, and transportation information available to new students and their parents, and we've seen geographically based virtual communities partnering with local companies to offer business directories.

GUEST COLUMNISTS ADD SPICE

Bringing guest columnists onboard can add variety and diversity to the editorial content of your community. Even if the intention of your community is to spark controversy, a unique perspective is sometimes necessary to add a breath of fresh air. And since guest columnists are usually paid by the column, you aren't bound to a fixed expense as you are with an in-house staff.

In its Career Makeover section, About Work invited Hope Dlugozima to write about Susan Molinari, a legislator who became a CBS anchor, in a feature article entitled "Blueprint for Change" (see Figure 4.12). Since they rely heavily on hot

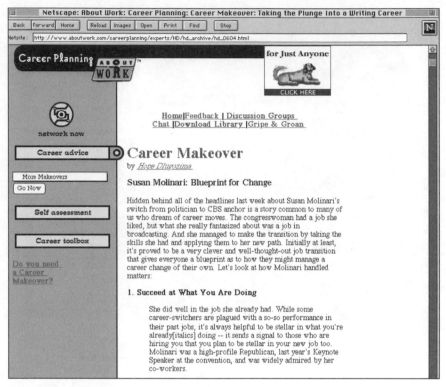

Figure 4.12 Hope Dlugozima, guest columnist for About Work, writes about making a career move.

topics of the day, About Work utilizes this method often. Bringing in an "expert" adds to the caliber of the content. And, to create a synergistic effect, the guest columns are typically linked to discussion boards and/or "ask the experts" sections.

Who Should You Invite?

Look beyond the obvious. If your site is devoted to the political environment within Chicago, it would certainly be appropriate to ask Mayor Richard Daley Jr. to write a column about the Democratic National Convention. But it would be equally informational, and maybe even more revealing, to ask a cab driver or a homeless person to give his or personal experience and insights about this same topic.

MATERIAL ADAPTED FROM OTHER MEDIUMS

Looking for content that would satisfy the growing needs of their readers, About Work cast their eye on *Fast Company*, a groundbreaking magazine documenting and speculating about the revolutions in business. About Work made a wise decision in "going out of house" to obtain an article entitled "Getting Out Of The Corporate Red Box." The material is timely, innovative, and of great importance to the members of About Work. On a side note, if you're in business and you don't read *Fast Company*, now is a good time to start (**www.fastcompany.com**).

Don't Forget The Permission Slips

Make sure you CYA ("Cover Your Avatar")—send out a permission slip to be signed by the author or publisher of the content you wish to reprint. Of course, be sure to check with a lawyer before you send anything out.

Where To Find Material

You're in luck—the Web is one big virtual archive, with terabytes (that's a thousand gigabytes) of potential content that you can use on your site. Start checking magazines, both digital and print, for ideas. Search through the scholarly works at academic institutions; thesis papers and reports often prove valuable. (In fact, we used this tactic to find content for Chapter 7.) Nonprofit organizations, such as civic groups, are a gold mine of information. And the biggest content generator of them all? The U S government. Here's how you can get *free* content from the government to publish on your Web site.

Government Documents In The Public Domain

It's a little-known fact that documents generated by governments (local, state, and federal) are in the public domain. After all, we Americans paid for them with our tax dollars. So if your community has a political theme, it's certainly okay to post the Declaration of Independence or the latest congressional bill on your Web site. If there's a .gov at the end of a URL, the content at that site is yours.

Beyond The Written Word

With the Web, you can go beyond print and develop some really creative content using multimedia. There are many great ideas online for nonwritten-word content, and we'll explore some of the most popular ones here.

YOU'RE ON THE AIR WITH REALAUDIO

Think about producing a "streaming audio" radio show. RealAudio servers are made for both commercial and personal needs, and if your ISP won't allow you to serve these files, some ISPs are offering hosting services just for RealAudio. Most of them charge a monthly fee plus a variable rate, depending on the size of your files.

FROM YOUR BASEMENT IN AURORA, ILLINOIS

Feel like taking the next step to video? You could put your own version of Wayne's World on the Net. You'll need a digital video camera, a video capture card, conferencing software, and a realtime server if you decide to broadcast live. For basic Internet video, U.S. Robotics markets an excellent line of "Big Picture" products that pro-vide everything you need (except for the realtime server) in one package. Connectix's tried and true "Quick Cam" products are also worth checking out, and a trip to any of the major retail computer stores will reveal a growing range of other choices.

About Internet Video

Actual video on the Internet (we're talking about full screen video at 30 frames per second) is still in the future. The technology and bandwidth required are simply out of reach for almost everybody, so don't plan on simulating television on your Web site just yet. Uncompressed NTSC (television) video delivers roughly 100 megabits of data per second. Optimizing this signal for Internet connections would demand a compression ratio of 5,000:1.

On the other hand, the technology available for what is called "streaming video" can provide a reasonable imitation of NTSC video. It can be choppy, and the image is small, but it comes through in realtime with reasonable sound quality.

Progressive Networks (**www.realaudio.com**), the creators of RealAudio, have recently gained notoriety for RealVideo, which can optimize traditional .avi files to simulate realtime video. RealVideo compresses an .avi video file at a ratio of about 250:1, and a browser with the RealVideo plug-in can play the file on the fly, as it downloads. This would allow surfers to access video from your site, or you could broadcast live. To learn more about these possibilities, visit the Progressive Networks site to learn about their server solutions for delivering streaming video.

Of course, there is always a competitor, and in RealVideo's case, it's VDO (**www.vdo.net**). VDO's streaming video solution is another viable product; it's a Netscape plug-in, but it can also serve as a standalone application. Although VDO's technology is older, it appeared on the scene at about the same time as RealAudio. RealAudio gained rapid market penetration, however, and when they released RealVideo early in 1997, they managed to steal some thunder from VDO. The real differences between the two lie in the image size and in the algorithms for bandwidth optimization. VDO works well for low-bandwidth surfers, but RealVideo offers about 30 percent more picture area, and is optimized to perform better at the higher bandwidths that are becoming much more common.

THE RIGHT TOOL FOR THE JOB: SOFTWARE LIBRARIES

Providing useful tools like software can benefit your community members greatly. Suppose your community serves the hordes of people tracing their genealogical roots. Lots of family-tree software, both commercial and shareware, is warehoused on the Internet. Although searching and locating all the potential software is a time-consuming process, the resulting software library would probably be of great value to your members.

It's possible to link externally to the files you find, through a simple **<A HREF>** tag. Simply insert the address of the file you want to make available to your members, and when they click on the link, the file is accessed and downloaded. However, there are two problems with this approach.

The first problem is that if the directory structure of the site you link to changes, you'll have a broken link on your site, and Web surfers hate broken links. That's not good for your reputation. The second problem is more insidious. When you link directly to a downloadable file via an outside server (especially without the permission of the outsider server's administrator), you create additional hits on that server—but those surfers who are downloading the software will never see the content or ad banners on that server. For Web sites that still pay per hit, this can be costly.

To keep peace with your Web neighbors, we suggest you use a different approach: House files locally that you want your members to have access to. Contact the author of an application and ask permission to "mirror" the file, placing a copy of the file on your server. Many freeware and shareware authors will accept, since an arrangement like this will increase the distribution of their product. Be aware that some commercial applications will require a fee, and be sure to maintain communication with the developer in the event that changes or updates are made.

You'll find many general-audience software repositories on the Net. We've listed a handful here to get you going with your research:

- Filepile (**filepile.com**)

- Shareware.com (**www.shareware.com**)

- ZDNet Shareware Library (**www.zdnet.com/downloads/**)

- Jumbo (**www.jumbo.com**)

- Windows 95 (**www.windows95.com**)

- University of Texas Mac Archive (**wwwhost.ots.utexas.edu/mac/main.html**)

- Stroud's Consummate Internet Apps List (**cws.internet.com**)

Linking Files With Filepile

Filepile stores over 1.2 million shareware and freeware files for Windows, Mac, and even OS/2 platforms. Because they exist to serve the community of shareware authors and vendors, they encourage other sites to link to their site for free. They provide free banner graphics (shown in Figure 4.13) and helpful HTML code to cut and paste into your page.

For example, if your community is geared towards astronomy buffs, you might want to provide an educational astronomy program. Skymap 3.0 is a shareware

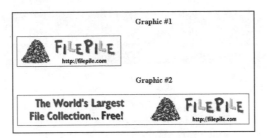

Figure 4.13 These banners help point your site's visitors to a vast software library.

file, available from Filepile, that fits the bill. Filepile offers an advanced method of linking directly to any of their files; because their directory structure changes as files are added, they use a dynamic linking method that prevents broken links. Check out the FAQ on the Filepile home page (**filepile.com**) for details on linking a file or files to your site.

COOL SITES OFFER COOL STUFF

People love playing with gizmos on the Web, from watching Webcams pointed at fish tanks, to playing with the virtual Etch-a-Sketch (**www.codepilot.com/~kbenell/ netsketch/netsketch.html**), to tattooing a digital paperdoll named Mildred (**www.mildred.com**). About Work added some "cool tools" to their arsenal by offering a unique selection of electronic greeting cards. We've seen these cards implemented in a number of ways, but none have been as well done as About Work's version, seen in Figure 4.14. The users not only type in their messages, but they can also select the font style. The postcard is then generated on the fly by a custom CGI script. It's interesting to note that the user's message is created as a graphic, rather than ASCII text, giving the card a highly polished, professional appearance.

DEVELOPING A ONE-TO-ONE RELATIONSHIP WITH YOUR MEMBERS

Don't you feel warm and fuzzy when you enter a Web site and the greeting says, "Hi, So-and-so, glad to see you back for a visit"? A personalized message like this builds a more intimate relationship between you and your community members. Why is this important? First, intimacy deepens the bonds of your community. Second, you want to minimize "churn," the turnover of people within your

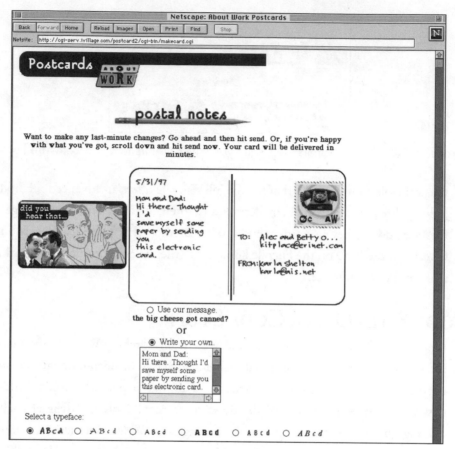

Figure 4.14 About Work offers its members fun and technically innovative electronic postcards to send to coworkers and friends.

community. The online services like AOL battle this problem every day, because it's expensive to constantly be recruiting new members. If you're in the community-building process as a profit-making venture, this is an issue you'll need to pay attention to. Third, as mentioned in the last chapter, solid relationships reinforce continuity. And fourth, relationships build value. All this adds up to keeping people coming back to your site.

CGIs

CGI (Common Gateway Interface) is a technology that allows your Web server to "talk" to a visitor's computer. Powerful scripts enable users to submit forms, interact with image maps, search databases, and even build Web pages online. CGIs also allow you to build personalized content for the end user, like the "Hi So-and-so" example mentioned earlier.

Tracking Visitors With Cookies

Cookies: not tasty snacks eaten with a cool glass of milk, but a system of tracking information about a visitor to a Web site. Netscape, the primary creator of this technology, looked at it this way: "We know that security concerns on the Internet will not allow us to keep information about visitors at our site—but we can build something into our browser so that the browser itself can remember some information (by writing to a predefined cookie file), and then the browser can, on request, pass all that information up to the server at one time."

Let's clarify this with an example. When you visit the 777-Film Web site (**www.777film.com**) for the first time, you fill out a form that includes your zip code. The server generates a cookie and feeds it to your browser, where it will be stored from then on. The next time you enter the 777-Film site, the server asks your browser, "Got any cookies for me?" The browser responds, "Yes, I've been here before; here's my file." What does this accomplish? 777-Film provides local movie times and locations to Web surfers who want to get out to the big screen for the evening. Based on the zip code provided by the cookie, the server "knows" which theaters are in the surfer's area, and can generate a tailor-made list of movies and show times accordingly. Compare this experience to having to wade through page after page (virtual or newsprint) just to find out when the latest action adventure flick is showing, and you have a good argument for letting servers store information on your computer. In this scenario, cookies are good.

But some people don't like cookies. Many critics charge that privacy is compromised with cookies, which may be true, or at least debatable, depending on the type of data stored in the cookie. Another concern is that cookies threaten security by raiding the user's hard drive, or by retrieving email addresses. This is simply a rumor. We aren't sure how this paranoia got started, but it has no basis in fact. On the whole, we prefer cookies to the alternative approach of storing user data on the server side.

If you decide to integrate cookie technology, you need to look at how the technology can assist your end users. If cookies provide no obvious benefit to your community members, than they're not really worth dealing with. Merely using cookies to track a visitor's path through your site is not a sound reason to use them; neither is attempting to track down broken links. And there will be users who will resent the intrusion, especially in social settings. So stay focused on the needs of your community members when deciding whether to integrate cookie technology—after all, your goal is to build relationships and trust.

Weaving A Web With Function And Form

Many people have no tolerance for poorly designed Web sites. We're not talking about flashy graphics; indeed, there are still many users who surf with the graphics mode turned off in their browsers. What we're talking about is the organization and navigation of your site. One anonymous user stated, "The more well-organized a page is, the more faith I will have in the info." Furthermore, many Web surfers insist that they will abandon a server and never return if the server returns too many errors or "under construction" signs. As another surfer put it, "Either the information is there or it is not; don't waste my time with stuff you are not going to give me."

Clearly you don't want to anger your audience. What can you do to avoid their wrath? Contrary to popular myth, surfers care about organizational and navigational issues. Provide smart design along with good content, and they will cheer.

Before you start building your Web-based foundation, think about what we discussed in Chapter 3—who is your audience? What is your mission statement? The answers to these questions will drive what you say and how you say it.

LOOK AND FEEL (DEVELOPING A SENSE OF STYLE)

"Look and feel" is a commonly used phrase that describes the interface of a software application. It encompasses not only the appearance of an application, but the way it is used as well. The concept has been extended not only to Web design, but to all visual design industries, including print and television. In the next sections, we discuss the factors that lend themselves to creating your own look and feel.

The Psychology Of Color

Many designers don't take into consideration the powerful feelings that colors can invoke. Orange makes you feel "energetic," yellow conjures up "caution," green is "refreshing," and "peaceful." Or are they? These associations are typical to the American psyche. Some of them may cross geographic and cultural lines, but for the most part each culture has its own associations. You may want to localize elements of the user interface, such as graphics or the colors of text, in versions of your application designed for different regions or different languages. Consider this when planning your color schemes, especially if you're actively reaching out to a global audience.

Geographic Origin Of Community Members

When you design your community's Web site, remember that color, graphical icons, calendars, and text represent different things around the world. For example, in the United States, we use flat file folders with tabs that indicate the folder's contents. In Europe, on the other hand, folders resemble narrow cardboard boxes.

Graphics can enhance your Web site, but be careful not to use cultural icons that could offend surfers in different cultures. For example, in some parts of the world, the owl signifies wisdom, but in Central America that same nocturnal predator has come to symbolize black magic. We're not suggesting that you make yourself crazy trying to be "politically correct" in every culture; that would be impossible, and it's often not necessary. Also, we humans tend to be biased toward our own familiar culture, and try as we might to be sensitive to foreign cultures, we often fall flat on our faces. If yours is a small community, try to be as aware of these issues as you can, and correct errors when you realize them. (Big corporations, on the other hand, often have serious concerns about multiculturalism, and employ people to pay special attention to these cultural sensitivity issues.) If it suddenly becomes obvious that you have a huge following in some foreign country, then you can use the Web to research that culture and design your site appropriately.

A Great Use For Cookies

You already know that cookies can tell you where a surfer is surfing from. Let's say red is the basis of your community's color scheme, but suddenly you have an influx of visitors from Moldavia (the fictional country depicted in the long-running series, *Dynasty*) where red is associated with the evil God of Death. You can create a set of pages where instead of red, the scheme is green, a color associated in Moldavia with the Goddess of Goodness. The cookie can tell the server to serve green pages to surfers in Moldavia, and red pages to the rest of the world. (Of course, we never said this would be easy.)

Keep Pages Short

Short pages are better than long pages. People are less likely to read a long passage of text than a short one, especially if they have to make an extra effort, like scrolling, to do it. Onscreen text is more difficult and time consuming to read than hard copy, which makes people even less likely to thoroughly read long sections of text on a computer.

Age Range

Consider carefully your target audience's age. A children's site will use bright, cheerful colors, large text, interactive graphical features, and maybe embedded MIDI files for music. Kids love to be entertained, and they love to learn, but above all, they love to participate, so a site for kids should feature plenty of interaction.

The needs of teens and young adults change every few months, but in general, they are attracted to darker colors and they like plentiful graphics—but they hate to wait, so make sure your graphics are small and fast-loading. Also, be careful not to talk down to teens online. They are a savvy bunch; they hate to be treated like children, and they can smell patronization a mile away.

From a technical point of view, adults are easier to please. They want clear and concise information, no more graphics than necessary, and a subdued color scheme that's easy to look at but not drab. Content-wise, they can be demanding. Most sites with an adult audience will be driven heavily by the quality of their textual content.

Computer Experience

If your core community members have a high level of experience, you may want to utilize Shockwave or Future Splash animations, RealAudio sound files, or even streaming video. On the other hand, if many of your members exhibit entry-level skills, you'll probably want to keep your pages basic.

Bandwidth

Even with the existence of high bandwidth Internet solutions such as the 56K modems, ISDN, and ADSL, it's surprising how many Internet users still surf at 14.4Kbps. To make your site painless for everyone to access, you should plan on a maximum of 50K per page, including text and graphics.

Tips For Maximizing Efficiency

Here are several tips to increase the overall efficiency of your Web pages. Much of this information is drawn from Apple Site (**applenet.apple.com**), a good place to visit for all kinds of useful information about Web publishing. Another good source of data is Lynda's Homegurrrl Page (**www.lynda.com/index2.html**).

- *Minimize the file size of graphics.* To achieve this, use as few colors as possible. Gradations of color and 3D effects tend to expand the size of images.

- *Use small images to limit graphics file size and increase performance.* If you really need to display a large image, put it on a separate page linked to a thumbnail image on the main page. This gives users a choice of whether or not to take the time to load the large image.

- *Repeat images whenever possible.* When a graphic can be accessed from the local memory cache instead of being downloaded, performance increases. Some images that can be easily repeated include bullet characters, title banners, logos, and separator images.

- *Specify the width and height for graphic images in their HTML tags.* This makes your page appear to download faster, because browsers determine page layout before downloading graphics. Consequently, the text on your page is displayed immediately, so surfers can begin reading content rather than idly waiting for graphics.

- *Choose GIF and JPEG graphics wisely.* The JPEG format offers better compression, and images load faster. It's an efficient format for photographs; however, JPEG compression does lose some of the original image quality. GIFs, on the other hand, don't lose image data when compressed. GIF images are better for line drawings and solid-colored graphics.

Advertising Banners

If you decide to pursue advertising on your site (which we'll discuss in Chapter 12), you'll want to seamlessly integrate ad banner content into your page layout design. This should be well thought-out beforehand; even large companies like Microsoft can goof. Various Microsoft content areas, such as MSNBC, Mungo Park, and Slate, incorporated differing ad banner sizes: Some were rectangular. Others were square. Some were large. Others were small. Not only did the salespeople and traffic coordinators find this system unwieldy, but advertisers complained as well. After industry standards were developed in the latter part of 1996, Microsoft spent months (and money) in site redesign incorporating the new advertising banner formats.

Monitors And Resolution

Despite the proliferation of 17- to 21-inch monitors and high-powered graphics cards available in the retail market, there are still a surprising number of 13- and 14-inch monitors in use, powered with simple 1MB video adapter cards. Therefore, it's no wonder that most surfers still set their screen resolution to the 640×480 mode and surf at a mere 256 colors. Plan for users that have a small screen size; to accommodate them, don't make your pages bigger than 640 pixels×480 pixels. Many people don't realize that they can use scrollbars to scroll down a page, so be sure to put critical information near the top, preferably within that first 480 pixels.

Another consideration is the size of the browser on the desktop. Users will reduce their browser size for many reasons; perhaps they are researching a term paper and want to share the screen between the browser and the word processor. In light of this, be sure to test your layout with different window sizes to see that critical data is viewed.

Charting A Course Through Your Pages

Designing a navigational philosophy can be a challenge. Think logically about the information you are presenting. What's the logical way to go through the site? Is it linear like a book? Is it a stream-of-consciousness-type site, like an online art gallery? How do you read a book? How do you walk through a gallery? Thinking about navigation issues in these terms will help direct you toward intelligent interface designs. Linear material will likely follow the book metaphor, using "previous" and "next" buttons to create a directional structure. Looser forms could lend themselves to something like a graphical site map, allowing surfers to lead themselves on a tour.

There is no one right way to organize a site, although we've seen plenty of wrong ways. To be sure your site works, let your content dictate design. The concept to remember in this case is "function over form."

Avoid The Back Button

Don't create situations where the only way to leave a page is by using the browser's "back" button. If there are users who don't know they can scroll on a page, there are likely to be others who don't know about the "back" button. Provide "previous," "next," and "top" buttons on each page to forestall problems. In those rare instances where you can't do that, be sure to boldly tell the user, on the page, to use the "back" button.

Create Easy-To-Follow Site Navigation

Your Web site undoubtedly has several key areas, like a home page, a table of contents, feature articles, "about" information, and probably other prominent areas. Under each of these headings will be found the associated content. A site map or navigation bar, preferably in or near the upper left-hand corner of the page, can be used to provide links to each content area. This navigation tool should appear consistently throughout the site, at least on the top page of each major section.

Most folks read top to bottom, so it's wise to provide a miniature set of these same links at the bottom of every page. As long as the navigation is easy, uniform, and handy, your site's visitors will be able to focus on content, which is after all what they've come for. Consistency is a key factor in your site design, and Web surfers place great stock in good site navigation.

A Table Of Contents

Assuming that each section of your site contains a great deal of information, a table of contents can be a great asset. The standard navigation tools easily move the casual browser from one section to another; however, many Web surfers know exactly what they're looking for. Like the table of contents for a book, a table of contents for a Web site allows these focused users to zero in on exactly the information they want. "No muss, no fuss," is their motto.

We're sure you're saying, "But I want the visitors to see everything, all my ad banners, all the articles, everything!" Well, we understand. But think about this: When you go to a Web site, if the content you're looking for is hard to find, what do you do? If you're like most people, you'll go somewhere else, and you won't come back to the site with the clumsy organization. Maybe it's true that people will use the table of contents, find what they want, and move on; but the next time they want something, they'll turn to your site first, again and again, as long as they find what they need. If you have good content and great organization, you will soon have a permanent new member of your community.

Provide A Search Mechanism

Basic navigation is fine for the simple site. Add a table of contents for a larger site. If your site is vast and teeming with content, a table of contents might even be too tough to follow, so add a third tool: a local search engine. This will allow your visitors to find exactly the data they need by keyword, and it will mitigate the navigational problems that arise naturally on sites with rich, expansive, and deep structure.

You Are Here

When you visit your friendly neighborhood shopping mall, you probably notice the large maps located throughout the mall. On each map is a big red arrow, pointing to a big red dot, next to big red letters that say, "You are here." Your navigation bar can play that same role on your Web site. On each page you can indicate what section of the site the visitor is in with a noticeable change in the navigation bar's graphics (an arrow, perhaps). This is very helpful to users who land in the middle of your site by following a hyperlink from another site.

As always, you can get fancy by using Javascript or pretty graphics, but while users like that, they don't demand it, so a simple approach to the "you are here" pointer will suffice. What users really demand, and we're sorry if we seem to be beating a dead horse, is function over form.

DESIGN RESOURCES ON THE WEB

If you've spent any time at all on the Internet, you know that if there is one type of information that is not in short supply on the Web, it's information about the Web. The self-reflective nature of the Net is a great benefit to new and experienced Web designers alike; here's a short list of the myriad Web development resources available online:

- Killer Web Sites (**www.killersites.com/1-design/**)

- Web Review (**www.webreview.com**)

- Clnet's Elements of Style Guide (**www.cnet.com/Content/Features/Howto/ Design/index.html**)

- Lynda's Homegurrl Page (**www.lynda.com/index2.html**)

- Project Cool Developer Zone (**www.projectcool.com/developer/**)

- Robyn's Road to Web Page Builder Resources (**robynma.simplenet.com/theroad/**)

- Web Mastery (**www.projectcool.com/developer/**)

- Pixelsight (**www.pixelsight.com:80/PS/pixelsight/pixelsight.html**)

- Kai's Power Tips and Tricks For Photoshop (**the-tech.mit.edu/KPT/Tips/ index.html**)

- The Warren Idea Exchange (**warren-idea-exchange.com**)

A Note About The Virtue Of Simplicity

We've discussed the value of simplicity and ease of use in this chapter, and we've also mentioned that many Web surfers are relative novices when it comes to the Internet (like those who don't yet know how to use scrollbars, for example). Newbies are often met with scorn in the Web community for their lack of Web "smarts," but we think it's important to look more closely at this issue. Many of us who work within the Internet community are blessed with having grown up around computers, and we have what seems to be an instinctive understanding of how to use the medium. To us, the interfaces and functionality of our browsers are completely intuitive, and we can't imagine how a person could lack the insight to be a Web guru. Sadly, we sometimes fall into the trap of considering our new virtual neighbors as "stupid," or "uncultured, ignorant slobs." We often hear statements like, "my pages look best at 800×600, and if they're too stupid to get a better browser and monitor, that's their tough luck." Be careful; this kind of thinking can lead to a traffic-free Web site. Many a designer has fallen victim to their own elitism and short-sighted biases.

Let's not forget that we are in our element. The Internet is still young, and it's growing everyday. Many new Web surfers are also new to computers; in fact, many may never have used a computer before in their lives. It's a big learning curve from pencil, paper, and telephone to a high-end computer with a sophisticated OS. Newbies aren't stupid; rather, think of them as very smart for wanting to learn to use and participate in this new frontier. By designing inherent simplicity and clear navigational structures into our pages, we aren't "dumbing down our sites;" instead, we are providing accessibility and empowerment to a fresh generation of Web netizens. We'd all do well to keep that in mind as we create the future.

Mastering Webmastery

So you've rounded up all this excellent content that will delight, inform, or educate your readers, and everything looks great, right? Well, maybe for the first few months or so, or even longer if you're lucky. But managing content can quickly turn into a crisis situation if you try to handle too much at once.

Some of the community developers we talked with said that their page volume has doubled in the last 12 months. Furthermore, they lament that they would update their content more often, or integrate more interactive community-building tools, if the process were simpler. Forrester Research, in a study entitled *Content Management Crisis* (January 1997), forecasts that no relief is near, since total pages online will more than likely triple in volume in 1998. And as you add pages, you encounter more content-management problems like:

- Not enough time spent on the approval process to check for errors or inaccuracies

- Slow integration of new types of community-building tools

- Too many resources devoted to managing broken links

- Too much time spent developing material across varying browsers, plug-ins, and platforms

As a growing community, you probably won't have warm bodies to throw at these problems, and that's not such a great solution anyway. Forrester's research points out that "sites performing 100 changes per week cannot solve their problems by hiring more people."

CONTENT-MANAGEMENT APPLICATIONS

Most community builders are using "home-grown" solutions, ranging from link-checking tools to HTML-validation applications, to deal with content management. These tools have worked well, but most of them were not really meant to manage a full-scale operation. Luckily, there's another way. In this section, we'll focus on solutions that will lighten the burden of content management.

Full-fledged solutions have hit the market to aid content managers in maintaining their Web sites. Here's an introduction to several key components that are not only desirable, but essential: versioning librarian, structural framework, approval and staging processes, JIT delivery, and performance optimization.

Versioning Librarian

You'll probably have more than one person developing and maintaining content, or you may even have more than one author working on a single project. Keeping track of edits and changes under these circumstances can become a logistical nightmare. To solve this problem, you'll need an application that supports *version control*. This functionality essentially keeps track of who is working on what document, and monitors the progress. Another handy feature is *multi-staging*, which allows multiple authors to develop content simultaneously and share their progress with others in the group before posting it to the Web site.

Structural Framework

The easiest-to-implement HTML-based templates provide a consistent structure for the look and feel, navigation, and page layout of a Web site. This is a great low-tech solution for a high-tech problem, especially if a site has multiple authors or content providers. While you can plug different elements into different locations on various pages, it's important that the structure be consistent throughout. If you start with a particular structure on your home page, every additional level of your site needs to conform to that structure. Templates, prefabricated or custom made, are great solutions for ensuring consistency.

Approval And Staging Processes

You'll never face a more embarrassing situation than if someone from your team posts a document that's full of errors, bad HTML, or worse. Formal approval processes can be instituted with a content-management suite. A system like this tracks the approval process for each document, and verifies when everyone on the approval list has signed off on it.

JIT Delivery

JIT (just-in-time) delivery allows pages to be assembled on the fly using Java applets, structured templates, and back-end databases. The latter is quickly becoming the standard for most large sites. The *Chicago Tribune* still employs authors to "hard code" each page in HTML (although they do use templates to simplify the process). However, when they designed Metromix (**www.metromix.com**), their new site, the *Tribune* shelved the old way in favor of a slick, shiny, new way—using a Java-based, object-oriented, custom database designed by the Leap Partnership (**www.leapnet.com**). Now pages are created instantly, and are fully customized to the preferences of the viewer.

Performance Optimization

Tools such as performance utilities (link checkers), usage simulations (check for server weaknesses), and traffic monitoring (stress testing), simplify any system administrator's job. After all, you don't want your visitors running into "404 Not Found" error messages or being rejected from the site because the server is too busy.

There are many content-management suites on the market, with many more scheduled for rollout. In Figure 4.15, we present a summary of the frontrunners in Internet application development.

Of course, purchasing a content-management suite is just one approach to finding a solution for your Web management woes. Furthermore, you can utilize some of the previously described functions without having to purchase a full-blown application.

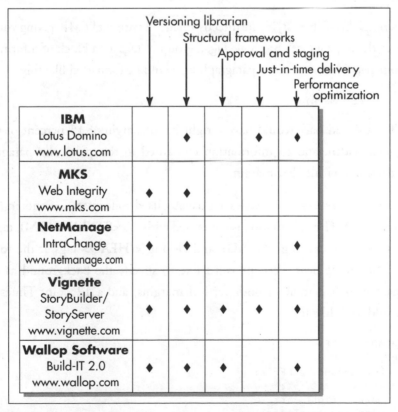

	Versioning librarian	Structural frameworks	Approval and staging	Just-in-time delivery	Performance optimization
IBM Lotus Domino www.lotus.com		◆		◆	◆
MKS Web Integrity www.mks.com	◆	◆			
NetManage IntraChange www.netmanage.com	◆	◆			◆
Vignette StoryBuilder/ StoryServer www.vignette.com	◆	◆	◆	◆	◆
Wallop Software Build-IT 2.0 www.wallop.com	◆	◆	◆		◆

Figure 4.15 The strengths and weaknesses of various suites.

For instance, the template solution is easily integrated with simple HTML. Even high-tech companies such as 3Com (**www.3com.com**) use this approach. You could also choose to use JIT delivery by selecting from a multitude of standalone database applications, which we'll describe in the following sections, along with other solutions for you to consider.

The Cascading Style Sheet Solution

Used in the graphic design industry for years, style sheets empower designers by giving them a great deal of control over the formatting and typographical layout of pages. This concept, brought to the Web through a recommendation by the World Wide Web Consortium (W3C, located at **www.w3.org**) in December 1996, has been implemented by Microsoft Internet Explorer, with Netscape promising to integrate it in version 4.0. Cascading style sheets can be implemented in three ways:

- *Inline styles*—These styles are directly included within HTML, giving you control over the appearance of a single tag, a group of tags, or a block of information on your page. For instance, a paragraph tag could be formatted like this:

```
<P STYLE="margin-right: 15%">
```

The finished page would have a right-hand margin of 15 percent of the total screen width, and all information contained in this particular paragraph tag would fall within that margin.

- *Embedded styles*—These styles are usually used to format elements in an entire document. The information is contained within a **<STYLE>** HTML tag, placed between the opening **<HEAD>** and closing **</HEAD>** tags at the top of the HTML document. Perhaps you'd like to specify the background as white, a margin of 5 percent of both vertical margins, and a 12 point Times font. It would look like this:

```
<HEAD><STYLE>
body {
    background: #FFFFFF;
    margin-left: 5%;
    margin-right: 5%;
    font-family: Times;
    font-size: 12pt;
}
</STYLE></HEAD>
```

- *Linked style sheets*—These styles are written into a separate text file stored on the Web server. The file is referenced by an HTML document through a **<LINK>** tag in the file's **<HEAD>** tag. Here's where content management becomes a dream—if you decide to change the look and feel of your pages, you merely need to change the styles in the style sheet text file, not the tags in the HTML pages themselves. The styles are then dynamically integrated whenever an HTML page requests the newly formatted style sheet document.

To find out more about cascading style sheets, take a look at these Web sites:

- Style Sheet Resource Center (**www.peavine.com/CSS**)

- The World Wide Consortium's (W3C) working draft on Cascading Style Sheets (**www.w3.org/pub/WWW/TR/WW-css1**)

- Web Review (**www.webreview.com/97/05/30/feature/index.html**)

- Support for Cascading Style Sheets—Microsoft Internet Explorer 3.0, Win32 version (**www.shadow.net/~braden/nostyle/ie3.html**)

- Support for Cascading Style Sheets—Microsoft Internet Explorer 3.0 for Macintosh (**www.cwru.edu/lit/homes/eam3/css1/msie-css1.html**)

Server Solutions

This year you may have 1,000 Web pages on your site; next year it could grow to 2,000, and then possibly to 6,000. Even if you have just a tenth as many pages, changing information as simple as a copyright date can be a chore, even with some of the cool find/replace gizmos. You can avoid this situation by using a server-side script: Enter the copyright and any other footer information (closing body and head tags) into a text file housed on your server. The content is then served dynamically as each Web page is requested by an end user. Now when December 31 hits, you won't have to spend New Year's Eve grinding out changes to several thousand documents; instead you can just amend the single text file on the server and be on your way.

 ### Don't Be Afraid Of Your System Administrator
Dynamically serving copyright information is just one example of the power of "server-side includes." Have a heart-to-heart with your system administrator to find out what other features your particular server allows.

The Dynamic, Database-Driven Solution

As stated earlier, more and more sites are switching from "hard coding" Web pages to creating pages on the fly using a back-end database. For standalone Web database solutions, take a look at these sites for more information:

- Lotus Domino (**www.lotus.com**)

- Informix (**www.informix.com**)

- Oracle (**www.sun.com**)

The Foundation Is Laid

To summarize: function over form, and simplify.

It's true, there's more to it than that, but those are two essential rules to keep in mind. Remember that the Internet is evolving and the rules change daily, so don't be afraid to be innovative. Be bold, be unique, experiment, but always consider the consequences of your design before you make any final decisions about implementation. Once you have your site ready to go, it's time to start adding more tools like chat applications, mailing lists, and discussion groups, among others. In the next chapter, we'll go beyond the Web site and look at the many exciting features you can add to set yourself apart from the pack.

Chapter 5

Beyond HTML: Integrating Community-Building Tools

Chapter 5

- Text Chat Options For Your Web Site

- Administering Mailing Lists

- Creating A Push Channel

- Guestbooks

BEYOND HTML: INTEGRATING COMMUNITY-BUILDING TOOLS

Chapter 5

Using The Tools

In its early days, the Web offered little more than text and graphics. It wasn't long, however, before the founders of the Web and its users alike began exploring what could be done with this new technology, and tools were rapidly developed to enhance the Web experience. Having a Web presence once meant a home page, with a picture of you and your cat and an article about your camping trip in the mountains. But as the words "publish" and "Internet" become more and more linked, each of us has the chance to be a bona fide "Web publisher." With the advances in HTML, and the introduction of Java, advanced browsers, and many other tools, content developers can now create high-quality Web sites with rich, dynamic, content. These tools are crucial to bringing together people within your Web site, since they allow for interactivity and two-way communication. And without this interaction, a virtual community really can't exist.

As a community developer, you have a plethora of tools to choose from. The choices aren't always easy, since feature sets among applications vary. So, the "perfect" solution for your community may not exist—yet. In this chapter, we present various tools and vendors for your review. We've also included the highlights of each vendor's feature sets in order to make your decisions easier. Let's start with text chat, the most popular realtime communication tool.

Text Chat

As you'll see in this chapter, there are plenty of text-based chat solutions to choose from. Which one should you pick? We suggest you start by studying the features available in each package. In Table 5.1, we've pointed out features that we consider "must haves"—that constitute the lowest common denominator acceptable in a text chat package. We've also identified some "would be nice to have" features that would enhance the chat experience of your community members.

It's important to ask yourself a few questions: How much administrative control do I want? This could include features such as obscenity filters, gag control, and kill commands. What type of "beyond chat" features do I want? Options may range from allowing file transfer among users to embedding hypertext links within "speech." What type of relationship-building tools does my community require?

Table 5.1 Feature sets of text chat systems.

FEATURE	MUST HAVE	WOULD BE NICE TO HAVE
Scalable	X	
Realtime Communications	X	
Seamless Web Integration	X	
Open Architecture	X	
Event Moderation		X
Rotating Ad Banners		X
Language Filters		X
Robot ("Bot") User Support		X
Email Links		X
User/Buddy Lists		X
Private Room Creation		X
Private Messages		X

Evolving features include such options as buddy lists, paging systems, member directories, user profiles, and more. Is scalability important? Some packages place a limit on the number of simultaneous users; a solution of this type won't grow with you as your community grows.

Equally as important as features, but more subjective in nature, is the quality and flexibility of your chat system's user interface. In order for chat to be successful, it needs to be user-friendly and have a small learning curve. A good solid interface should offer lots of user-controllable features; however, a feature that's intuitive to you, your system administrator, or your core group of site developers, may turn out to be cumbersome and confusing to your community members. The result? A really nifty feature that no one uses.

Since you'll probably devote considerable time and resources to implementing chat, you'll want to make the right choice for your community right out of the starting gate. One option is to conduct a usability test of several software packages, to see what works best with your audience. At Web Review (**www.webreview.com**), Keith Instone escorts you through five easy and inexpensive steps for conducting such a test. (You'll find this in-depth "how-to" guide at **www.webreview.com/97/ 05/30/usability/index.html**.) Instone also features an insightful walk-through of the Internet Travel Network site, including valuable tips for evaluating the usability not only of software, but of other graphical interfaces such as Web sites.

As we said, there are a lot of chat solutions out there to choose from. We'll take a look at some of them now.

CGI And HTML Chat Solutions

CGI- and HTML-based configurations allow just about any user to join in the conversation, without the need for a plug-in or any other type of software. However, solutions like these use a refresh statement to update the user's screen; while users have the option to reset the refresh interval, we found that the regular updating disrupted the flow of conversation. While these packages are definitely first generational, they are feature-rich and easy-to-use for both the end user and the administrator.

ichat ROOMS

ichat offers browser integration through ROOMS, an HTML/CGI solution. Client support is available for Windows 3.1/95/NT, Mac/Power Mac, Unix, and OS/2. In addition, ichat supports direct IRC connectivity within the user's Web browser. When an IRC link on the Web is selected, ichat transforms the browser window into an IRC client.

ichat's client list includes such communities as Yahoo, Universal Studios, ivillage, and Time Warner.

The Web Tour is one of ROOMS' most unique features. Tours enable users to browse the Web collaboratively, playing "follow the leader" through a Web site while carrying on their conversation in realtime. In addition, hyperlinks can be embedded within chat messages, and during moderated events, administrators can "push" URLs to the audience, updating the HTML frame in the users' browsers.

ichat also provides a user profile for chat participants to fill out, as shown in Figure 5.1. This can help build relationships among your community members.

If you'd like to add entirely new and unique features and functionality to your online community, ichat offers API support through C++ based extensions (servlets).

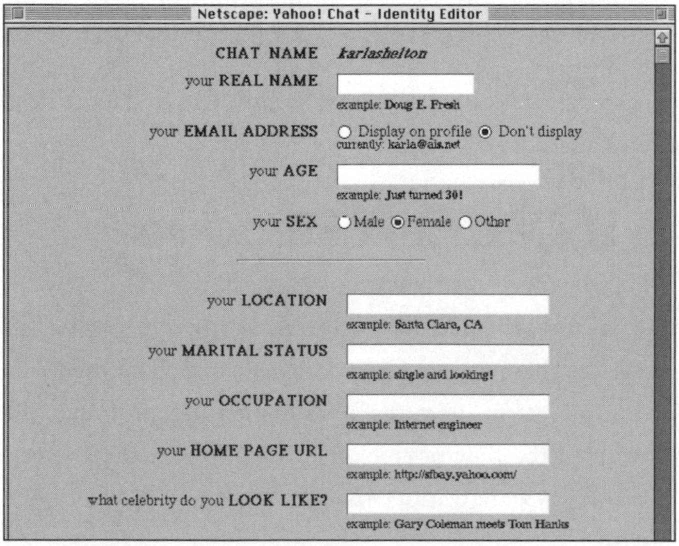

Figure 5.1   Your community members can let the world know who they are and what they like through a user-profile system.

The "bot" API makes it easy to create robotic (bot) users, allowing administrators to program bots that give presentations, greet new users, play games, and more. Other ichat features include:

- Rotating ad banners

- In-line avatar support

- Scalable to 50,000+ users

- Language filters

The ROOMS user interface is composed of HTML, making it easy for site builders to customize an intuitive interface for their community, like the one in Figure 5.2.

 A Closer Look

ichat: Not Many Barriers

iChat poses few barriers to entry by your community members. In addition to their HTML solution, ichat offers a client plug-in component for ROOMS. (Plug-in components operate directly within the browser in order to extend functionality of the browser.) The interface is

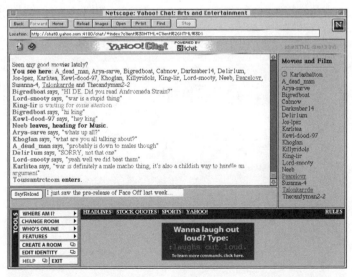

Figure 5.2 The ichat HTML interface is laid out using HTML frames, offering the user many controls such as room list, user list, user profile editing, and a help section.

similar to the HTML version, but the speech flows smoothly across the screen, with no irritating screen refreshes. The plug-in is available for the Windows 3.1/95/NT, and Mac/PowerMac platforms. ichat also permits users to log into ROOMS servers using Java. And of course, not wanting to leave anyone out, ichat is now offering a Microsoft Internet Explorer ActiveX component that system administrators may add to the client mix. ichat allows the end user to choose the method they prefer to chat with, as shown in Figure 5.3.

On the server end, ROOMS requires 32MB of memory, and is available for a variety of platforms such as SPARC, MIPS, Alpha, and PC with Pentium or better. It runs on several Unix flavors and on Windows NT, as well.

Contact ichat by phone at 512-425-2200, or by snail mail at 11100 Metric Blvd., Building 7, Austin, TX 78758. Or simply visit ichat at their Web site (**www.ichat.com**).

ChatWare 1.1c

Eshare produces ChatWare, an out-of-the-box solution that's not as robust as ichat, but a contender in the category, nonetheless. Their client list includes Jumbo

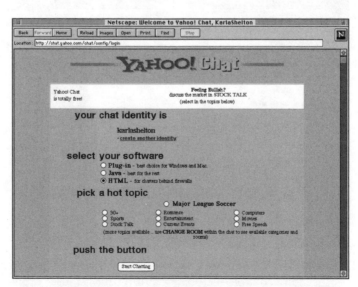

Figure 5.3 Using ichat technology, Yahoo allows end users to choose their method—HTML, plug-in, or Java.

Kids!, Universal Underwriters, Do It In Durham, Student Chat, Nursing.net, and the Military Network. And if you don't want to be bothered with the fuss of maintaining your own server, eShare works with UUNet (**www.usa.uu.net**) to provide a hosting solution.

One of ChatWare's interesting features is a library of small images that participants can include in their messages, as shown in Figure 5.4. Your administrator selects the library of images, and can add, delete, or modify them. Other important features include:

- Scalability

- Seamless Web integration

- Event moderation

- Rotating ad banners

- Language filters

- Hyperlinks (email only)

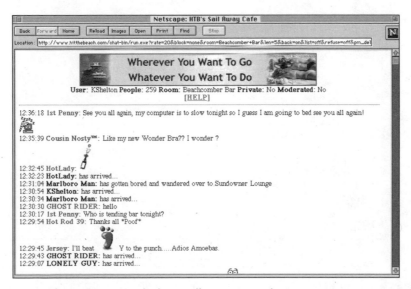

Figure 5.4 Chatters may include small images in their message to punctuate emotions or ideas.

- Private room creation

- Private messages

- User-definable setup (users may turn the user list on and off, adjust the number of messages on screen, "ignore" specific individuals, and choose to refuse or accept messages)

ChatWare allows limited control over the user interface, as shown in Figure 5.5. As an administrator, you may select a color from standard choices during set up, or you may choose from a more comprehensive color set after installation, using the ChatWare Administrator submenu. Other choices include adding or deleting rotating images.

ChatWare 1.1c is currently shipping for Windows 95 and NT, Sun Solaris 2.x, SunOS, and SGI IRIX 5.x.

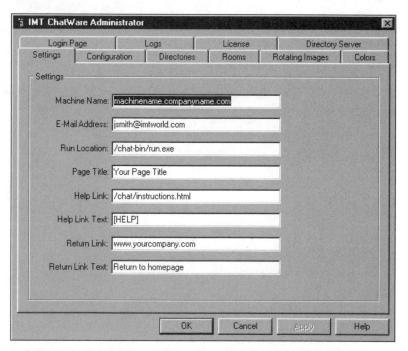

Figure 5.5   Changing preferences is easy, but rather limited in scope, with eShare's ChatWare.

System requirements for Windows 95/NT are: a minimum of 32MB RAM, 15MB available hard disk space, and a TCP/IP stack (Internet or intranet access); Unix installation requires at least 32MB RAM, 10MB available hard disk space, and a TCP/IP stack (Internet or intranet access), as well.

Contact eShare at 1-888-ESHARE4 (U.S. only) or 1-516-864-4700 (international), or by snail mail at 51 Mall Drive, Commack, NY 11725. You'll find their Web site at **www.eshare.com**.

ChatBox

ChatBox by EmeraldNet utilizes server-push technology to display the chat area. Currently ChatBox works with Netscape 1.1 or higher, Microsoft Internet Explorer 3.0 or higher, and even WebTV 1.0 or higher. As shown in Figure 5.6, the interface is strictly utilitarian, consisting of only two elements: the message field and the chat area.

EmeraldNet offers two options: ChatBox 2.0 and ChatBox Lite. ChatBox Lite is a one-room, 10-person, limited licensed server. Because it's free, EmeraldNet doesn't offer technical support, but they have created a newsgroup (**chatbox.server.general**)

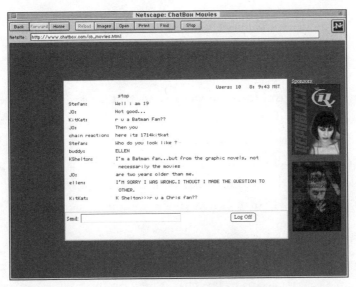

Figure 5.6 Chatbox's user interface is strictly utilitarian.

where ChatBox Lite administrators can help each other out. ChatBox 2.0, on the other hand, is a commercial release that includes full tech support and enhanced features such as multiple rooms.

The ChatBox client list includes Atlantic Records, The Verve Pipe, Counting Crows, Skold, Rhino Records, The Arizona Diamondbacks, and The Ultimate Taxi.

The minimum server requirements for ChatBox 2.0 are a Pentium processor running Windows NT 4.0 with 32MB of RAM, although EmeraldNet recommends 64MB.

Write EmeraldNet at 1718 E. Speedway Blvd. #315, Tucson, AZ 85719, or call a representative at 520-318-1993. On the Web, request information by email at **info@emerald.net**, or visit their Web site at **www.chatbox.com**.

Other HTML/CGI Chat Applications

Check out these options as well:

- The Chat Server (**chat.magmacom.com**)

- Chatalyst (**www.chatalyst.com:8080**)

- Keep Talking (**www.keeptalking.com**)

STANDALONE CHAT SOLUTIONS

Another option to consider is a standalone chat application. A client software download is required for the chat participant, since it is not integrated directly within the Web browser. Instead, it operates as a "helper application" alongside the Web browser. Typically, the look and feel (and usability) is similar to popular chat applications featured on commercial online service providers, such as America Online. The benefit? Ease of use for your community members.

Global Stage

This application from Quarterdeck gives community members using the Global Chat client program access to live chat using two methods. Members can either connect to any public Global Stage proprietary server, or they can connect to any one of the hundreds of IRC servers on Undernet or EFNet. Global Chat also supports standard IRC "slash" commands. Other features include:

- User-created channels

- Restricted channels

- Moderated and unmoderated channels

- Unlimited number of simultaneous channels

- Up to 1000 simultaneous users

- Ability to record transcripts

- Ability to send realtime advertisements to users in chat

- Integration with a broad range of Web-based member databases

- Custom enhancements available

Within the standard Global Stage package, site developers have little or no customization control of the interface. However, if branding is important to you, Quarterdeck will design a special interface for an additional fee.

Global Stage supports Solaris, Sun OS, and SGI IRIX platforms on the server side.

Contact Quarterdeck at 13160 Mindanao Way, Marina del Rey, CA 90292-9705. Or contact the sales office at 800-225-8148 or by email at **gchat@quarterdeck.com**. The Web site is at **www.globalchat.com**.

JAVA CHAT SOLUTIONS

Definitely a next-generation technology, Java brings chat into the 21st century. Let's start off with a brief description of Java: Java is a cross-platform, portable language that allows programs to be downloaded over the Web, and then executed by the browser on the user's machine. Java is a very powerful tool, and it allows community builders to make complex functionality and features available to the end user with a minimum of barriers.

Sun Microsystem's Official Definition

Java: A simple, object-oriented, network-savvy, interpreted, robust, secure, architecture-neutral, portable, high-performance, multi-threaded, dynamic language.

Developers are constantly writing and improving chat applets. Critics of Java applets say that most of them tend to load slowly—and this was certainly noticeable during our extensive review of chat applets. Considering that most Internauts are still surfing at 28.8Kbps or less, slow loading can present a barrier to entry. However, Java is still in its infancy, and speed improvements are coming. If you're planning for the long term, or your community members are early adopters of new technology, a Java chat solution may be what you're looking for.

Some developers offer applets as freeware, while others license their chat applets for a small fee. And some companies are rolling out in-the-box solutions. If you're looking for Java applets to test out, head on over to Gamelan (**www.gamelan.com**), *the* repository for Java, JavaScript, VRML, and other cutting-edge technologies. Java authors display over 110 applets for text-based chat there, ranging from simple to complex in regard to feature sets and the user interface. We'll share a couple of the solutions we found.

ConferenceRoom

Webmaster, Inc.'s ConferenceRoom technology uses Java to marry the Web and IRC in an open standard solution. Visitors may participate in your community's chat areas either by using a Java-capable browser, or by logging in through an IRC client.

Webmaster's client list includes NBC and the Second Annual Internet LIVE Mardi Gras Compucast.

Webmaster's line includes several packages to choose from:

- Personal Edition: up to 100 users; single server configuration

- Professional Edition: up to 1,000 users; networking; channel management

Beyond HTML: Integrating Community-Building Tools

- Developer Edition: complete with source code to the Java client

- ConferenceRoom Enterprise: up to 10,000 users; event server

Although feature sets vary somewhat across the packages, most of them include the following:

- Channel management

- DALnet compatibility mode

- Full IRC compatibility

- Private messages

With the ConferenceRoom Enterprise solution, you have complete control over the interface. However, the standard interface, shown in Figure 5.7, is quite intuitive.

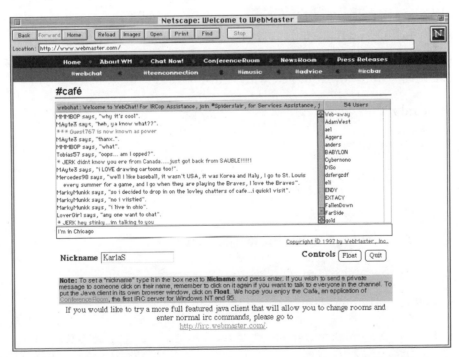

Figure 5.7 The ConferenceRoom chat client uses Java to interface with the network of IRC servers.

To run Webmaster's Conference Room server, you'll need a 486 CPU or better, running Windows 95 or NT with 8 MB RAM (16 MB recommended) and 2MB free disk space.

You can reach WebMaster at 1601 Civic Center Drive, Suite 200, Santa Clara, CA 95050, or by phone at 408-345-1800. You may request additional information by email at **info@webmaster.com**, and their Web site is at **www.webmaster.com**.

ENTER:Active Chat 3.0

eaCHAT offers a full range of serving solutions, starting with a personal license that includes unlimited simultaneous users, technical support throughout the setup/installation process, free software upgrades for one year, and documentation. eaCHAT even offers short-term leasing of servers for special events, as well as channel leasing for personal Web pages.

ENTER:Active Software developers have designed their solution to include "modules," which will extend the functionality of eaCHAT. Currently in the planning stages are the EnterRC Module, which will create a gateway between eaCHAT and IRC, and the Trivia Module, which will turn a chat channel into a fully automated live trivia game show, complete with virtual host.

Standard features include:

- Private messages

- Who's Online list

- Private rooms

- FIND command to locate friends (if they're online)

- Ability to ignore one or more users

- Full HTML/multimedia support (configurable by channel)

- Extensive administrative controls including the ability to KICK and BAN problem users

The user interface is straightforward, and your site developers have some control over layout and design. For instance, since the page is laid out in HTML, your designers could change the layout of the frames, or change the color of the background or text. You could even add a branded frame to tout your virtual community.

As eaCHAT is written in C, it can run on any Unix server. The application requires approximately 1MB of drive space. A Pentium 100 or higher is required for a moderately sized chat site, and ENTER:Active recommends at least 64MB RAM for a medium to large chat site

Contact ENTER:Active Software at 10804 Quail Plaza Drive, Suite 100, Oklahoma City, OK 73120. You can also reach them by email at **chat@eachat.com**, or by phone, 405-752-1194. Visit the Web site at **www.eachat.com**.

RENT-A-CHANNEL CHAT

If you're just getting started, and you don't want the headache or expense of setting up a dedicated chat server, or working out technology issues with your ISP, you may want to considering "renting" a chat channel. Some companies, usually developers of Java technology, will lease a chat channel, maintaining the server and software and handling most of the administrative duties. The chat room then becomes accessible from your Web site. Some of the services we investigated will even help you customize your interface, set up specific administrative controls, and list your site in a searchable directory. Prices, features, and user interfaces vary, so check out each site yourself to determine which solution fits your specific needs.

TalkCity

Talk City (**www.talkcity.com**), a popular virtual community in its own right, offers individuals, business, and organizations the ability to "rent" a Talk City chat room. Individuals can apply for a Personal Connection (personal chat room), while businesses and organizations—in fact, any virtual community with a site dedicated to a particular topic—apply for a Publisher Connection. And the program is free!

A chat room on Talk City provides a number of benefits and services, including:

- Twenty-four hour community standard advisors, who help create a "clean, well-lighted" atmosphere within Talk City's community model.

- Talk City's chat infrastructure, and the critical mass of thousands of moderated weekly conferences to build community on your site.

- A permanent Channel for use by you and your friends, associates, or customers to discuss topics of your choosing.

- Administrative control over your own chat room.

Chat Planet

Chat Planet (**www.chatplanet.com**) offers a wide variety of chat plans, ranging from a free service to a fully customized channel. To get started, you must first choose a plan that fits your needs. The first plan, shown in Figure 5.8, is free, but there are a few drawbacks: your community members must be exposed to Chat Planet's advertising, the number of users that can chat varies according to the

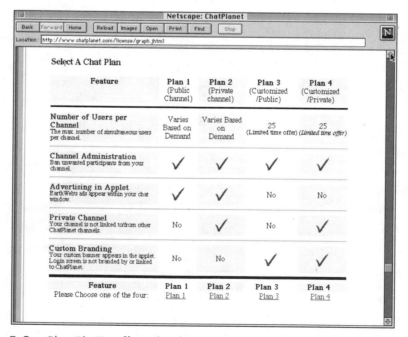

Figure 5.8 Chat Planet offers chat hosting services that you may license.

demand on Chat Planet's servers at any given time, and your room is located on a public channel. If you upgrade to Plan 2, you may move your site to a private channel, while Plan 3 guarantees access to 25 simultaneous users and you may integrate your own advertising program. Plan 4 is similar to Plan 3; however, the chat room is located on a private channel.

After reading and accepting the terms of license agreement, and submitting your registration, you may select the look and feel of your chat interface, as shown in Figure 5.9.

Next you select the category, such as Society and Culture, Computers & Technology, or Entertainment, that best describes your community. After review, your site may be placed in the Chat Planet directory. Chat Planet also offers promotional support through a chat event calendar. To post your event, visit the administrative area at **www.chatplanet.com/channel_admin**.

Adding the chat feature to your Web site is easy, even if you don't know HTML very well—simply cut the HTML code from the email sent by Chat Planet, and paste it into the source code of your chat Web page.

Figure 5.9 Three chat interfaces offered by Chat Planet.

IRC Chat Solutions

Although IRC seems like a low-tech solution, there are many communities that use it. As you'll recall from Chapter 3, IRC means Internet Relay Chat; it's a network of global servers that handle nothing but chat. Shareware clients are available for both the PC (mIRC 5.2 is the most popular) and the Mac (Homer is the preferred choice). Good IRC clients allow users to search the network for other users, list available chat rooms, and conduct file transfers.

At **www.sna.com/wray/mirc.html** you'll find Steve Wray's mIRC Page, an excellent example of the many user-based pages about mIRC. There's also excellent information there about IRC in general. Mac users can visit **www.aye.net/HomerFolder/HomerMac.html** for information concerning the Homer IRC client.

What's So Low Tech About IRC?

IRC simply lets you create a channel, register the channel name, and have "operator status" over the channel. It doesn't connect directly to your Web site, but you could advertise meeting times on your community home page and then meet on an IRC channel. In spite of The Palace, the many Java chat clients, and VRML apps becoming available, IRC remains remarkably popular, partly because it's fast and easy to use. For a FAQ on IRC, check out **www.kei.com/irc.html**.

The Lowdown On IRC

There is a lot of hubbub in the media these days about pornography on the Internet. IRC is the one place in the whole Internet where it may seem that porn is truly prevalent. If you're going to use an IRC channel on a popular network like DALnet or UnderNet, remember that IRC is unregulated and uncensored. This is a good thing in terms of free speech, but it also limits your audience, as some surfers don't want to mix with an unfettered crowd that can include a lot of unsavory characters. Personally, we wouldn't want IRC handled any other way, but if you want to enforce specific community standards, you might be better served to choose another chat method, like Palace or a Java client.

Discussion Groups

Like chat solutions, there are many discussion or conference packages to choose from. Again, our advice is to study the features available in each package. In Table 5.2, we highlight features that are must haves—a feature set that constitutes the least you should consider in selecting a package. And, as with the chat table, we also identify features that would be nice to have.

Like any other Internet tool, the user interface is critical. An interface must be easy to use and quick to understand. The principles you would apply to selecting a chat interface will apply here, too, and be sure to consider ease of use as you review message-base options.

WebBoard

This zippy conferencing system by O'Reilly & Associates, which supports threads and messages in a logical hierarchical table structure, is one of the highest-rated commercial conferencing packages available. *Infoweek, Web Week, New Media*, and *Web Review* magazines have all given a positive nod to O'Reilly & Associates for this entry into the Web-based discussion forum application market.

Table 5.2 Feature sets of discussion groups.

Feature	Must Have	Would Be Nice To Have
Scalable	X	
Seamless Web Integration	X	
Open Architecture	X	
Intuitive Navigation	X	
Threaded Messages		X
Rotating Ad Banners		X
Embedded Hypertext		X
Email Links		X
User Profile		X

WebBoard's chat features allow users to have JavaScript-based, realtime, interactive discussions with other participants visiting the WebBoard. Administrators have the option to enable or disable chat rooms for each conference created.

WebBoard 2.0 can display advertisements within chat, allowing communities to charge sponsors to display their ads. Advertisements can contain anything from simple formatted text to hot-linked, clickable images that take users to the advertiser's Web site.

Other features include:

- File attachment support

- Frames support

- Email notification and tracking for new messages

- Spell checking

- CGI and ISAPI WebBoard 2.0 System Requirements

- Public/Private/Moderated/Read-only conferences

- Anonymous message posting

- Cookies support

- HTML postings and support for active links and images in messages

- User location and keyword searching for topics and messages

- Automated message archiving and message archive retrieval

- Cross-platform support for Netscape Navigator and Microsoft Internet Explorer

- Remote administration

WebBoard sports an easy-to-use interface, as shown in Figure 5.10. You can search for messages or see a list of active participants, and you can also embed HTML tags in your messages. Tags that can be embedded include URLs, images, and 24 WebBoard-specific tags, such as users' email addresses. You can hold up to 255

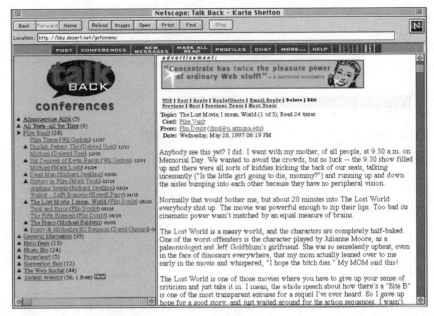

Figure 5.10 O'Reilley & Associates' WebBoard, one of the highest-rated Web-based conferencing applications, supports several unique features like realtime chat and banner advertising placements.

different conferences, which can be either public or private, and you can customize the user interface for each conference.

The requirements for serving WebBoard are as follows:

- 486 (or higher) Intel-based system

- VGA video display adapter (SVGA recommended)

- CD-ROM drive

- 5MB of free disk space for the program (more needed for your conference and user database)

- 24MB RAM (32MB recommended)

- Network card or modem (14.4Kbps minimum modem, 28.8Kbps recommended)

- Windows 95 or NT

- Fully qualified domain name and IP address

Contact O'Reilly & Associations at 800-998-9938 or 800-889-8969. You can also reach them by email at **software@ora.com**, or by snail mail at 101 Morris St., Sebastopol, CA 95472. Visit O'Reilly's Web site at **webboard.ora.com**.

NET.THREAD

Another product from eShare, positioned as a complete "out-of-the-box" solution, net.Thread lets you create online discussion forums that may be managed, even from remote locations. net.Thread's features include:

- Hierarchical discussion organization

- Simple user interface and navigation

- Auto-formatting of plain text messages

- Support for hypertext links, images, audio, video, and forms within user posts

- Removal of old messages and deletion of specific messages

- Password protection of individual discussion groups

- Forum moderation

As shown in Figure 5.11, the interface allows the user to navigate forward and backward within a thread, or to advance to the next thread. A compressed list of all threads is available, and the user can configure various controls by selecting the "settings" button.

net.Thread supports a number of platforms, including Windows NT, OSF/1, Irix, SunOS, Solaris, AIX, HP-UX, BSD, and Linux. It is compatible with Netscape, Microsoft Internet Explorer, Mosaic, Lynx, and all other HTML 2.0 and 3.0 browsers, as well as with all CGI-compliant HTTP servers (NCSA, CERN, and Netsite).

Contact eShare at 1-888-ESHARE4 (U.S. only) or 1-516-864-4700 (international), or by snail mail at 51 Mall Drive, Commack, NY 11725. You'll find them on the Web at **www.eshare.com**.

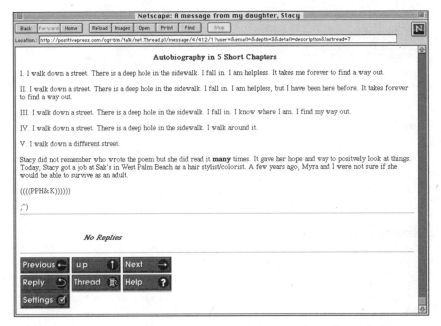

Figure 5.11   Positive Press has incorporated the net.Thread technology into its Web site.

WEB CROSSING 2.0

Web Crossing 2.0 is a customizable solution by Lunden & Associates. As a value-added service, the sales staff (at **sales@lundeen.com**) will assist you in finding a host if you prefer not to operate the software on your own system.

Web Crossing's client list includes Salon Table Talk, shown in Figure 5.12, the Star Tribune Talk Section, Excite Talk!, and the New York Times.

When posting to "threaded" discussion groups such as Usenet, you typically either add to the main thread or "respond to a response" (thus starting a nested thread). The end result of this process is a complex tree of messages. Unlike Usenet, Web Crossing uses a linear flow for each topic, making the interface much simpler.

You can also choose to customize the look and feel of every thread, by controlling banners, footers, and background color on a folder-by-folder basis. All of the buttons, icons, and help messages can be replaced. You have flexibility in laying out headings, folder items, and more; simple-to-use templates make this custom

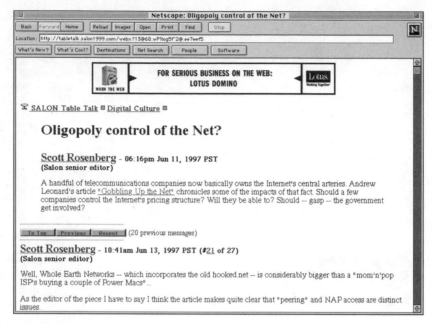

Figure 5.12 Salon, the ultra-chic digital magazine, uses Web Crossing 2.0.

control easy to facilitate. And all customization is achieved from your browser through HTML-based forms.

This application uses Web Crossing Template Language (WCTL), which allows you to customize every page you serve. WCTL is a server-side scripting language that affords the Webmaster a great deal of control, even allowing you to create custom macro definitions.

Web Crossing operates on Windows 95/NT, Macintosh, and Unix systems, including AIX, BSDI, Digital Unix, FreeBSD, Irix, Linux, Solaris, SolarisX86, and SunOS.

Web Crossing for the Macintosh requires 4.5MB of RAM, System 7, MacTCP or Open Transport (Open Transport required for chat), and a Web server that supports the 'sdoc' AppleEvent for CGI. The server must have a full TCP/IP con-nection to a LAN, for local serving, and/or to the Internet for serving on the Web.

Contact Lundeen & Associates at 510-521-5855, 510-522-6647 (fax), or by email at **sales@lundeen.com**. You'll find their site at **www.lundeen.com**.

WELL ENGAGED

Mentioned in Chapter 2, The WELL established itself as one of the first virtual communities. Many industry insiders attribute The WELL's success in part to its conferencing system, called WELL Engaged. Looking for additional revenue streams, The WELL now offers hosting solutions to communities who are not interested in serving or administering a full-fledged conferencing system in-house. The software runs on WELL Engaged's servers, and system administration is handled by an in-house staff, without delay or interruption to conferencing. WELL Engaged provides several report options, arming you with detailed statistics about participation in your conference(s). This is handy data to have when making decisions about content, or keeping advertisers abreast of how their ad banners are doing.

WELL Engaged is used by CMP Media Inc.'s TechWeb, Electric Minds, Play Boy, Quote.com, The Wall Street Journal Interactive Edition, and Golden Gate University. Features include:

- Users' controls customize the system to display and sort conference information.

- Posting presented in a linear, chronological fashion that resembles real-life conversation.

- Ability to embed hotlinks to Web pages, email addresses, and other conferences and topics, without knowledge of HTML.

- Ability to bookmark favorite conferences, topics, and postings.

- Internal search engine allows searches by numerous criteria within one or across multiple conferences.

- Profile pages allow users to provide biographical information.

- Scalable.

- Moderated or unmoderated conferencing.

- Conferencing data stored in relational databases, such as Oracle and Sybase.

- Detects the user's browser type and preferences, and tailors the user interface to match the user's computer and software.

Contact Sylvia Lacock, Partner Development at 415-332-4335 x210 for pricing or email **lacock@well.com**. The Web site is at **www.wellengaged.com**.

Mailing Lists

Mailing lists generally serve two purposes: They keep your community members informed about news, special events, and promotions, and they allow your community members to communicate among themselves.

MAILING LIST FEATURES

The most popular kind of mailing list is the discussion list, which is designed so that every subscriber can post messages to everybody on the list. Discussion lists facilitate open discourse and conversation for the list's subscribers. You can use this kind of list to promote one-to-one customer support if you are a business, or to engage in topical discussions if your community is an affinity group. Mailing list subscribers can trade recipes, argue about sports, or keep abreast of medical research, depending on the list topic. The following section details some of the issues you'll need to think about when starting a mailing list.

Open Forum Or Closed Club?

Most mailing lists are open, which is to say anyone with an email address can join. This is great if you're going for numbers, but if you have a target audience, like C++ programmers or veterinarians, for example, you might be best served by a closed list, where all subscription requests require your approval.

Moderate Or Debate?

If the list is unmoderated, postings will be sent to all subscribers as they are received. In the case of a moderated list, on the other hand, postings are reviewed first by a moderator (usually the list owner), who'll approve and possibly edit messages before forwarding to the list. Moderated lists are generally straight to the point. Off-topic postings, spam, or general silliness will not survive the judgment of the moderator. Subscribers of more serious, or information-oriented, lists prefer this. On the other hand, moderating a list takes lots of time and dedication.

Automatic Problem Solvers?

Many list-management programs can anticipate and correct common problems. It's certainly tempting to allocate repetitive tasks to the software, but the more you automate, the less likely you are to be aware of serious problems, should they arise. That's why it's important to find a host that uses sophisticated and reliable list-management software.

Into The Archives?

Many list-management applications will archive your list. This can be useful, particularly for lists that are rich in technical or detailed information. It will, however, consume a great deal of disk space on your server.

HOSTING THE LIST

After you determine which features you want, you need to determine how to host your mailing list. Options include using an Internet service provider or a list hosting service, or you could even host your list yourself.

As a list owner, you need to work with host system administrators to understand the list software, set up the list, and deal with problems that may arise. Typically you'll be responsible for daily list management, while administrators will handle the technical issues.

Internet Service Provider

Many ISPs don't offer mailing list hosting because of the drain on server resources that lists can cause. However, most ISPs are willing to offer services beyond the advertised standard services to clients who are important to them, so it might pay off to chat with your system administrator about that. Remember, too, that email can be accessed anywhere in the world; as long as you have a local POP, your mailing list host doesn't have to be local.

Mailing List Hosting Services

Of course, there are services dedicated strictly to the hosting of mailing lists. These services are devoted to maintaining mail servers on a full-time basis. They are often able to supply a more feature-rich mailing list solution.

Where To Find Mailing List Hosting Services

*Internet Mailing List Providers, housed at **catalog.com/vivian/ mailing-list-providers.html**, is a brief list compiled by Vivian Neou. This site is a great place to start looking for a host.*

*Internet Mailing List Providers (same name, different site) is a text document showing organizations that will host your list, including some that may do so for free. Go to **www.cs.ubc.ca/spider/edmonds/ usenet/ml-providers.txt** to download a copy.*

*SkyWeyr Technologies hosts full-service mailing lists. Visit the site at **www.skyweyr.com/skylist/list-services.html** to learn more.*

*Internet-Tools is another mailing list hosting service maintained at **www.internet-tools.com/it_html/mail_list.html**.*

If you decide to pass off the administration of your mailing list to a third-party host, the features that are available to you will depend on your host's choice of list-management software. Over 20 different mailing list software packages compete with each other, so it's important to know what features you want so that your list service provider can match your needs to the software. Before you decide on a host, consider the following:

- *What software does the host use?* This is the most important factor. Find out whether the host's list-management program accommodates the features you want.

- *How involved is the host in the administration of the list?* If you are very technically minded, you might prefer a host that merely sets up the list and lets you administer it by sending commands to the software via email. Other hosts provide full-service support. They will set up the list, deal with daily administration, and send you regular status reports. In either case, be certain that the host performs regular backups of its mail servers.

- *How much does it cost?* Mailing lists are a bargain. You can expect to pay a hosting fee of about $15 per month. Find out whether the host charges extra for archive storage space, regular archive backups, or for a high-traffic list.

- *How good is customer service?* Mailing lists serve a number of people, and if something goes wrong, you'll hear about it. You need a host who is there when you have questions or need help.

SETTING UP YOUR OWN LIST SERVER

To set up your own mailing list, you need to get the gear. Freeware and commercial versions are available for these products:

- L-Soft International, LISTSERV (**www.lsoft.com**)

- The Shelby Group, Ltd., Lyris (**www.lyris.com**)

- Leuca Software, Majordomo (**hofdi.med.cornell.edu**)

RUNNING YOUR LIST

Obviously, the first step is to name your list. The name should be one word, but hyphens are allowed. For example, a list on gardening may be the Green Thumb list if it's spelled "green-thumb." Many lists use these conventions: "topic-talk" for discussion lists, such as "aquarium-fish-talk," and "topic-announce" for announcement lists, like "martian-invasion-announce."

Testing, Testing, 1-2-3

Once you've chosen your host and have the basic list set up, beta test it. Post messages to the list. Ask friends to subscribe and unsubscribe to the list to be sure those functions work correctly. As soon as you know it works, unveil it on your Web site so the subscriptions can begin.

Write A Charter And A Welcome Message

Not unlike a mission statement, a charter lays out the list's purpose, scope, and rules. A charter needs to include the standard "who" (who is the list for?), "what" (what is the list about), and "why" (why are you starting this list?). Simple rules of conduct, to clarify what's an acceptable post and what is off-limits, will be needed. It isn't that you're being draconian; you're simply saying, "this list is about this, and not about that," so that potential subscribers will be making an informed decision about whether to join.

Most list-management applications will automatically send a welcome message to new subscribers. This message should include the charter, instructions for posting, where to get help, how to unsubscribe, and how to send comments to the list owner. As always, keep the message simple and clear. The QuickTime VR Mailing List provides an example of such a message.

The QuickTime VR Mailing List

First, the list owner, Joel Cannon, welcomes members to the list:

"This document describes how to be a happy member of the QTVR developer family. Think of this mailing list as an informal conversation around the dinner table. Ask relevant questions, or just sit and listen. Break the rules and you will be excused from the table. And, as with the dinner table, if you want to leave, you must ask to be dismissed. ;)

"This list server is an informal means for everyone interested in QTVR to share information. It is intended as a means to promote the technology, not an official source of technical support from Apple. The official option is to contact <devsupport@applelink. apple.com> for paid technical support."

Then, Joel lists the table of contents:

(1) The Rules
(2) Important Addresses, URLs, and Other List Servers
(3) Server Commands

Joel's rules are worthy of inclusion here; they are complete, but simple:

"To avoid utter chaos and anarchy, the List Mom wears the pants around here. Break the rules and suffer the penalty. If you have a complaint about a posting, tell the List Mom. If you are caught bickering on the list, you will both be sent to your rooms without dinner. Make the List Mom angry, and your access privileges will be (at least temporarily) suspended.

1. *No Flaming—online or offline. "Just Be Nice."*

2. *No cross-posting. If you have multiple subscriptions, pick the most appropriate mailing list for your email.*

3. *Do your homework. Please read any relevant FAQs or manuals first.*

4. *Stay on topic. No "for sale" or "want to buy" ads, and NO chain letters or political endorsements.*

5. *No copyrighted materials.*

6. *KISS—Keep It Short and Simple. Trim quoted material, and keep your signatures short.*

7. *Use an appropriate subject. Summarize your post in the subject. Descriptive subjects get more attention.*

8. *Use discretion. Post prudently, and send private email when appropriate."*

Start A FAQ

A FAQ, pronounced "fak," is a Frequently Asked Questions file. When you send a FAQ to new subscribers, or publish it on your Web site, you'll minimize the number of newbie questions on the list. As you encounter repeat questions, add them to the FAQ. Most seasoned Internet surfers use and appreciate FAQs.

Create A Companion Web Page

Part of your virtual community is the Web page, but since you've added a mailing list, you should add a few pages to the main site about the list. Include one page for subscription information, and perhaps a page for the FAQ.

ADDITIONAL MAILING LIST INFORMATION

Many resources are available for you to learn more about mailing lists. Try some of these sites:

- International Federation of Library Associations and Institutions Internet Mailing Lists: Guides and Resources (**www.nlc-bnc.ca/ifla/I/training/listserv/lists.htm**)

- Email Group Discussion: Discussion Lists, Interest Groups, Listserv, and Mailing Lists (**www.mwc.edu/ernie/lm-net5.html**)

- Mailing List Management Software FAQ (**ftp://ftp.uu.net/usenet/news.answers/mail/list-admin/software-faq**)

- Majordomo FAQ (**www.math.psu.edu/barr/majordomo-faq.html**)

- Majordomo User Group Mailing List Archive (**www.enfo.com/MailLists/majdom/index.html**)

- Usenet (**comp.mail.list-admin.software**)

Creating A Push Channel

As we discussed in Chapter 3, a push channel allows you to broadcast information about your virtual community onto the desktops of your community members. Why would you want to do this? For two primary reasons: it allows your members to describe exactly what information they want to receive, and it permits your members to browse your content offline.

Push technologies range from the incredibly easy to the amazingly complex. In the following sections, we'll take a look at two points along the continuum.

Beyond HTML: Integrating Community-Building Tools

POINTCAST CONNECTIONS

PointCast was pretty cool when the first beta arrived on the scene in early 1997. At that time, you could download the free client and "subscribe" to major news sources, like the *New York Times*, CNN, and more, and you could have these updated regularly. Now PointCast Connections provides Webcasting: You can broadcast your community bulletins directly to PointCast users, and there are over a million of them so far. You'll create a Connections channel, and your community members can subscribe to it and receive regular updates alongside *Wired*, Pathfinder, the *Chicago Tribune*, and other channels. In addition, you can have your community listed in the Excite PointCast Connections Guide, shown in Figure 5.13, which includes a "Best of Connections" listing and reviews of popular Connections channels.

Private Communities Are Secure

You can still take advantage of Connections even if you have a subscription-based community. Connections supports password protection via standard http authentication.

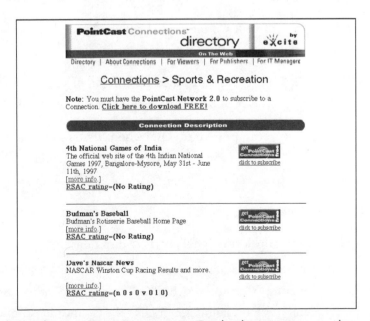

Figure 5.13 The PointCast Connections Guide showcases a number of emerging channels, created using the Connections Builder.

Creating Your Own Channel

Using PointCast's authoring tool, Connections Builder, creating a channel is a simple and quick 1-2-3 process; we'll demonstrate how in a minute. Connections Builder uses your existing Web pages for generating editorial content, and PointCast also offers the Studio tool for creating snazzy animations.

Animations And Commercials

Interested in including animated features in your channel? Somewhat more time-consuming than adding text to the channel, adding animation is still a breeze. The Connections Studio has built-in design templates to create animations quickly and easily, and Studio also includes a set of animation effects, including dissolves, wipes and peeks, stretches, and doors and blinds.

Before you get started, make sure you have all the materials:

- A list of the Web pages you want to broadcast and the URLs for those pages.

- A short description of your Connection channel. This description will be used in the Directory and during the subscription process.

- The URL to a Web page with a detailed description of your Connection (optional). A link to this description will be included with your Directory listing.

- Access to a Web server to post your Connection. If you don't have access to a Web server (and therefore cannot specify a valid Connection URL), you can still preview a test Connection.

- PointCast Network version 2.0.

To create your own channel, simply follow these directions:

1. After you've downloaded and installed PointCast 2.0, launch the Connections Builder by selecting "Connections Builder" from the Windows Start menu. Under Programs, click on PointCast or click the Connections Builder button in the Connections Personalize dialog in the PointCast Network 2.0.

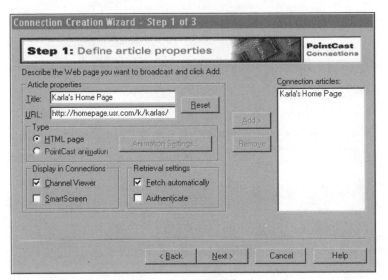

Figure 5.14   First, enter the URLs of the Web page content you wish to broadcast.

2. Enter the URLs of the articles you want to broadcast, as shown in Figure 5.14. (Don't use pages that have frames, Java or JavaScript, or ActiveX.) We recommend entering from three to eight articles, with a max of 150K per channel.

3. Next, name your channel. Then, as shown in Figure 5.15, enter the following information:

    • Channel description

    • URL

    • Update schedule (6 hours to 31 days)

    • Password authentication and SmartScreen (informational screen saver) options

    • Content ID (assigned by PointCast) and rating (assigned by the Recreational Software Advisory Council, RSAC) options, which are required by corporate viewers

4. To see a preview of your Connection, as shown in Figure 5.16, just select the preview button.

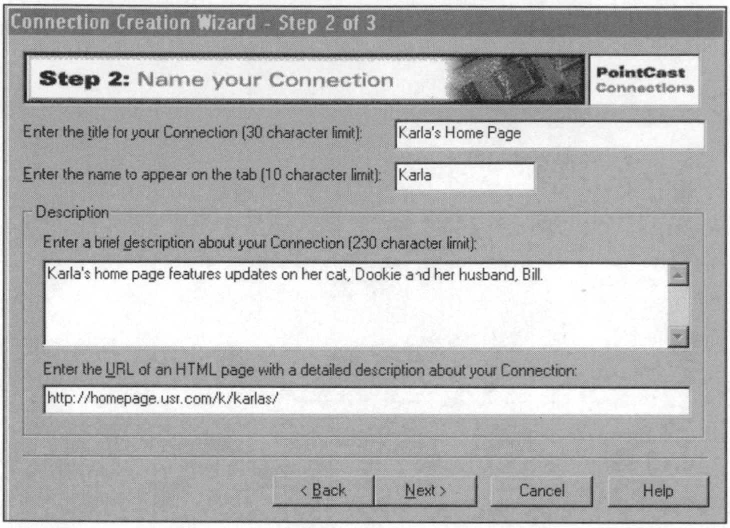

Figure 5.15   Next, enter the name and parameters of your channel.

Figure 5.16   Last, select the preview button to see what your channel will look like.

That's all there is to it. Connections Builder then creates a PointCast Connections file (CDF) that you upload to your Web site, along with two other required files. This identifies the channel content to be broadcast. When a viewer subscribes to your channel (via the Connections superchannel or by clicking on a Subscribe button on your Web site), your channel is cached on the viewer's computer. It's then automatically updated, based on your schedule.

To learn more about creating a channel, visit PointCast's Guidelines for Connections at **pioneer.pointcast.com/connections/webcaster/**.

 ### Tips For Managing Your Connections Channel
First, don't change the location of your CDF or the Subscribe Jump Page on your Web server; doing so may break the links. Second, to ensure visual consistency with your Web site, modify your Subscribe Jump Page to include your Web site's header or navigational system.

BackWeb

At the other end of the push spectrum, BackWeb originally forced Web site content developers to construct original content. However, BackWeb now allows developers, through an automated API, to create a bridge between existing Web content and BackWeb content.

BackWeb offers three types of InfoPaks for pushing content to your subscribers:

- *InfoFlashes*—InfoFlashes contain information of interest to users. BackWeb keeps you up-to-date by sending presentations from channels to which you've subscribed. When new information arrives on your desktop, a small interactive graphic appears, alerting you that new information has arrived; you have the choice of whether to click on it or not. If you do click, a second level of information appears; if you don't, it goes away.

- *SoftwareFlashes*—SoftwareFlashes will download software or software upgrades to a user's system in the backround. When downloading is finished, an interactive graphic appears. Clicking the install button displays your inbox, and from here you install the new software. Of course, you're in control of what's installed. You don't have to install anything on the fly, and that gives you a chance to run a virus scanner, or find out more about the software before you commit to it.

- *Wallpaper and Screen Savers*—As we said in Chapter 4, people love playing with gizmos like electronic postcards, and Backweb offers lots of gizmos. Wallpaper and screen savers can be broadcast and updated regularly to your desktop. This can be fun, and many users like having different wallpaper and screen saver options.

OTHER PUSH RESOURCES

Push technology is hot, hot, hot! You probably can't pick up a computer or Internet magazine without seeing some reference to it. Amazingly, however, the subscriber base is still comparatively small, roughly a million. But forecasters are projecting big numbers for this medium, so you'll want to educate yourself about all the contenders out there before making a final selection:

- *Active Desktop*—A Microsoft product, Active Desktop will be integrated into Microsoft Internet Explorer 4.0. Content providers may utilize CDF technology, much like PointCast, to build push content. For more information, see **www.microsoft.com**.

- *NetCaster*—Netscape leaps into the push fray with NetCaster. Available with the newly released Communicator, NetCaster pushes content via Live Sites, which again is similar to PointCast's Connections technology. Check it out at **www.netscape.com**.

- *Castanet Tuner*—Basically for high-end power users, Castanet, by Marimba, Inc., updates Java applications and content. A mover and shaker in the industry, Marimba is forging deals with Apple, IBM, and Lotus. More information can be found at **www.marimba.com**.

- *Intermind Communicator*—This software is definitely easy to use, thus attracting hundreds of small publishers. That's why The Palace, Inc., adopted this technology. Again, Communicator functions similarly to PointCast Connections. Check out their site at **www.intermind.com**.

Even More Resources

- Airmedia Live News Catcher (**www.airmedia.com**)

- Datachannel (**www.datachannel.com**)

- Domino Broadcast (**www.net.lotus.com**)

- Downtown (**www.incommon.com**)

- Headliner (**www.lanacom.com**)

- Incisa (**www.wayfarer.com**)

- Intelliserv (**www.verity.com/intelliserv**)

- NetDelivery (**www.netdeliver.com**)

- Newscast (**www.wavephore.com**)

- WebCast (**www.astound.com**)

TIPS FOR INTEGRATING PUSH TECHNOLOGY

Unless your community members actually subscribe to and use your push channel, you're wasting precious resources. PointCast encourages their publishers to place the "Get PointCast Connections" button right on your site's home page to direct visitors to subscription information.

But once you have subscriptions in place, you need to generate the right kind of content, or you'll churn, churn, churn your subscription base. Read on...

Generating The Right Content For Push Mediums

While push technology makes it possible to broadcast virtually any page or set of pages from your Web site, we strongly advise that you give special consideration to the content you push to your community members. These viewers will have different expectations when content arrives on their desktop than they do when visiting your community Web site. Make sure the content:

- Is useful and relevant

- Is timely and updated frequently

- Minimizes bandwidth requirements

What Information Is Valuable To Community Members?

It may seem obvious, but consider the profiles and interests of people who visit your Web site. Also think about the new surfers you want to attract. Surfers may want information pushed to them if it's newsworthy and it appeals to them based on their affinity group. Consider these points when selecting compelling content.

What Value Will Push Subscribers Get?

People subscribe to a push channel to receive information. Successful push content providers will take the opportunity to provide a special service to their audience. If you just push your Web site home page to subscribers, they aren't going to be happy about it. Community members also get annoyed by excessive links back to your Web site, rather than articles utilizing links sparingly to provide secondary information.

How Frequently Will You Refresh Your Content?

If your content never changes, your viewers will have no incentive to continue subscribing to your push channel. When setting up your channel, select the articles that change most frequently, and be realistic about the time and resources required to keep the information up to date.

We recommend that your channel include three to five full articles that are updated at least weekly. While these articles can have links back to your Web site, they should provide enough information to be valuable without needing to click to get more information. (If you're building a channel for subscription-based content, or content that requires user authentication, consider using brief abstracts to attract your viewers to the full-text articles.)

Guestbooks And Feedback

Guestbooks and feedback forms are not only great ways for you to glean important information from your community members, but they're also an excellent way to start a one-to-one dialogue with them. Guestbooks come in many shapes and sizes, so the look and feel is totally dependent on your Web designer and programmer. However, before we move on, you should be aware of the features to look for in guestbook programs.

- Do you want your guests to be able to preview their entry before submitting it?

- Do you want comments to be automatically posted to a Web page for public viewing, or do you want an editorial staffer to review entries before they're posted?

- Do you want email addresses or phone numbers validated before being processed? This will save your database manager from having to "scrub" a dirty database.

- Do you want to post the time and day that the user submitted his/her comment?

- Do you want the author's name to appear as a mailto link when the entry is posted to your Web page for public viewing?

Now that you know what features to look for, let's take a look at some guestbook options.

CGI

A Perl-based CGI script is the most popular method of handling data gathered from a form. A script collects the data and either posts it to a database, or more commonly, forwards it via email. FormMail, a freeware script, is a generic WWW form-to-email gateway that parses the results of any form and sends it to a specified user. This script has many formatting and operational options, most of which can be specified through the form, and best of all, you don't need to know any programming to implement the script.

If you don't have access to a CGI script, it's possible to use a simple HTML trick as a low-tech solution: embed a mailto hyperlink as the **METHOD** of the **<FORM>** tag. The code for the **<FORM>** would look like this:

```
<FORM METHOD="post" ACTION="mailto:karla@ais.net">
```

Please keep in mind that this solution, although workable, is rather unreliable. In addition, you may be blocking access by many users whose browsers do not support the mailto option. This could include not only America Online users, but many corporate users as well.

JAVA

Why Java, when the CGI solution is tried and true? As stated earlier, Java adds some powerful features that can take guestbook or feedback forms beyond the ordinary. Take a look at Figure 5.17. This window opens independently from the browser upon clicking the "sign on the guestbook" button. You could include other enhancements like "graffiti walls" (shown in Figure 5.18), scrolling text, and animation. Your community members could even attach a photograph of themselves to go along with their comments.

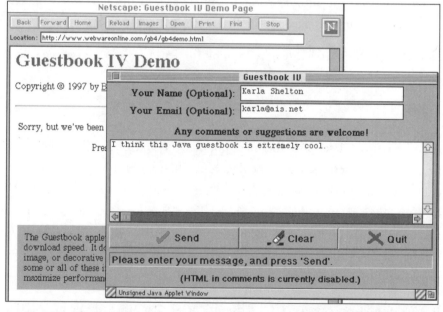

Figure 5.17 The Java-based guestbook at **www.webwareonline.com/ gb4/gb4demo.html** opens in a separate window from the Web page.

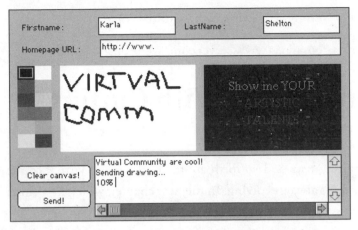

Figure 5.18 Guestbooks get even funkier with graffiti boards.

HOSTING SERVICES

Looking for someone to set up and manage your guestbook for you? Quite a few services emerged when the popularity of personal Web page development surged. Often the "vanity plate" Web page builders, although proficient in HTML, simply didn't want to learn CGI scripting. And many ISPs don't offer generic guestbook/feedback form scripts to their customers. This has turned many users' attention to hosting services, and today, even mid- to large-sized sites are utilizing these services.

One of the first services out of the starting gate was Lpage (**www.lpage.com**). This company started in 1995 as a hobby, on a borrowed home PC sitting in a spare bedroom. Now, Lpage is incorporated and has moved into bigger digs, complete with a provider that has multiple T3 lines. With revenue streams coming in from advertising and sponsorships, Lpage has beefed up their CPU power and hard drive space, making it a viable guestbook hosting solution.

Other Hosting Services

Check out other guestbook hosting services at:

- Dreambook (**www.dreambook.com**)

- Paradise Guestbook Server (**www.pergatory.com/paradise.mirage**)

- Sign This (komy.nethosting.com/signthis/)

- Server Corporation (www.server.com/WebApps/)

Moving Ahead With Cutting-Edge Chat

Chat, mailing lists, and so forth are the backbone of virtual communities. But the Internet is always evolving. In the next chapter, we'll take a closer look at The Palace. This new and unique software can seamlessly integrate into your Web pages to provide a new level of community interaction and intimacy, and many Palace sites have combined other Internet tools to create a comprehensive community experience.

Chapter 6

Building Community With The Palace

Chapter 6

- How Palace Pushes The Chat Envelope

- Your Friends, The Smileys

- The Hierarchy Of Palace

- Palace History Lessons

BUILDING COMMUNITY WITH THE PALACE

Chapter 6

The Next Logical Step In Community Evolution

In the previous chapter, we dealt with several chat clients. We know that interactivity, like realtime chat, is what really binds a community together. But until now, chat has been entirely text-driven, and text can be cold and impersonal, which is why so many conventions exist, such as add-on scripts for mIRC, to add elements to chat that help facilitate a greater degree of interconnectivity. The smileys, hugs, LOLs, and other conventions of text chat add many levels to chat except one: a sense of space and physicality. That's why we believe that the Palace represents the next logical step in chat evolution, and subsequently, community. At a Palace site, as we saw in Chapter 3, you are represented by an avatar and can move about and interact in virtual physical space with others, more like having a room full of people than a screen full of words. In researching this book, we took particular note of the increased level of communication exhibited on the Palace. Palace users tend to talk more freely and with fuller sentences and completely expressed thoughts or ideas. Not that this isn't done in text-based chat, but in graphical-based chat, it's easier and feels more human.

Around The World In 80 Clicks

On an average weekend evening, you'll find about 350 Palace sites up and running. These sites target just about any interest or hobby. On one weekend night, we toured the Palace site directory at **www.thepalace.com/directory**. We found sites with orientations ranging from music (Beatles, punk, orchestral), to travel (Hawaii, France, England, Mexico, New Orleans, New England), to gaming (Marathon, Duke Nukem). Whether it's science fiction, religion, law enforcement, education, animals, or the environment, there's probably a Palace site out there for you. (If not, it's time to build it, isn't it?)

More than 300,000 client versions have been downloaded, and over 1,000 commercial and privately hosted Palace communities have been built. Granted, this is a small list in comparison to the number of chat rooms available on behemoth services such as AOL and CompuServe, but what's fascinating here is that the majority of these sites are running on personal computers in the homes and schools of people just like you.

According to Mark Jeffrey, co-creator of the Palace and now director of commercial marketing, the Palace enhances the social experience by amplifying the sense of *presence* with other users. We interviewed Mark to explore in-depth the community-building philosophy of The Palace, Inc. (TPI). Read on to learn about the Palace's vision and what the future holds for virtual communities.

Who Is Mark Jeffrey?

Prior to joining the Palace Group, Mark Jeffrey, shown in Figure 6.1, headed the 20th Century Fox lot office of what is now called iGuide. He also managed online service/Web site production for 20th Century Fox Film, Fox Television, fX Networks, Fox Interactive/Video, and Infiniti Broadcasting radio station KROQ FM. In addition, Mark produced the first on-air/online auction, "The fX/X-Files Auction," featuring collectible memorabilia from the hit Fox television show, "The X-Files."

Figure 6.1   Mark Jeffrey, director of commercial ventures for The Palace, Inc.

A PALACE VISIONARY, MARK JEFFREY

On February 17, 1997, we asked these online interview questions of Mark Jeffrey. What follows is the result of that interview.

K & T: What is TPI's virtual community vision?

Mark: We want the Palace to be invisible in your consciousness as you use it. You should forget that you're looking at a computer screen and think you're sitting in a room with seven other people. When you watch television, you don't think "That cathode ray tube is creating scan lines on a phosphor from patterns of electromagnetic waves vibrating nearby." Instead, you become absorbed in the drama unfolding before you. Palace endeavors to be the same kind of thing—to be the tool you use to go places and see people from your armchair, instead of "that neat technology."

The Web is like a great microfiche reader into the greatest library ever built. But you can't talk to anyone else who is out there with you or see that person. Interacting with others is, of course, the next logical step.

Online services such as AOL, Prodigy, and CompuServe show what the Internet would be like in microcosm. The most popular and useful thing you can do on them is chat and email. Ted Leonsis, a vice president at AOL, said, "The only reason we have content is to give people something to talk about." Seventy percent of time spent online on these services is accounted for by chat and email. The amazing thing is that the Internet is only content and email; the chat component has only begun to appear! People are far more interesting than content.

Of course, you want to have online conversations and interactions with people who share some common ground—generally referred to as an affinity group. TPI is introducing several innovations into the Palace product to help people of like interests find one another and form communities—and for people to find established communities they would be likely to enjoy.

K & T: What is the most important ingredient in building an online community?

Mark: The Queen Ant. You need someone to nurture the community, care about it, put time into it, meet and greet people and help them meet other people. It's like dancing; no one will move out onto the dance floor until there are people out there. You need those first dancers and the people who will keep dancing—even during terrible music—for the sake of keeping the party going.

K & T: What tools do you think will be needed in the next two or three years to grow communities?

Mark: A resource that profiles, targets, and matches people and communities together dynamically. Palace will accomplish this later this year.

People are the most important tool. The strong communities will be the ones with the "Queen Ants," as Jim Bumgardner, co-creator and chief technology officer likes to put it.

The auditorium will be a great help. People need to have group experiences to form a common frame of reference on which to found a community. The Palace auditorium will allow large groups of people to watch one interaction while participating in another interaction. AOL got this right with their concept of rows in their Auditorium concept—giving you the "Mystery Science Theater 3000" kind of experience of watching with others. We're augmenting this with a visually engaging environment.

And in two to three years, all online communities will be avatar-based for the most part. The larger group of the population will not tolerate a dull text interface in the same way they would not tolerate the linear and confusing DOS and waited for a graphical user interface such as the Mac or Windows. Also, text does not do much for the sense of *being there* that a graphical environment does.

K & T: How is the Palace differentiated from other community-building software or chat clients currently on the market?

Mark: It is fairly alone in its space right now. Others have focused on 3D chat. It introduces huge distortions into the socialization process, which get in the way of communicating, and actually stunts it. Other than that, there are text chats—of which there are several—which are trivial to build in Java or whatever, and are not very compelling to most consumer-level people.

We are differentiated from both groups [3D chat and text chat] in the sheer size of the user base and number and quality of Palace servers that are up right now; no one else comes close. We will be introducing other services and Palace space-wide capabilities, which will closely tie Palace servers and users together in a very useful and interesting way.

Most importantly, people *love* Palace in a way they usually do not love anything having to do with computers. It has enormous grass roots appeal that is hard to quantify. For example, my mother, who hates computers, loves Palace and uses it. And believe me, it's not because I'm involved with it; there have been plenty of those (projects) she's hated. Palace is cozy and not computery. This is about the closest I can come to giving you a one-liner.

K & T: What advice would you give to Palace-builders?

Mark: Clear your schedules and learn how to call into work sick; you know, practice the fake cough, know names of sicknesses you supposedly contracted, etc. (Just kidding.) Nurture your Queen Ants when you find them; they are gold. Treat them well and give them whatever they want. Well…except your Palace server, that is.

K & T: Where do you think virtual communities will be in five years?

Mark: Hard to tell in this business what will happen next. It's so surprising. However, I believe they will be a dominant feature of the Net—demarcating advertising profiles, forming natural channels for products to be marketed to and sold through. There will be these little clusters of related affinity groups that will loosely overlap and there will be traffic bleed between them, creating co-competition between groups defining a category.

Establishing Proactive Skill Sets Based On Community Interaction

Kids Nation, shown in Figure 6.2, is a voluntary, collaborative, nonprofit effort headed by a Palace user known only as Cyberia. It was created to meet the need for a safe, educational, and fun site for children. Many people in the teaching field came together with talented artists and programmers to make this project happen. Read on to learn more about this unique and compelling site in our interview with Cyberia.

T & K: Describe a typical visitor to Kids Nation.

Cyberia: Visitors to Kids Nation are usually children between 8 and 12 years of age. Many parents visit the site as well. During the day, a teacher may come in with a group of students. (See Figure 6.2.) The class is usually hooked up with several computers to connect to the site. We also have students from a deaf school visiting. They find this a great way to communicate with other children. We get over 1,000 visitors a week to Kids Nation. We have gotten incredible feedback from teachers, students, and people who work with children.

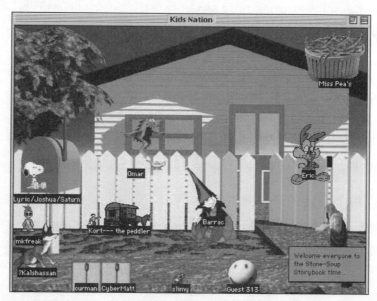

Figure 6.2 Kids Nation, a collaborative effort among teachers, programmers, and artists.

T & K: Who is managing Kids Nation now?

Cyberia: Administrative duties are controlled by Chris Lucasey, a Palace mentor, and myself, with consultants in the teaching industry. Kids Nation, Inc. is a non-profit organization.

T & K: How many rooms have you developed? Could you describe one of the rooms and tell me why it has been so popular?

Cyberia: When I first created this site, I made an outline of rooms I wanted to see. My idea was to have a home atmosphere connected to educational rooms and other activities that would all become part of a virtual educational village. I have done some of the graphics, and with the help of many others, I am glad to say that all I envisioned has come to exist at Kids Nation. So many of the rooms are popular at Kids Nation. The planetarium, language rooms, tree house, and many others…. There is so much to be found by just clicking the links.

T & K: What type of events do you hold now? What future plans are you developing?

Cyberia: One of the most popular events is Story Time, put on by Kids Nation's Stone Soup Storybook Team. A crowd of over 20 kids comes to hear a different story each week. The stories are fun and enhanced by the prop changes of the storytellers. We are in the process of developing a new workshop called "Kids on Broadway." The general idea is to encourage kids to use their imagination and interact in creative ways—with props, stories, and other exercises. In the future, we would like to have contests for kids designing rooms for Palace. We are also planning on having guest speakers come talk to kids on a variety of subjects. There is so much than can be done in this virtual world.

T & K: What advice could you give to other Palace builders?

Cyberia: It's best to start with a theme, put up 10 basic rooms, and go from there. Ask others to help with graphics and scripts because the Palace community loves to be a part of developing a new site. It also takes dedication and patience to make a good site. Take your time and think about what people would enjoy and what would make them want to return.

Chapter 6

Getting Back To Cybernature

The Forest was developed by three friends who go by the nicknames Firebird, Gromp, and Lisa who met on TPI's Palace Main site. At first an experiment to see if they could "really do it," the Forest site was a special challenge because these three people have never met in real life. Firebird lives in Singapore, Gromp in London, and Lisa in Pennsylvania. Through email, file transfer (FTP), and chat, they collaborated as a group from concept to finished product. In the following interviews, we find out exactly how they did it.

K & T: How did you begin planning your Palace?

Firebird: I went to over 200 sites to take a look at what works and what does not. I decided on a forest theme because I noticed that folks generally go for holiday scenes or outdoor environments with lots of greenery.

K & T: How did you manage the development process?

Firebird: This was done through detailed planning and visualizing the theme as a whole. I would get an idea, and then communicate it in minute detail (by email) to the artists: colors, textures, style, flow, positioning of objects, and shapes. We would then go through the drafts and amend as we went along, until it was perfect.

K & T: Who visits your Palace? And how many people visit per week?

Firebird: The forest attracts a universal crowd of *all* ages. We get over 1,000 to 2,000 folks coming per day, so I would say about 10,000 to 15,000 per week.

K & T: How many rooms are in your Palace?

Firebird: We have over 50 rooms, including hidden ones. Many are prop rooms. Some rooms can be used as meeting rooms, others as places to relax. All rooms are designed to be fresh and fun. They take into account the users and how they interact with their environment. This will range from how a user sits in a chair, climbs a tree, or perches on a tree branch.

Impressed with the overall appearance of the site, we approached Gromp with questions about the creative strategy of the Forest.

K & T: Tell me about how you designed the graphics.

Gromp: We decided to have the artwork give the illusion of being three-dimensional. A lot of Palaces are designed in 3D programs. Despite the abilities of these applications, I was very often unhappy with the sterility of the pictures. Some Palaces use photographs, and while they offer a great amount of realism, they usually appear flat. So, I tried to combine all the different techniques. The Frontroom is the best example. The basic layout was done in a 3D program. Photographs were used to map a wooden surface on the floor and walls. The rest was painted onto the 3D model.

Space is very important. The foreground and background need to be clearly defined. This is why the Cottage—in the entryway (see Figure 6.3)—has trees on both sides leading the eye into the scenery. The trees in the background have significantly less detail than the ones in the foreground. I find that a disadvantage of 3D programs is that everything is in focus, thus taking away from the illusion of space. Scaling is another factor. Objects should be in scale with the size of an average avatar, so that people can sit comfortably in chairs, climb the trees, or walk through a door. In that respect, the angle of the view is important, too. It must allow people to anchor their avatars to a certain point in space so that their

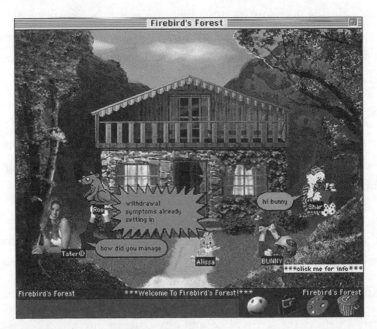

Figure 6.3   Firebird's Forest entryway.

position in the room is clearly defined. A person just doesn't place his or her avatar on the screen; they stand by the fire, lay on the carpet, or perch on a rooftop.

K & T: What are your future plans?

Gromp: We are constantly expanding and improving the site as a community. Many fun events are in the works—jokes night and a treasure hunt to name a few. We want the Forest to stand as an example of what we have done. It is a showcase of the talents and quality of our work. We hope to develop more sites for commercial purposes, so we formed a new company, Asaph Creations.

Apparently, someone believes in the talent of this group. A philanthropist, who shall remain nameless, offered to host Firebird's Forest site on a dedicated Unix server with a high-speed connection to the Internet.

Turkette's Frustration Is Your Pleasure

Turkette created a Palace site and called it Turkette's Frustration. She is a young woman, majoring in chemistry, attending a university in Kentucky. Although she's been online and owned a computer for quite some time, she doesn't consider herself a "geek." So, why did she invest the time, resources, and sometimes the frustration to build a site? Read the following interview to find out.

T & K: Why did you build your Palace site?

Turkette: I originally started my Palace as a place to store my important props and as a place to experiment with various Palace tricks. After getting it set up though, I thought, "I could really do a lot with this place."

Several of my friends were also excited by the possibilities, so I decided to keep it up and give myself and my friends a place to experiment and learn. I now believe that with more work, my little Palace could really be a worthwhile place to visit.

T & K: How does your site build a sense of community?

Turkette: I believe the sense of community that my site offers is the chance for people to get to know one another outside of the mainstream Palace sites. It is a lot easier to get to know someone when there are fewer distractions. I also believe that for my friends and I to be working and learning together towards a common goal helps immensely with the feeling of closeness and friendship. I have also made several new friends directly because of my involvement in creating a Palace.

T & K: How did you manage the creative development?

Turkette: The creative development of my Palace is directly due to a very dear friend of mine who is a struggling graphic artist. I believe that my Palace offers him a place to show his work without any restrictions; he is free to be as creative as he likes. I also hope that by having his art in my Palace (see Figure 6.4) he may eventually get the recognition he deserves for his work.

T & K: Who visits your site?

Turkette: The primary audience for my Palace right now are friends and people needing advice on the creation of their own sites. When my Palace is finished, I believe the appeal will be towards people that appreciate surreal and entertaining environments.

T & K: What types of relationships have you formed by building your Palace site?

Figure 6.4 Turkette's frustration, a surrealistic view.

Turkette: The relationships I have formed during the creation of my site have been great ones. It really seems to bring a sense of closeness when you are able to share common interests. In the process of creating my Palace, I have both received and given a lot of advice. This seems to create a link between people. When you are able to help someone, both people feel good about what they are doing.

T & K: What advice or help could you give to other Palace builders?

Turkette: What I would recommend to anyone starting a Palace is to do as much research as he or she can on the process and to ask other people for advice. Most people love to help others by sharing what they have learned while creating their own sites. Another good place to look for help is the Palace home page; there are many links to helpful advice. Most of all, I would recommend that they have fun with it. Creating something uniquely yours can be very enjoyable.

Hangin' With The Smileys

What types of people will you find at the Palace? I'm not talking about personalities here—after all, people are people. I'm referring to the social stratification of the Palace community.

GUESTS

The guests are low people on the totem pole. Guests haven't paid any money to register their software, but they do have trial membership status. As a guest, you are allowed three free hours of member privileges at the Welcome Palace (shown in Figure 6.5), where you may specify a nickname, create and wear an avatar, run scripts, and generally do anything that registered members can. Overall, the Palace community is very supportive of and friendly to new users.

MEMBERS

Members occupy the rung above guests in the hierarchy and make up the largest segment in the Palace community. They have *full citizenship* in the Palace, and can visit member-only sites, create custom avatars, define their nicknames, and other cool stuff. Members usually hang out in smaller Palace sites. They may be tired of

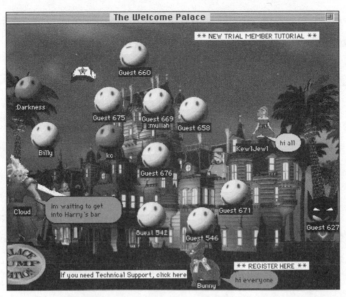

Figure 6.5 Entryway at the Welcome Palace (**palace://palace.thepalace .com:9998**)—a friendly place for new users.

the crowded atmosphere of Main and are looking for more solid relationships; Main, at times, can feel like a pick-up bar. Or maybe they've found a site that suits their particular interest, such as one of the gaming or computer sites.

Members fit into one of two categories: they're either satisfied with their station in life, or they aspire to be wizards. You'll usually find people in the latter group hanging out at one or two specific Palaces, hoping to get noticed by the wizards or gods.

WIZARDS

The creator of a Palace site can grant special powers related to safeguarding the site. Some sites may only procure a handful of wizards, while others, such as Kids Nation, employ 40 or more. Upon entering many Palace sites, you'll be welcomed with a "the wizards have been paged" sign. This script lets the wizards know that someone has entered the site; if one is free, maybe he or she will pop in and say hi. And if you're having problems of a technical or social nature, call a wizard to assist you. You'll recognize them because they wear an asterisk (*) before their nickname.

Wizards are also known to create, update, and change a site. Sometimes wizards have special abilities that make them attractive to a god: artistic talent, technical abilities, or outstanding small group communication skills. Wizards typically hang out on the Palace user group mailing lists and discussion boards.

 ### Wizard Politics
Many wizards are lobbying for stricter structure. They would like to see decisions to create voting procedures, establish rules of order, and establish punishments and jails for "crimes."

GODS

Gods are the creators of a site. They have total control over how the site is managed, and are the equivalent of Webmasters on the Web or sysops on bulletin-board systems. You probably won't run into too many gods—they're usually too busy in the background, making changes or working with scripts, to come to the foreground.

MAGI

Magi are devoted to helping the Palace community. These people, all Palace experts, have banded together informally to create a Web site, a Palace site, a mailing list, FAQs, tutorials, Palace bus tours, special events, and more. From technical help to marketing, the magi are a wealth of knowledge. One of the most helpful items they've created is an informational bulletin board, shown in Figure 6.6.

Jim Bumgardner sees specific trends evolving within the Palace community. Stratification, as described previously, will continue. Cliques have formed. And, as with any society, rules of behavior and communication will become much more complex. Not like it isn't already; chat on the Internet (and in Palace) is full of cute little abbreviations and conversational shorthand.

Important Lessons From Palace History

Actually, these lessons can apply to any type of community in cyberspace, but since they happened on the Palace, this might be a good time to reflect on them. These stories were extracted with permission from *Conception to Toddlerhood—A History*

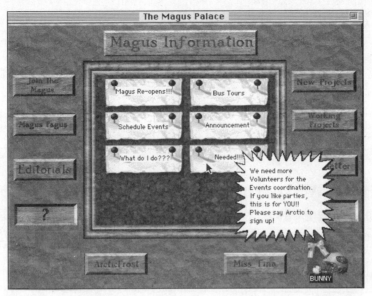

Figure 6.6 Magus information bulletin board (**palace://arcticfrost .com: 9997**).

of the First Year (or so) of The Palace (January 1997) by John Suler. By the way, John's article was published on the World Wide Web (**www1.rider.edu/~suler/ psycyber/palhistory.html**).

THE SKEEZIL INCIDENT

Skeezil was a well-respected, talented, and devoted member of the Palace community. He was given supervisory responsibilities at some Palace sites, and even placed in the position of Vice Chairperson of the newly formed Palace User Group (PUG). Much to the surprise and dismay of some adult members, Skeezil turned out *not* to be the 26-year-old computer programmer he claimed to be, but rather a 14-year-old dishwasher/busboy with lots of computer time on his hands.

What Did We Learn From Skeezil?

Cyberspace is a level playing ground, where appearance and status from the *real* world fall to the wayside. "Unimportant" people can be heard and recognized just like the "important" people. Yet, in cyberspace, people are not always who they seem to be.

THE DEATH OF ROBIN

Robin was a regular at the Palace. Many people knew and liked her. However, many of her online friends didn't know that she suffered from a very painful and destructive version of MS, until she died. Some people wished they had known more about her condition so they could have helped her. A memorial service was held at one of the Palace sites, and a Web page describing her life was posted. At the Main Mansion site, Robin's Garden was erected in her memory.

What Have We Learned From Robin?

Disabilities are not always visible online. In some ways, that may be a good thing. In other ways, it may not. Palace is a community like any real-world community, with all the same triumphs and losses.

Taking The Next Step

In this chapter, we looked at what the Palace is, why it's an essential component of your virtual community, and how the Palace culture functions. When you first start managing your Palace site, if you choose to build one, you'll find it challenging and you'll likely make mistakes. Network with other Palace wizards, gods, and magi, and call on their collective experience to help you. After all, that's the great thing about a community; you can draw on the many human resources out there for support. You'll want to use the Palace extensively, look at what the many Palacians are doing, and make new cyberbuddies. In Chapter 7, we'll show you how to create your own avatar. Then you'll be all set to venture forth into the world of Palace building in Chapter 8. See you there.

Chapter 7

The Construction And Psychology Of Avatars

Chapter 7

- PSYCHOLOGICAL AVATAR PROFILES

- LEARNING A NEW LANGUAGE WITH AVATARS

- AVATAR ETIQUETTE

- AVATAR CREATION AND GRAPHICS APPLICATIONS

THE CONSTRUCTION AND PSYCHOLOGY OF AVATARS

Chapter 7

All About Avatars

It's pretty easy to get hooked on the Palace, and as soon as you pay the registration fee and get your serial number, you'll be able to unlock the secret power of avatars. As a community leader, if you think you want to go through with this and build your own Palace site, you'll need a distinctive name and look. Well, you have to supply the name yourself, but we can help with the avatar. We can also help you with the unique props that you'll litter your Palace site with and share with your new community minions. Of course, to build an avatar, you'll need a grasp on the psychology of avatars.

Avatars And Props—Which Is Which?

Avatars. Props. What's the difference? Sometimes these words are used interchangeably, but there is a difference. *Avatars* refer to pictures, drawings, or icons that users choose to represent themselves. *Props* are objects that users add to their avatars (say, a hat or a cigar), place in a Palace room, or give to another person (say, a can of soda or a bouquet of flowers).

Figure 7.1   Here's a picture of Dr. Suler. He kinda looks like a psychologist, doesn't he?

To help us out with the psychology of avatars (or avs) and their interaction at Palace sites, we'll turn the floor over to our esteemed colleague, John Suler, Ph.D. John (shown in Figure 7.1) is professor of psychology at Rider University in New Jersey, and a practicing clinician. His interests include psychoanalytic, existential, and Eastern psychology, with current research focusing on the psychology of cyberspace. His Web publications include "The Psychology of Cyberspace" (**www1.rider.edu/~suler/psycyber/psycyber.html**), "Teaching Clinical Psychology" (**www1.rider.edu/~suler/tcp.html**), and "Zen Stories to Tell Your Neighbors" (**www1.rider.edu/~suler/zenstory/zenstory.html**).

Suler On The Types Of Avatars

STANDARD AVATARS

Avs fall into two overall categories. The first are the standard set of "smileys" that come with the Palace program. These faces are available to all users, including unregistered guests. They come in a set that displays basic human emotions and behavioral signals—happy, sad, angry, winking, sleeping/bored, blushing, head-nodding, and head-shaking. The user also can change the color of the face or add to it one or more props, such as hats, wigs, scarves, devil horns, a halo, a glass of beer, a bicycle, etc. [See Figure 7.2.] Because the faces and props can be mixed and matched, users have at their disposal an almost infinite array of combinations to express themselves. Want to drink a beer and smile? Do it! Want to poke at someone who made you angry. Put on that frown and pitchfork!

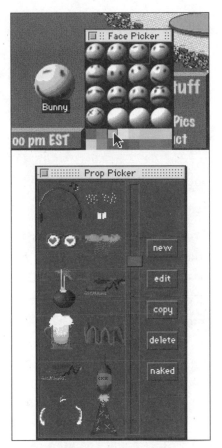

Figure 7.2 The various colors, facial expressions, and accessories for the standard smiley avatars.

As such, the standard set of avs are designed very cleverly and offer a wide range of behavioral and emotional expression. Because you quickly can shift among a variety of facial gestures to convey your emotional state, one member, Heyoka, told me these smileys are her avatars of choice. She is the exception rather than the rule. Most registered members of Palace rarely use them. In fact, some of them *hate* the smileys. "They're dorky," one member told me, "I wouldn't be caught dead wearing those tennis balls."

CUSTOM AVATARS

This leads to the second major category of avatars—those created by the members themselves. Only after paying the registration fee can the user unlock the prop creating/editing feature of the Palace software. This is the key to what is perhaps the most fascinating aspect of the Palace. Visually, you can be any-thing you want. Only your graphics skills and imagination limit you. Early in the development of the Palace, Bumgardner noticed that people preferred the custom faces over the more anonymous smileys. In cyberspace, most people don't want to be totally anonymous. But they *do* like control over how their identity is expressed. They like it a lot. Hang out at the Palace for any length of time and a seemingly endless parade of avs of all shapes, colors, and styles pass before your eyes.

We social scientists love to categorize the phenomena we study. So allow me to indulge my professional inclinations. I'll outline here several different types of custom avatars. By no means is this list definitive or exhaustive. There are many ways to slice a pie. I've chosen these categories partly because some of them are fairly obvious, and partly because each one conveys interesting psychological and social themes.

Animal Avatars

Animal avatars [see Figure 7.3] are some of the most popular at the Palace. Some members come as their pets. Because animals symbolize certain traits or attributes in myth as well as popular culture (e.g., strength, loyalty, grace, independence, cunning, transcendence), the animal chosen for an avatar probably bears psychological significance to the user—perhaps representing some real aspect of the member, or some characteristic admired by the user. Thinking in the tradition of the Native American, we might even regard an animal avatar as being a member's "totem."

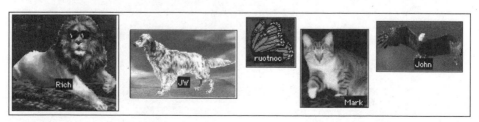

Figure 7.3 Examples of animal avatars.

Cartoon Avatars

While younger users (adolescents) may be more inclined to don cartoon costumes, older members frequently use them as well. The psychological significance of the cartoon character probably affects the choice made by the user. People select characters with whom they identify or admire. Rather than relying on childhood cartoon figures, some adults wear cartoon avs of a more sophisticated style—some of these classified as "anime." See Figure 7.4. The psychological tone of these avs tend to be more seductive, whimsical, or mysterious.

Celebrity Avatars

Celebrity avatars [Figure 7.5 spotlights celebrity avs] tend to follow trends in popular culture. There may be a variety of motives behind the use of these avs. People may use them to express personality traits or social issues that are associated with the celebrity's image (sensuality, intelligence, power, corruption, rebellion, etc.). The user may identify with, desire, or be poking fun at these attributes. They may hope to bolster their self-esteem and identity by establishing their connection to the celebrity. They may simply wish to display a knowledge of current events in pop culture. Celebrity avs also advertise one's specific interests in entertainment in order to find like-minded users: "Hey, I like Seinfeld! Anyone else out there like Seinfeld?"

Figure 7.4 A variety of cartoon avatars.

Figure 7.5 Look who's popping up as celebrity avatars.

Evil Avatars

Everyone has a dark or "evil" side to his or her personality. The definition of "evil" varies from person to person, although usually it has something to do with malicious, aggressive fantasies and/or feelings of guilt. Note how many Halloween costumes fit this category. As a form of sublimation, evil costumes allow people to safely—and even creatively—express their dark side. While some members may wear an evil av [like those in Figure 7.6] as their facade for the evening (which may reflect their mood at the time), others may "flash" it as a momentary cue to others. Mess with wizards, for example, and they may flash their evil av as a warning that they're getting annoyed and may pin, gag, or kill you. On one occasion, I witnessed a male come on to an attractive female member wearing a real face prop. When her attempts to brush him off failed, she flashed a nefarious looking skull at him. He quickly backed off.

Real Face Avatars

Most users do not use pictures of themselves as their primary avatars. People prefer the partial anonymity. Or they simply enjoy the creative fun of experimenting with new identities through their avs. In more rare cases, members find the use of real face avs to be an uncomfortable, disassociative experience. "I have a picture of myself in the prop file, but I really don't like to use it any longer than it takes for me to show it to a new friend," said River, a wizard. "It is a little disturbing to sit here at home and see myself speaking in cartoon balloons in a non-reality. Whew!!!!"

When users do present pictures of their real faces [check out revealing Figure 7.7], it may be a gesture of honesty and/or intimacy—a sign of friendship,

Figure 7.6 Feeling naughty? Try an evil avatar.

Figure 7.7 Reveal yourself with real face avatars.

or even romance. Showing one's real face av can be a very poignant experience. Several members have described to me encounters when an intimate conversation culminated in their companion showing a real face av. "That moment will stay with me for a long time to come," one member stated, "The value I placed on that particular moment was friendship, trust, a sense of oneness."

Idiosyncratic Avatars

These avatars [showcased in Figure 7.8] become strongly associated with a specific member—almost as if it is that person's trademark. In some cases the avatar may be highly unusual or creative. Sometimes it is quite simple. Yet its association to the particular user is so strong that others experience it uniquely as that person. While trading props is a common practice, the owner of an idiosyncratic av rarely gives it away. It would be like giving one's identity to someone else to use. Conscientious members also don't "steal" (i.e., screen capture) an idiosyncratic av and use it as their own. They respect its integrity. If someone does steal and attempts to wear an "idio" av, they must be willing to put up with criticism by the friends of the owner.

Figure 7.8 Idiosyncratic avatars are unique to individuals.

Figure 7.9 Users of power avatars show their strength.

Power Avatars

Power avatars are symbols of…well…power [see the strong Figure 7.9]. Who wouldn't want strength and invulnerability? In some cases the power theme is benign. Sometimes not, which may be a variation of the "evil" avatar. Because competition invariably accompanies displays of power, members seem to vie with each other in creating the most "awesome" power av.

Seductive Avatars

Frontal nudity, including uncovered breasts, are not permitted at the [Main and Welcome] Palace. Some users create avatars of partially naked or scantily clothed figures. A seductive, sexy, or simply "attractive" avatar can have a powerful impact on other members. One member described how his prop of a cartoon animal didn't seem to be getting him much attention from females. Most of them wouldn't talk to him. Curious about whether he could alter this situation, he searched the Net and found a picture of Brad Pitt which he turned into an av. The result? Lots of attention. If he happened to be wearing his cartoon prop and found that he was being ignored by a woman, he would move to another room, switch to Brad Pitt, and then return. Or he would switch to Pitt right in front of her. Nine times out of ten, he said, the woman would strike up a conversation with him even if he hadn't said a word. He even established a relationship with someone who eventually wanted to meet him face-to-face. "The pic got her attention," he concluded, "but in the end it was me that won her over."

Suler Discovers How Many Ways You Can Say "Hi" At The Palace

We type "hi lucy" and hit return. Now if Lucy is a good friend, we've committed a bit of a *faux pas* here [see Figure 7.10]. This salute is rather lukewarm. It's perfectly appropriate as a polite greeting to strangers and casual acquaintances, but for a friend it's a weak gesture. First of all, without even one exclamation point, or caps, there's very little evidence of enthusiasm. The fact that we didn't even bother to capitalize Lucy's name (or the "H" in hi) might be taken as a sign of indifference or laziness. Lucy may wonder why we seem a bit distant and formal.

So let's try again. Lucy appears in the doorway, only this time we type "Hi Lucy!" That's better. Caps, an exclamation point...some enthusiasm! An unspoken norm at the Palace is that one's degree of enthusiasm is loosely correlated with the number of exclamation points in the greeting. The more, the better, unless your exclamations start piling up in an ostentatiously long row and spill over to another line of typed text [see Figure 7.11]. That might be considered overkill...overly eager enthusiasm (or a perseveration indicative of an underlying organic mental disorder).

For a slightly different interpersonal effect, we might use a "spikey"—also known as an "excited balloon." It indicates, obviously, that we're excited to see

Figure 7.10   A lukewarm welcome to Lucy.

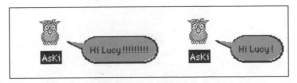

Figure 7.11   Some more enthusiastic welcomes to Lucy.

Lucy. The enthusiasm here is a bit different than simply using exclamation points. The very electric-looking spikey [shown in Figure 7.12] has a more visceral impact. It will be more quickly noticed by Lucy than a standard text balloon. It also will be quickly noticed by other users. We're making it very clear to everyone in the room that we're saying hello to Lucy and are elated about seeing her. It also takes a bit more keyboarding effort to create a spikey, which suggests that we went out of our way to show our enthusiasm for Lucy. A spikey with just "LUCY" (in caps) is like jumping up out of your chair while shooting your arms into the air with surprise and delight. As with abundant exclamation points, a spikey greeting will cause others to think that we must be good friends with Lucy. But if you use too many spikeys (or exclamation points) with too many people, others will assume that you're putting on an act and being a bit disingenuous.

Maybe we want to show emotion other than enthusiasm when Lucy arrives. Maybe we want to show warmth, affection. For quite some time in many chat environments, this affection has been expressed by the use of brackets or parentheses that "hug" the name of the fellow user [as shown in Figure 7.13]. It's interesting that this technique rarely is used at the Palace. It's hard to say why. Palatians do like to think of their culture as unique—especially its graphical features. So widespread habits from other virtual communities may be viewed as a bit hackneyed when applied at the Palace.

Figure 7.12   Wow, it's Lucy!

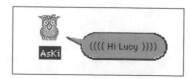

Figure 7.13   Expressing warm fuzzies to Lucy.

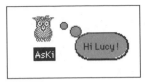

Figure 7.14 Mind reading with Lucy.

A "thought balloon" greeting also is rare because it doesn't have an equivalent in the real world [contemplate Figure 7.14]. Could we think "Hi Lucy!" and expect her to know that we were saying hello? Not in real life. Not unless we're a schizophrenic afflicted with delusions of thought-broadcasting. For that very reason, our "Hi Lucy!" in a thought balloon would look quite strange at the Palace. People might think that we simply mistyped, don't understand how to use Palace commands, or deliberately are trying to under-emphasize our greeting to Lucy by playing our cards close to our chest. They may wonder if we're muttering to ourselves, or expect other people to read our mind. They may simply *wonder* about us...and why Lucy has this effect on us! Lucy probably will be thinking the same things.

The beauty of the Palace compared to text-only chat is that we (or rather, our avatars) can *move*. When Lucy arrives we could "run" to her side. She most likely will notice this and take our gesture as a sign that we feel close to her. With exclamations punctuating our hello, we are showing bursting enthusiasm that may cause people to take notice. We obviously like Lucy because we scream and run to her side when she arrives. Running to Lucy with a spikey would magnify this effect even more, though it might be a bit over the top in expressing enthusiasm.

Running to Lucy with a simple "Hi Lucy" *without* exclamations or spikeys can take on a very different meaning. Lucy most likely will know that we ran to her, but in a crowded room other people probably won't notice this. It's a more subtle, private, even secretive way to express our hello. If it's an uncrowded room, people will surmise that we are close to Lucy. They may even think that we are an "item" and are not hesitant about letting others see that.

Top 10 Ways To Master The Palace

Well, now that Dr. Suler has given us the lowdown on the psychology of social interaction with the Palace, you're probably ready to get started with your Palace experience. These tips will get you well on your way:

1. *Do* join a Palace User Group discussion group or mailing list. You can find more info at the Palace's Web site at **newbie.thepalace.com/D100.html**.

2. *Do* move closer to another person during a one-on-one conversation, to show that you're interested in what the other person is saying. It's not polite to shout across the room.

3. *Do* create your own avatar. It's fun. See the instructions later in this chapter.

4. *Do* help each other. In Palace culture, karma rules. It's unlike most archetypes of chat that came before in that its close-knit structure inspires cooperation. Give and you shall receive.

5. *Do* learn how to use the 16 common sounds to add flavor to your conversations, but save them for "dramatic effects." (See number 7 in "10 Tips For Not Getting Your Av Kicked.")

6. *Do* use emoticons to punctuate your speech with virtual body language. If you want to use the "smiley" emoticon, use a double ":" mark. The first creates a thought bubble, while the second creates the eyes of the smiley.

7. *Do* explore different rooms; you may find hidden objects or games to play. Palace is more than just chat—it's an experience.

8. *Do* clean up after yourself. If you're trading props, painting, or playing games, put everything back where it belongs before you leave.

9. *Do* use the menu bar. Great options await you—finding other users, locating rooms, and saving your log to a text file.

10. *Do* take a Magus bus tour. Tours to Palace sites leave every Saturday; contact **mstrsst@soho.ios.com** for details.

10 Tips For Not Getting Your Av Kicked

All right, you know what to do to get into Palace society and Dr. Suler should have given you an insight into the culture, roles, and accepted modes of behavior at the Palace. But if you're still unclear or if you're thinking about causing some trouble, here's your last chance to learn how to behave:

1. Do *not* sit on people or treat them as objects. Guest 2772 in Figure 7.15 is a first-time Palace user. Not only did he sit on Shelli, but he made overt gestures towards her—notice the star-struck eyes? Believe me, Shelli was extremely annoyed by 2772's behavior, and called him a "snert"—a snot-nosed eros-ridden twit. Had 2772 stuck around much longer, she would have paged a wizard to reprimand him.

2. Do *not* wear a prop that you wouldn't really wear in public We have personally witnessed members ostracized for their attire, so go easy on the Hunk/Babe-of-the-Month artwork. Don't be too literal with this rule, after all the chocolate rabbit avatar worn by Bunny (Karla) is fine on The Palace, but obviously would not go over well at the office.

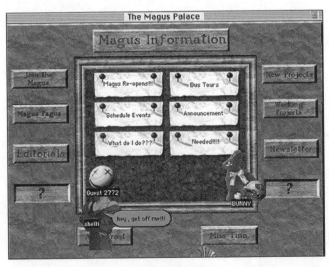

Figure 7.15   A rude guest at the Magus Palace.

3. Do *not* oversize your av. A large image is a burden on the server. Remember, bigger is not better.

4. Do *not* steal props.

5. Do *not* steal nicknames.

6. Do *not* impersonate someone else. Stealing an av is one thing—donning some-one else's nickname is another—but both at the same time? Blasphemy! It makes you a double snert.

7. Do *not* flood the server. Every time you enter a line of text or command your avatar to change, you are sending data to the server. If you send too much data too fast, you cause the server to work harder and subsequently you slow down the system, and that in turn slows everyone else down. They will be really mad at you for it.

8. Do *not* allow your av to turn into a "sleeper." If you feel the need to check your email or surf the Web, be considerate of others and put up a "be right back" sign. Or just disconnect for awhile.

9. Do *not* ask people to repeat themselves. If you fall behind in conversation, refer to the record of the current chat session in your log window, which is available in the Options menu.

10. And *never, ever* ask to become a wizard. If a god thinks thee worthy, he or she will bid thee participate.

In short, treat others the same as you would in meatspace. Even though you're using avatars, it's easy to forget that you don't really have the subtlety of body language going for you.

Palace Avatar Generators: The Cheap And Easy Way To Get An Avatar

The easiest way to get started is to use an avatar that someone else has made. Many Palace sites offer avatar and prop generators where you can try lots of avs on for size, just like shopping for clothes at the mall. Palace in Wonderland (**palace://wonder.lag.com**), operated by Cyberia, offers a plethora of storybook images, ranging from Cheshire cats to Humpty Dumpty to mad hatters. Being partial to rabbits, we clicked on the "cool rabbit" avatar. Doesn't Bunny look spiffy? (See Figure 7.16.)

Many sites are adding the generator feature, each with its own twist in functionality. For instance, at Electric Minds (**palace://minds.com**), you can choose such components as bodies, eyes, ears, legs, and arms. This makes custom avatar creation fun and easy. Of course, you might just want to create your own avatar from scratch, so read on in the next section to learn how.

Karla And Her Bunny Avatar

Avatars are made of graphic blocks. To store this avatar, Bunny dragged the pieces (using her mouse) into her prop bag (or suitcase), located on the Palace interface. After all the pieces were in the suitcase, Bunny was naked. When an avatar is naked, it just means it has turned back into a smiley, or tennis ball as it's sometimes called. To reassemble the rabbit avatar, Bunny clicked on the pieces in her prop bag and saved this as a macro. Currently, the Macintosh

Figure 7.16 It looks like Bunny really likes her new outfit.

client and the Windows client are slightly different as far as saving avatars is concerned. For a thorough explanation, see "Saving Your Avatar" at the end of this chapter.

How To Create Your Own Custom Avatar

Although you might look pretty good in an avatar assembled from another site, most members want to make one of their own. Here's an easy guide to get you into fancy threads in no time.

GET AN IMAGE

To begin with, you need an image to make an avatar. Unless you're an *artiste extraordinaire*, you'll probably want to use existing images. With the wide variety of options available, you won't have a problem finding something you like on the Web. Once you find it, it's easy to save the graphic to your hard drive: Position your mouse over the image. Windows users, right click on the image. Macintosh users, hold down your mouse button. Now go to "Save this image as" and select the directory in which to save your image. We suggest putting it in the Palace folder.

Here are some places on the Web to look for images.

Image Generators

The Web has a few image generators not specifically tied to the Palace. At these sites you can customize features. Later, you can resize the resulting graphic to meet the Palace avatar standards that we'll talk about in the next section. We tried Cartoon-a-matic (**www.nfx.com/cgi-bin/livingart**). We tweaked the controls for face, ears, mouth, and nose, and then we customized the size and placement of the features, as shown in Figure 7.17.

Clip Art Libraries

Photodisc is one of our favorite sites (**www.photodisc.com**). This company publishes over 50,000 high quality images, both online and on CD-ROM, for graphic

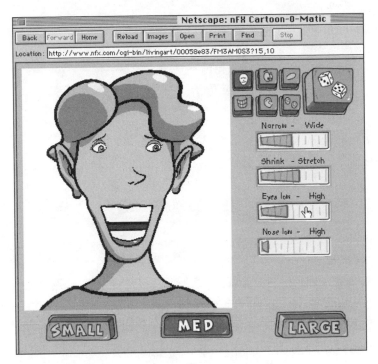

Figure 7.17 Generating an avatar at Cartoon-a-matic.

designers, advertising agencies, desktop publishers, and other enthusiasts. These images are royalty-free, but you must purchase a basic license (about $19.95) to use them for your Web site or avatar. In Figure 7.18, you'll notice we found an image by searching for the word "bunny."

You'll need to register before you download images. Payment is negotiated through an online credit-card system on a secure server, but if you're nervous about giving out credit-card information online, call 800-528-3472. You'll receive a Starter Kit containing a CD-ROM with nearly 10,000 complimentary images, complete with keyword searching, 20 bonus high-resolution images, and two resource books.

Art Today contains over 550,000 images in JPEG, GIF, EPS, BMP, and PICT file formats (see Figure 7.19). Art Today (**www.arttoday.com**) is like a club—you can join for a day, a month, or a year. As long as you're a member, you have unlimited use of the Art Today collection. Check out the Web site for pricing information. Or if you want an art collection on CD-ROM, check out the Best of Art Today CD-ROM bundle for about $49.95.

Figure 7.18 Searching for images on the Photodisc Web site.

Figure 7.19 Searching for images on the Art Today Web site.

If you're not into shelling out bucks for graphics, there are plenty of freeware libraries to check out. One of the most impressive sites is FILEZ (**www.filez.com**), where you can search through mountainous FTP sites for images. We executed a search for "bunny," and in minutes over 100 hits were returned. Figure 7.20 shows just a few examples of these high-quality images.

Figure 7.20   A sampling of the files found through FILEZ.

Be sure to read the Disclaimer And Limitation Of Liability on FILEZ before you use an image from this site.

Other clip art libraries you may want to check out include:

- Clip Art Connection—**www.ist.net/clipart/index.html**

- The Clip Art Directory—**www.clipart.com**

- Clip Art Review's Search Engine—**www.webplaces.com/search**

If all else fails, go to a search engine and type in a keyword, followed by the GIF or JPG extension. We used bunny.gif and thousands of hits came back in Wired's Hot Bot (**www.hotbot.com**).

Scanned Images

Here are some general recommendations for scanning images:

- Choose a high quality flatbed color scanner.

- Choose scanner software that allows you to adjust the resolution, as well as the orientation, of the image to be scanned.

- Non-glossy images produce the best scanned results.

- Choose scanning software that will compress your image as small as possible.

- In order to create the smallest file size possible for your pictures, adjust the resolution of the image before you scan it. For avatars, you should typically scan at 72 dots per inch (dpi).

IMAGE PROCESSING: SCALING, REORIENTING, AND CROPPING YOUR IMAGE

Most images will not be exactly the size you want. Here are some rules of thumb for sizing and scaling pictures.

- It's better to use a larger picture and reduce it in size than to enlarge a smaller picture.

- If you must enlarge a smaller image, scan it in with a higher resolution. This will enhance the image in the enlargement process.

- Remember, the larger the picture, the larger the file size.

In addition, the image you've chosen may not be facing the direction you want it to. There are two simple solutions:

- If the picture did not fit the physical dimensions of the scanner one way, but did fit the other way, you can still use the image by simply rotating it after it's been scanned.

- If you scanned a picture in upside down, or facing the wrong way, you can reorient the image to the correct position.

Often a scanned image includes background or other unwanted material. To crop it, select the desired area and cut out the rest.

Obtain An Image Editing Program

To make the changes described previously, you'll need an image editing program. Most graphic designers prefer Photoshop, which has a street price of about $395. If you have a scanner, you may have Photoshop Lite already. If neither of these programs is a good option for you, there are several good shareware programs on the market. In the following sections, I'll explain how to carry out the required steps in two shareware programs: Paint Shop Pro and Graphic Converter.

 ### Important Safety Tip

Before you begin creating your avatar, be sure to create a backup copy of your original image. Avatar creation isn't too difficult, but it does take some practice, and we all make mistakes!

Resize Your Image

There are two types of avatars that you can import into the Palace: single tile and multiple tile. A single-tile avatar is 44×44 pixels, while multiple-tile avatars may be as large as 132×132 pixels. In terms of on-screen performance of the avatar, there is no real difference between the sizes, but obviously one is much bigger than the other. Remember that big avatars can crowd a room, so try to be reasonable when deciding how big your avatar is going to be.

1. Open your image from within your image editing program.

2. Change the width and height of the image.

Paint Shop Pro: In the menu bar, choose the Image|Resize command. Specify the Custom Size option, and in the dialog box, select the Maintain Aspect Ratio option (this will maintain the proportion of your image while you are adjusting width and height). Now resize the image until both width and height are less than 132 pixels. (See Figure 7.21.) Click on OK.

Graphic Converter: In the menu bar, select Picture|Size|Scale. In the dialog box that pops up, select the Proportional checkbox, then click on the Size radio button. Now, resize the image until both width and height are 132 pixels or less. (See Figure 7.22.) Click on OK.

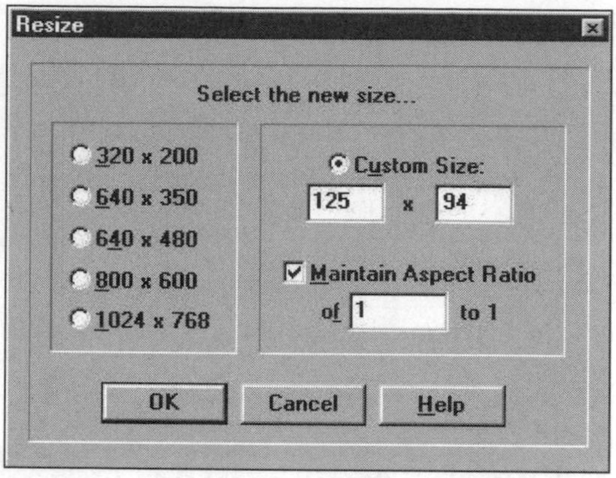

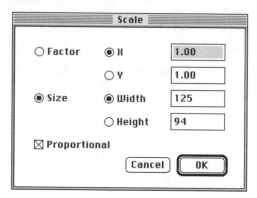

Figure 7.21 Resizing an image with Paint Shop Pro.

Figure 7.22 Resizing an image with Graphic Converter.

CONVERT YOUR IMAGE TO THE PALACE CLUT FORMAT

CLUT stands for "Color Look Up Table." This is a fancy way of specifying which colors you have to play with, and how many of them you can use within an image (otherwise known as a *palette*). If you don't convert your images to the Palace CLUT, weird things will happen—colors won't appear accurately or your image will look fuzzy and "dithered." The Palace CLUT, which can be found in the Palette folder on the CD-ROM included with this book, uses 236 colors, which makes it different from the Windows and Macintosh color system palettes. (See Figure 7.23.) Copy the appropriate files to your hard drive. Most designers store CLUTS in a single place, usually in a folder labeled CLUT or Palette within their image editing program.

Figure 7.23 The palette used in the Palace.

Here's how to make sure your image is using the Palace CLUT:

1. If your image is a GIF or grayscale image, convert it to RGB first. If it is a JPG,
   PICT, or BMP, skip to Step 2.

Paint Shop Pro: In the menu bar, go to Colors|Increase Color Depth|16 Million
Colors.

Graphic Converter: In the menu bar, go to Picture|Colors|Change to 16.7 Million
Colors.

2. Load the Palace CLUT.

Paint Shop Pro: Go to the menu bar and select Colors|Load Palette. Now, locate
the CLUT (named Palace.PAL). Three options are available for using the Palace
CLUT in your image. If you select Nearest Color Matching, Paint Shop Pro will
change each color in the image to the color in the Palace CLUT. The Error
Diffusion Dithering method will attempt to maintain the image's appearance by
dithering colors. Selecting the Maintain Indexes method option will assign each
color in the palette a sequential index number. The same routine is then performed
for the colors in your image, and finally each color in the image is changed to a
like-numbered color in the palette. Choose the option best suited for your graphic—
you may have to try each option to determine which is best. Click on OK.

Graphic Converter: Go to Picture|Colors|Options. In the pop-up dialog box, select
Use Custom Color Table, then click on the Open button. Now locate the CLUT,
named "Palace CLUT.PAL". If you check the Dither option, your image will have
attractive tonal gradations; you'll also end up with a larger file size. Now click on OK.

Preparing Your Image For A Transparent Background

An avatar with a transparent background has a specific color set to "invisible," so the room art shows through wherever that color appears in the avatar. Look at the bunny avatar in Figure 7.24. The image is actually a rectangular 44×44 pixel image, but the background has been made unobservable by "erasing" it, leaving only the bunny image visible. The image in Figure 7.25 is 132×132 pixels. None of the background has been erased—it is non-transparent.

If you'd like to make your background transparent, it helps to start with an image that has a solid color background. My avatar started with a white background. Dr. X, who runs the House of Props and Bots (**www.rahul.net/natpix/**) recommends changing this background to a bright neon green, which will make it easier to erase the background after the image has been converted to GIF format.

Here's how to change your background to neon green:

1. Change the color selection in the Background icon.

Paint Shop Pro: In the Tool Box, double-click on the Foreground icon (See Figure 7.26.). A dialog box will appear. In the Red field, type 51; in the Green field,

Figure 7.24   A transparent avatar.

Figure 7.25   A non-transparent avatar.

Figure 7.26   Changing the color selection in Paint Shop Pro.

type 255; in the Blue field, type 0. The new color selection is the neon green recommended by Dr. X. Click on OK.

Graphic Converter: In the Tool Box, double-click on the Foreground icon. (See Figure 7.27.) A dialog box will appear. Choose the Apple RGB icon. Then type 51

Figure 7.27   Changing the color selection in Graphic Converter.

in the Red slider percentage box; 255 in the Green slider percentage box, and 0 in the Blue slider percentage box. The new color selection is the neon green recommended by Dr. X. Click on OK.

2. Change the background color on your image.

Paint Shop Pro: In the Tool Box, select the Paint Bucket icon. Position your mouse pointer, which has changed into a bucket, over the area of the background of your image and click your mouse (see Figure 7.28).

Graphic Converter: In the Tool Box, select the Paint Can icon. Position your mouse pointer, which has changed into a paint can, over the background of the image and click your mouse (see Figure 7.29).

You'll notice the background of your avatar has now changed to neon green.

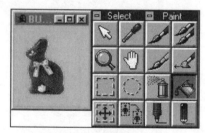

Figure 7.28 Changing the image background color with Paint Shop Pro.

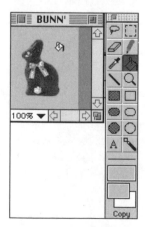

Figure 7.29 Changing the image background color with Graphic Converter.

SAVING YOUR IMAGE AS A GIF

Here's how to save your image as a GIF:

1. Change the image to GIF format.

Paint Shop Pro: In the menu bar, select Colors|Decrease Color Depth|256 Colors (8 bit). In the dialog box, select the Optimized radio button; then select the best reduction method, Nearest Color or Error Diffusion. Experience and trial and error will be your best teacher here.

Graphic Converter: Select Picture|Colors|Change to 256 Colors.

2. Save image as GIF.

Paint Shop Pro: Go to the menu bar and select File|Save As. Click on OK.

Graphic Converter: Go to the File menu and select File|Save As. A dialog box appears. Select GIF in the Format drop-down menu. Name your file and select a folder to save it in. Click on OK.

COPYING YOUR IMAGE INTO THE PALACE PROP EDITOR

Here's how to copy your image:

1. While you are still in your image editing program, copy your image.

Paint Shop Pro: From the menu bar, select Edit|Copy.

Graphic Converter: In the menu bar, go to Edit|Select All. You'll notice that an army of "red ants" are now surrounding your image. Next, go back to the menu bar and select Edit|Copy.

The Prop Editor Overview

The material in Table 7.1 is summarized from the Palace User's Guide. For further details, please refer to this guide. It is available online at www.thepalace.com, or call 1-800-796-6110. The guide costs $9.95.

Table 7.1 Prop Editor icons and their uses.

Icon	Name	Uses
	Pencil	Drawing or editing details. To fine tune the control over the pencil, hold down the Shift key while drawing. To "pour" color into an area, use the paint bucket, by pressing the Alt key (Windows) or Command key (Macintosh).
	Selector	Moving or deleting sections of a prop. Position your mouse at one corner, click and drag to the desired area, then release. To remove the section within the are, hit the Delete key.
	Eraser	Erasing parts of an avatar or prop. Erased portions automatically become transparent. To "pour" transparency into a solid-colored area, hold down the Alt key (Windows) or the Command key (Macintosh).
	Line Sizer	Changing the line width of the pencil and eraser. To increase, click in the upper-right corner. To decrease, click in the lower-left corner.
	Palette	A swatch of colors. Selecting a color with the eyedropper makes this color "active."

2. Launch the Palace client. You don't need to connect to a Palace site to paste and edit your avatar.

3. Open the Prop Window by double-clicking on the satchel icon in the lower-right corner of the Palace opening screen.

4. Paste the image in the Prop Editor: Go to Edit|Paste Multiple Props if your image is larger than 44×44 pixels; if not, select Edit|Paste.

5. In the Prop Picker window, click on the Edit button to edit a tile of the avatar (see Figure 7.30).

CREATING A TRANSPARENT BACKGROUND

After you have copied your image into the Palace Prop Editor, you can erase that neon green background you created earlier.

The Construction And Psychology Of Avatars

Figure 7.30   The image is now in the Prop Picker, in six separate tiles.

1. First, name your prop in the Prop Editor. Notice we've named this prop "Bunny 1" in Figure 7.31. This will come in handy if you want to refer to this image in a script when you set up your own Palace server.

2. Next, specify the type of prop you are creating. In this case you may want to specify a Head prop. The standard smiley will float in the background to give you a frame of reference for positioning tiles in a multiple-tile prop.

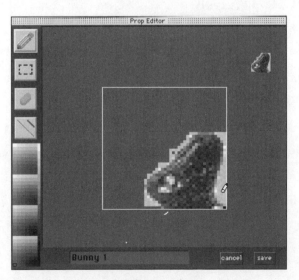

Figure 7.31   Erasing the image's background to create a transparent background.

If you are using a PC, place an "X" in the Head checkbox.

If you are using a Macintosh, go to the Menu bar and select Prop Edit|Face Prop.

3. Click on the Eraser icon.

4. Select a line width in the Line Sizer icon. Clicking on the upper-right corner increases line width, while clicking on the lower left reduces it. Select the width that's best for editing your avatar, and begin erasing. The neon green background makes it easy to distinguish between the parts you need to erase and the parts you want to keep. As you erase, you can preview your work in the lower-left portion (Windows) or the upper-right portion (Macintosh) of the Prop Editor screen. If you make a mistake, go to the menu bar and select Edit|Undo.

5. When you are finished, click on Save.

 ### Another Helpful Tip

If you have problems, you may want to connect to a Palace site and ask for assistance. Many sites have prop editing rooms, where you can work quietly or ask a wizard for help. The Palace community is known for its collaborative efforts and for helping new users to master essentials.

PAINT YOUR AVATAR

Editing your avatar is easy. Obviously, the bunny avatar is missing a nose. We think a bright pink candy nose would look divine. Here's how to edit your avatar:

1. Select an avatar tile. In this case we're choosing the tile that contains the head of the bunny.

2. Click on the Edit button.

3. Highlight the Pencil icon and, using the Eyedropper, choose a color in the Palette.

4. Select a line width in the Line Sizer.

5. Begin painting (see Figure 7.32).

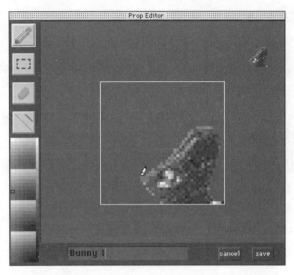

Figure 7.32 There, now the bunny has a cute button nose.

Some Advanced Avatar Advice

For advanced avatar creation techniques, check out Web Publisher's 3D & Animation Design Guide for Windows *by Mary Jo Fahey (Coriolis Group Books, 1996). Mary Jo goes in-depth with color correcting tips in Photoshop and quick masks to isolate images from a complex background. Online, Dr. X has a veritable feast of advice. Check out his advanced tutorial (**www.rahul.net/natpix/ppix.html**) for creating antialiased avatars (getting rid of those jaggy, hard edges outlining your avatar).*

SAVING YOUR AVATAR

Here's how to save your avatar:

1. Click on each tile of your avatar.

Follow these steps if you are working on a Windows platform (version 2.5, 32 bit, as shown in Figure 7.33):

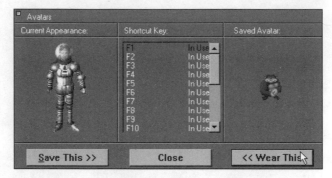

Figure 7.33   The Avatar menu within the Palace client.

2. Go to Avatars|Avatars.

3. Select a shortcut key.

4. Click on the "Save This" button.

Now, whenever you hit your "F" key assignment, your brand spanking new avatar will appear.

Follow these steps if you are working on a Macintosh platform:

2. Go to Macros|Macros.

3. Select a number from 1 through 9 to represent this avatar.

4. Select "Save Macro".

Equipped with a fancy, customized avatar, you're now ready to tread upon new territory—your own Palace server.

Chapter 8

Your Own Palace Server

Chapter 8

- ISSUES TO CONSIDER CONCERNING PALACE SERVERS

- INTERVIEWS WITH PALACE PROS

- SITE NAVIGATION, TOURS, AND SCRIPTS

- PALACE RESOURCES ON THE NET

Your Own Palace Server

Chapter 8

So, You've Decided To Build A Palace

Congratulations! The Internet needs more Palace sites and as we've learned in previous chapters, chat can be an integral part of your community. What you're about to do is going to be a lot of fun, and it will allow you to be far more creative than standard text chat will allow. There's a bit of a learning curve, but technical help is very easy to find, not only on various Web sites and The Palace, Inc.'s own home site, but also on actual Palaces. Many Palace users are also well versed in the technical details of the software and most are only too happy to help.

Before we dive in, we'd like to thank the many Palace gods, wizards, and users who have provided us with help along the way. We'd also like to offer a special thanks to Mark Jeffrey, director of commercial marketing at The Palace, Inc., who has been very helpful to us in the preparation of this book, and who gave us *carte blanche* to reproduce text from the Palace documentation.

In the following sections, we'll look at some of the technical details of setting up a Palace site, and then we'll talk with some knowledgeable people about their experiences with Palace design.

Finding An ISP To Host Your Palace

Currently there is only a short list of ISPs actively advertising that they host Palace servers:

- HotCity (**www.hotcity.com**)

- WorldSite (**www.worldsite.net**)

- SRT Enterprises (**www.srtenterprises.com**)

- Generation Net (**www.generation.net**)

We received this list from Robert McDaniel of The Palace, Inc., with the comment that, "most ISPs would probably be willing to host Palace servers. With the fierce competition among ISPs, and the flat-rate pricing, most are eager for additional revenue streams. Usually, the best place to start inquiries would be with your own ISP."

If you're thinking of running a server from your standard ISP dial-up account, you should be aware of several matters, which we'll discuss in the following section.

Hosting With Dial-Up Accounts

Every computer on the Internet, including the one that you use to surf the Web, has an IP (Internet Protocol) address. There are two types of IP addresses: static and dynamic. As suggested by the name, a *static* IP address is always the same. Servers are assigned unique static IP addresses, so that they can be found easily. Each time you connect to your ISP, you are assigned an IP address too, and for the vast majority of us, that IP address will be *dynamic*, which is to say it will be a different address every time you log on.

So if you're thinking of running a server from your standard ISP dial-up account, there are a few potential problems to consider.

- The server can only be up while you are connected. Maybe this won't be a problem for you; for example, if you meet with 11 other pals every Monday at 7:00 P.M. for a re-enactment of *12 Angry Men*, you obviously don't need a permanent server.

- The IP is always different, making it impossible to be found. A simple solution would be to email everyone on your community list, telling them your current IP address each time you launch your server. (Consult your ISP or operating system documentation to determine how to find your dynamic IP on your system.) However, this is tedious and time consuming. The Palace, Inc., has addressed this situation, making it easier for your community members to find you—even if you have a dynamic IP address. Each time you launch your personal server, the Palace software "pings" a server at The Palace, Inc., Your Palace name, description, and IP address are logged into a realtime database, which is searchable via the Web at **www.thepalace.com/cgi-bin/dirsearch.pl**.

- A dynamic IP cannot be assigned a domain name like www.yourdomain.com. It will always be a string of digits, like 123.456.789.10.

If these issues don't present a problem for you, then hosting a Palace from your machine (with a dynamic IP address) may be fine. If, however, you want to establish a 24-hour community, you'll need to host your Palace from an ISP's servers, or consider setting up a high bandwidth (ISDN or T1) dedicated line.

THE HOST MACHINE

You'll need two key ingredients to make a good host machine: plenty of speed and plenty of RAM. Slower computers will not support as many users, because each additional user acts as an additional burden on the system, resulting in serious latency, or lag—and Palace guests hate lag. It's also a good idea to run your server on a dedicated computer, because additional activity from other applications will slow down all the programs including the Palace Server, which brings us back to that lag problem. The Palace, Inc., recommends 16MB of RAM to run the Palace Server, and you'll need more if the machine is also serving Web pages. This is not just a rule of thumb, it's a hard and fast rule: There is no such thing as too much

RAM. This is not a plug for the people who make RAM, but we advise you to buy lots and lots of it. It's good for you and it's good for your computer.

What About Hard Drive Space?

The Palace Server itself only needs about half a megabyte, but the additional graphics that make up rooms, props, sounds, and avatars can add upwards of 20MB to your hard drive. Naturally, what this means is that the server software does not need a lot of space, given that most hard drives are at least 500MB these days.

How About Operating Systems?

The Palace Server runs on the Mac 68K or Power PC with System 7 or better. It also runs on the PC with Win 3.x, Win95, or WinNT. In fact, the Palace Server software is available for almost any flavor of OS you care to use, including Linux and the various shades of Unix. The only exception that we are aware of is IBM's OS/2 Warp.

Windows Users, Take Note

The 32-bit Palace Server client will run on any *true* 32-bit Windows environment. However, unless your system is truly 32-bit (Win95 or NT), your server may exhibit some odd behavior. The 32-bit Palace Server will perform adequately under Windows 3.X with win32s, but this is not the recommended platform; you should use the 16-bit client with Win 3.x.

Installation On Your Machine

The Palace Personal Server is included in the client software package, and the server was installed on your computer automatically if you chose the "Full Install" option during the initial setup of your client. If you previously selected "Custom Install" and have only installed the client, you'll need to run the Install program again. Simply double-click on the Palace icon on your desktop to launch the installation process, select Custom Install once more, and when prompted, select only the Palace Server checkbox. (Installing the client again will overwrite your client's prop file, destroying all the nongeneric props in your satchel.)

The Technical Stuff

We've provided you with some general knowledge concerning the Palace server. The nitty gritty how-to details, however, are not going to appear here. One great benefit of the Palace is that it is amazingly well-documented. Complete documentation and technical support information is available for free at The Palace, Inc.'s Web site, in both HTML and Adobe Acrobat PDF format. The documentation is complete and easy to understand, so repeating it here would be redundant. Instead, we'll concentrate on advanced tips and tricks and design issues, talking with some successful gods and wizards to learn from their experiences.

Three Palace Gurus

We spoke to three Palace experts, two gods and a wizard: Arctic Frost, The Man In Black, and Uncle Saturn. While these names may sound like they belong to notorious hackers, all three of these Palace denizens are in fact well-known personalities within the Palace community. They've all been around as long as Palace itself, and they agreed to share some of their insights with you, to help you develop better Palace sites.

PALACE DESIGN

Designing a Palace site is not completely different from designing a good Web site, because of the visual nature of the Palace and because of its ability to incorporate hyperlinking techniques. Like a Web site, clarity and function are essential, but in the case of Palace, form is much more important than it is on a Web site. In the Palace, clarity and function must be integrated into the form completely. Therein lies the challenge.

ARCTIC FROST TALKS FUNCTION

Lisa Herschbach is a Palace god. She serves as a wizard on a number of established Palaces and she serves as a co-god for U.S. Robotics' Towne Square 2000 Palace site (**usr.thepalace.com**). In the Palace community, she is known as Arctic Frost. Lisa says that functionality is extremely important for success with a Palace site.

"Keep your downloads small. Palaces that make you download enormous rooms usually fail." The reason, of course, is clear: Every time you enter a new room in a Palace site, you need to download the graphics that make up that room (which are then stored on your hard drive for subsequent visits). If the download time is too long, guests become impatient, and will scurry to another site. Lisa suggests 70K as a good target size for graphics files.

"There are programs out there that make files smaller. Some are part of art programs [like Corel 3D Dream or Adobe Photoshop]. I use error diffusion to get my files smaller." Lisa explains that error diffusion reduces the size of GIF files by stripping out, or thinning, excess data from a file. You can turn a 100K file into a 50K file using this feature on most advanced art programs.

Navigation

Navigational concerns on the Palace are not unlike those for Web sites, except that the logical paradigm that you extrapolate from is 3D space. Lisa says, "You want your floor plan to make sense. Willy-nilly planning will work very much against you. Having a good floor plan lets you follow where the traffic goes, and allows you to get information to people by herding them to a certain room with the floor plan." She adds, "If you are going to have rooms that really don't have a path to them, you want to make sure they have easily recognized names on the room list."

Towne Square 2000's front door is called "Dock Port." It has a futuristic theme, with buildings that rise into the sky. Notice in Figure 8.1 how each building in the artwork represents a place to go, from The Beanz Café to the Mayor's Office. Guests logging on here are almost always inclined to move into another space, leaving the port free and uncluttered. Also, new arrivals very quickly become aware of what type of content is available, as it's all clearly marked.

If your Palace's "front door" or "entry" doesn't feature clear indicators, like a path to doors or some representation of physical markers to other rooms, then visitors to your site will typically crowd into the front door and never explore further. All the hard work you put into prop rooms, chat rooms, game rooms, and other features will be for nothing.

Figure 8.1   Towne Square 2000's navigation is visually intuitive.

As an alternative to clear paths, you could design scripts that force traffic flow to certain areas. On that subject, Lisa says, "Some Palaces have scripts that force you to other rooms, but I don't recommend that. The basic desire of a person is to sit at the gate. You want to encourage people to move on by making graphics that will capture their interest. No one likes to be forced to do anything." Of course, she goes on to explain, using scripts to force movement isn't always a bad thing. There may be instances when, to achieve a certain effect or to clear a particularly bad bottleneck, a script may be employed; but be sparing in the implementation of such scripts, as scripts make for bad traffic cops, tending simply to anger people rather than helping them.

We asked if one should consider redesigning their graphics before adding a script, and her advice was, "[That] depends on your resources. If you have a good artist spitting out graphics for you, go the graphics route first. But if you don't [have a reliable artist], go the script way, or you'll wait forever while everyone promises to make you a new room."

Prop Rooms

Prop rooms are a must. Every Palace should have at least one, and the props should be unique to the Palace. Lisa suggests that you opt for scripts to distribute props, because just placing props in a room causes high maintenance and extra work for the server. Remember that efficiency and functionality are critical to Palace management.

Some Palaces have secret spots or areas that automatically award you a prop whenever you place your avatar on a specific spot. Do guests like that? Lisa says, "Those can be cool, but they can be annoying too. If they are cleverly placed yet not too burdensome, then that can be a very clever thing." She adds, "It depends on the room. For instance, this room we are in now [we were in a chat café at the Towne Square 2000 Palace]: It used to give you a prop when you entered. But cafés usually become the chat room of choice of most Palaces, and people would get mad when the most popular room constantly changed their prop."

When a guest logs into Towne Square 2000, they are automatically adorned with a prop that looks like a little flying saucer. As we saw above, the Dock Port features large futuristic buildings; notice in Figure 8.2 how the saucer's scale matches up with the buildings. Lisa explains, "At the gate we have [a script to] put a prop on people; that's good, and it's a cute prop that fits the theme. It's a good prop that goes with the dimensions and style of the place. If you are going to put a prop on someone, make sure it matches the scale of the room."

The Conversation Room

Most of our discussion with Lisa took place in the Beanz Café, shown in Figure 8.3. She explained the thinking that went into the design of the room:

Figure 8.2 The flying saucer looks right at home at the edge of the Town Hall.

"The conversation room is absolute genius here because it's got a big floor for props to sit on. It also has a chair that people wearing props can fit into. It also has wall space for flying props. Many different sizes of props can be in here and still fit. Having things in the room that people can sit on is something you want to keep your mind on. If your background images cannot be played with, they are useless and you'll find people won't hang in those rooms. You want to take care not to overcrowd the room; you have to imagine it full of people and props when you are designing it. If you do have scripts [in the conversation room], make them GIFs that flash or Web page links. Nothing that forces the user to do anything. People want to be left alone in a chat room."

The Censorship Script In The Beanz Café

Wizards and gods use scripts to keep vulgarities out of conversation. These are called censorship scripts, and they simply recognize certain strings of characters and block them. There's one running in the Beanz Café. About that script, Lisa says, "Censorship scripts are used to screen out vulgarities, but they can work

Figure 8.3 The conversation room functions just like a real café.

against you when foreign languages come into the mix. You want to be careful using censorship scripts. You want to decide if they are really necessary. In a site like this, they are because it has a company name to it."

Packing Them In

Palace is still young and hasn't been adopted as widely as text chat yet, although there are many Palace sites and the software is easy to use. If you cruise through a generous sample of sites, you'll find that some are full of guests, and some are like ghost towns. Lisa has some comments about that. "Gods can help their own sites. What cracks me up about those empty sites is that I'll be on Mansion or Welcome Palace and gods will sit on Mansion or Welcome all day whining how empty their site is. But they won't sit on their site. That's exactly why their site will fail. No one will come to your site if you don't. If you do, you'll have lots of people there."

THE MAN IN BLACK'S MYSTERIOUS TOUR

There's a mysterious man who hides out at a Palace site called Marathon (**palace:// marathon.lag.com**). Online, he's known as The Man In Black or MNB for short. We have it on good authority that in real life, he works at a well-known computing company and is known as Curt Lewis. He built the Marathon Palace, which takes its name from the 3D action game Marathon, and which attracts many Palace members interested in computer gaming. Curt says he focuses on having fun, rather than on gaming, but he likes having the gaming audience visit his virtual home so frequently.

We spent the bulk of our talk with Curt lounging about in his Space Bar, seen in Figure 8.4. This room, Curt pointed out, has been featured on Clnet and tv.com. The room is also featured on an "automatic" tour, one of the coolest features on several Palaces. A script allows visitors to explore the Marathon through a guided tutorial.

About deciding what to include on the tour, Curt says, "Well, for our tour I thought it out this way…is it a room that would be commonly inhabited? Like the bar here. By including it in the tour, they [a new visitor] have downloaded the files already and gotten a spiel on it from our script." The spiels include information

Figure 8.4 This room is a regular hangout and a tour stop at Marathon.

about what scripts are in the room, what the room is used for, or some other interesting facts. "And," Curt points out, "if they come back later, they can drop right in without waiting on the technology." This is because once a room is visited, the graphics that make up the room are stored on the user's computer.

Curt's tour follows a VCR remote-control paradigm (see Figure 8.5), allowing users to be in control, as opposed to the fully automated tours that some Palaces use. "[On the typical tour] you click the button at the entrance and everything is timed like an amusement park ride. You don't get off until it's over. Geek [one of the Marathon Palace wizards], who did the script for the movement on the tour, thought that wasn't the best way. He suggested the VCR-type control panel so the user controls the tour. You can go forward, backward, or leave anytime you want, even skip the spiels if you've already heard them."

How long should the tour be? "Well, that depends on how fast the user goes. You can actually spread it out over logons. But if you just go start to finish at a

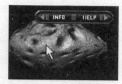

Figure 8.5 The tour interface is intuitive, like a VCR remote.

"normal" pace, I'd say 10 minutes, maybe 15. There are 10 rooms on our tour; rooms that are common for use, rooms that have interesting scripts, or rooms I considered fun."

Curt notes, "Having [the tour] also takes a load off the wizards. Without it, they have to personally escort those that are interested in touring." He is also quick to point out that, "but if visitors use the scripted tour and a wizard escort too, that's the best. The script says all the important stuff, and the wizard can give them [personal] attention instead."

So how many guests use the tour? "Maybe 10 percent, hard to say…Most users like to be free and just roam on their own, but the tour is there for information." Of course, if you consider that 10 of every 100 folks who visit will use the tour, then the tour is mighty handy. An interesting feature of the tour at Marathon is that if you are in a room where the tour normally goes, you will see the tour control buttons. So if a user is not taking the formal tour path, they can still access the tour information. "Our tour is complex; Geek is a programmer, and I'm a computer tech as well, so we put a blower and some mags on it, so to speak. For a brand-new site, the tour is more useful, I think, because everyone is a newcomer."

Another Plug For 2D Chat

We moved on to the Spa seen in Figure 8.6. As we chatted, the conversation drifted toward the pros and cons of 2D versus 3D chat. Curt had some interesting observations. "Palace isn't 3D, but it's fast enough for chat. You don't really need that much tech, especially for the sake of being tech. Tech has got to add to the experience. I haven't seen a 3D chat application that uses 3D for more than just being able to say it's 3D. No one has worked it well into the medium of chat. I think once hardware takes off some more, that someday, someone will use 3D well because it's easy to use and fun for the end user."

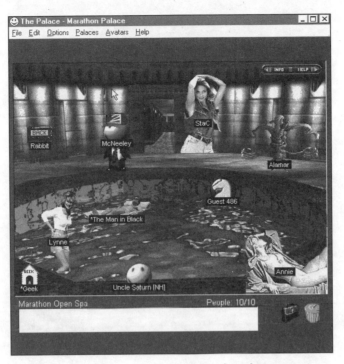

Figure 8.6 The relaxing Spa is a favorite Marathon hangout.

Naturally, we decided to ask what Palace innovations Curt was anxious to see. "I'm looking for a paging/notification system, file transfers, streaming audio for users, scriptable props, more third-party plugins." Of course some of these are on the drawing board now and others may soon be. Curt adds, "You could use streaming audio for tours, music, and events. You might be able to have concerts online, at the Palace, theoretically, by using a Webcast."

We wondered also if there are a lot of veteran IRC users waiting for those features before they move to graphical chat? "Possibly. I must admit that I'm stunned more of my old IRC friends haven't moved to Palace. I used to be very into IRC, but when I saw Palace, I felt it was considerably superior to IRC."

Eventually, we had to leave the Palace, but not before a relaxing chat on a remote island and a pool party at the Spa, as seen in Figures 8.6 and 8.7.

Figure 8.7 You can really get away on this mystical island.

UNCLE SATURN'S SCRIPTS SPAN THE PLANET

You might be under the impression that scripting for rooms on a Palace is hard. In fact, it's actually fairly straightforward. Scripts are simply little executable files that hide in the rooms of a Palace and activate when certain actions occur. For example, you could write a script that would apply a custom avatar to a visitor if that visitor clicks on a certain graphic or types a special word. When choosing whom to speak to about scripting, we went to one of the best. Online, you'll know him as Uncle Saturn, but in the real world, he's called Sean, and he's 13 years old. Sean is an aspiring computer programmer; at his young age, he has already mastered HTML, iptscrae, and the Internet. He serves as a wizard for Firebird's Forest (**palace://firebird.com**), and he's responsible for many of the scripts to be found there. While Sean is certainly a gifted young man with a bright future ahead of him, the fact is that his mastery of Palace programming skills could be achieved by anyone who puts some reasonable effort into learning the Palace scripting language.

Figure 8.8 Notice the postage-stamp pictures, the thread spool furniture, and the hand-held TV set.

The room where much of our conversation took place is called Ray Rat's Hole. It's a mouse hole, as you can see from Figure 8.8. When you enter the room, your avatar is placed near the graphic representing the hole in the floorboard of another room. Then a giant cat's paw comes through the hole, accompanied by a "meow" sound, and the avatar moves away, as if being chased by the cat. It's adorable, and it was scripted by Sean. "Well, it was assigned to me by Firebird, I just scripted it. He knew he wanted the cat's paw and the chasing script," says Sean modestly.

We wondered how long it took to script. "I'm not sure, maybe half an hour or so, longer than usual."

Wow, we thought, only a half an hour? That seemed like a mistake, so we restated the question to be sure we had an accurate response. "I'm not exactly sure, but I would say around that much." So there you go, it's not a terribly hard thing to do at all. In fact, Sean told us that the code that executes the script is only 20 lines long.

Of the type of experience you need to learn Iptscrae, Sean says this, "You don't really have to have much experience in anything, you gain the experience as you learn the Iptscrae. Anybody can learn it, you just have to be able to remember the commands, and think how they would process together and what they would do." But how do they process together? "Well, basically, scripting is run by event handlers, such as ON SIGNON. ON SIGNON, as you would expect, would activate the script when you sign on."

"So, all scripts are run by event handlers, like I said, and they are simple text files, essentially. Inside the event handlers are atomlists, or the little scripts that will execute themselves, these are the scripts themselves. That's basically how it works. Each script is tied to an event handler."

"Right now, there's no WYSIWYG type of Iptscrae editor, so it's all hard core typing, but really not that difficult, easier than Java for sure." Well, if it's easier than Java, we wondered where a good manual of iptscrae might be found. "The Iptscrae manuals are not much help when you are first starting, because they just basically are a dictionary of the commands. The secret is to look at scripts, study them, then read them over and over and over till you understand every command and how it works, and remember, don't say 'I don't get it' before even trying."

Of course, all programming languages have syntax and nomenclature, like a mathematical expression such as 1+1=2. Sean explained the syntax of Iptscrae. "There's the name of the event handler, then a left curly bracket, like this {...Each atomlist (aka script) is also enclosed in curly brackets { }...To finish off the event handler is a right bracket }. If you have a conditional script, the condition would follow the script. For example, let me show you a simple script here...

```
ON SIGNON {    { "A Big Howdy From Bob" SAY } USERNAME "Bob" == IF }
```

"Now, let me explain this. ON SIGNON is the event handler, telling you that it will execute when you sign on. Now there's a left bracket to open the event handler, and another left bracket to open the atomlist. Now look how the condition follows the first right bracket [which closes the atomlist]. So the script says to speak the words 'I'm here' which is what "A Big Howdy From Bob" SAY does, and the condition USERNAME "Bob" == IF simply means that the script will only execute if you have the name 'Bob.' So, when you sign on, the script will determine if you signed on with the username Bob, and if you have, it'll execute the script to say 'A Big Howdy From Bob.'"

We told Sean that what he explained made sense to us, to which he responded, "Does it really? (laugh) Took me a while to catch on at first…" Of course it might take a while for you, and us, to catch on in practice, but the syntax of a script is pretty straightforward, and a list of script commands can be found on the Iptscrae documentation at **www.thepalace.com**.

On the topic of favorite kinds of scripts, Sean said, "My favorite kinds? I couldn't say I have a favorite kind particularly. I say my favorite kinds are the ones not too complicated or laggy, the ones that are fun and will interest others when the script executes. I would say Palace scripts add a lot to a Palace; they provide the ability to do any kind of room picture animation. They also provide many other effects which are enjoyed by many users. One thing I consider [when writing a script] is lag. I don't want to lag the user too much. Another thing that's very important is if the script is faulty. To find out if the script is faulty, look in the log while executing the script and if the log says 'an error has occurred while executing the iptscrae script' or something like 'ixnay on the iptscrae' that's a sign that you have a faulty script. Most good scripts give you a choice of whether you would like it activated, too."

Sean then took us to a room called High Places. "High Places is a room where I have made a pretty popular script. The instructions for the script appear on the status bar when you enter the room. How it works is that you just stand at the bottom of the tree, and say [type] 'slide' to activate the script." Matamoras, a friend of Sean's at the Forest, gave us a demonstration of the slide script, featured in Figure 8.9 (a through d).

Figure 8.9a   Matamoras begins the slide.

Figure 8.9b   Mata is on the way up.

Figure 8.9c   Oh no! He's gonna fall!

Figure 8.9d   Whew… A safe landing.

More Palace Resources On The Web

If you're looking for help with your Palace software, a great place to look is The Magus Pagus at **www.xmission.com/~hapyface/magus/magus.html**. Here you will find the chief page for Palace Magi. The Magi are not associated with The Palace, Inc., but they are organized to help new users with Palace problems. They are like the AAA of Palace roadways.

Perhaps the favorite resource on the Net for Palace users is "Dr. X's House o Props n Bots" at **www.rahul.net/natpix/house.html**, where you'll find piles of great information for the new and veteran Palace user alike. There's data about how to create better avatars, the ins and outs of scripting, and a program called Bot Bot, which is a Palace favorite. Bot Bot will custom design scripts for you, and download them to you in one handy "cyborg" file to be used by your avatar when you log on. This file extends functionality to your avatar automatically; for example:

- saying "hello" to everyone in the room upon entering

- slamdancing and moshing across a room

- blowing a kiss to a specific area in a room

- firing a laser at everyone in a room

Finally, the Palace home page, at **www.thepalace.com**, is a wealth of knowledge. We've mentioned this page numerous times, so rather than rehash the information we've covered, let's add one more new bit: This site contains links to several mailing lists that were set up for Palace users, including The Palace Usergroup or PUG. You can subscribe directly from the pages here, and you'll find plenty of details to help you decide which list or lists are for you.

Invite Your Friends Over For A Grand Opening

So you've got your Palace site all set up and your graphics and custom props in place. Seems like a good time for a party! Of course you'll want to invite anyone and everyone you've met on the various Palace sites to come help you celebrate the grand opening. You can also announce your site opening on the Palace User Group Mailing Lists (don't forget to give 'em the address). We hope you're also using your community home page to let folks know about the festivities. The key here is to get as many folks as you can to look around your site and get to know the place.

Link Directly To Your Palace

Don't forget that you can embed a hyperlink to your Palace within the HTML code of your Web site. When a user who has The Palace software clicks on the link, their software is launched and they are transported to your Palace site. It's just like any other hyperlink. Here's an example:

```
<A HREF="palace://my.palace.com:9998">Click Here To Go
To My Palace</a>
```

By the way, don't miss this opportunity to indoctrinate some new Webheads into the Palace community. You know who I'm talking about. There's Jed from the mailroom who has AOL but isn't sure what's good online. There's your mom, who likes Recipe.com but hasn't figured out yet what's so "cool" about the Net. There's that fellow across the street, who just bought a computer and keeps asking you how to launch the Solitaire game. These people, and millions like them, are just waiting for that last friendly push into the world of virtual communities. Set them up with the Palace demo software and show them how it works, then be sure that they join your party, too.

Important Safety Tip

It goes without saying that software piracy is wrong, but remember this: Never use your Palace registration number to validate Palace software on another person's machine, even if it's just so that person can "try before they buy." If you try to connect to a Palace and that user is on with your number, you will be denied access, even if it's your site. The Palace was designed so that only one copy of a registration number could exist at a time.

Looking At The World In 3D

The Palace offers the best solution for chat in a 2D graphical environment. What about 3D? In the next chapter we'll take a look at what will become the next generation on 3D chat and Internet application. VRML technology is poised to re-revolutionize the Net.

Chapter 9

Put The Virtual In Your Community With VRML

Chapter 9

- THE HISTORY OF VRML

- PRACTICAL VRML APPLICATIONS FOR YOUR COMMUNITY

- AN OVERVIEW OF AVAILABLE VRML APPLICATIONS

PUT THE VIRTUAL IN YOUR COMMUNITY WITH VRML

Chapter 9

A Brief History Of VRML

VRML (Virtual Reality Modeling Language) is a language for describing multiparticipant interactive simulations—virtual worlds networked via the Internet. All aspects of virtual world display, interaction, and inter-networking can be specified using VRML. This language that mimicks HTML, but does something far different, was conceived of in 1994 by computer scientists Mark Pesce and Tony Parisi.

In 1993, Mark Pesce fell in love with the Web when he began using Mosaic (a Web browser) on his Sun-based SparcStation. Sensing that it would be easy to get lost on the Web, he felt a 3D interface would make the Web more intuitive to navigate. A specialist in both networking and graphics, his vision was to combine the two disciplines on the Web.

Late that year, Tony Parisi, an expert in computer languages, moved to Pesce's hometown of San Francisco. He and Pesce became friends, as well as partners in a visionary project. Their complementary backgrounds covered the three core components of VRML (networking, languages, and graphics), and they wrote the first 3D Web browser, Labyrinth, in February of 1994. (It took them about a week.) They were then invited by Tim Berners-Lee to the first World Wide Web Conference in Geneva, Switzerland, and VRML was born.

GETTING UP TO VIRTUAL SPEED

At the conference, Berners-Lee and Dave Raggett created a Birds-of-a-Feather (BOF) session to discuss virtual-reality interfaces on the Web. Some session attendees described projects currently underway to build 3D interfaces. They agreed that a common language for the Internet, like HTML, was essential for the success of Web-based virtual reality. The moniker Virtual Reality Markup Language (VRML) was coined, and "Markup" was later changed to "Modeling" to reflect the graphical nature of VRML. They also agreed that version 1.0 of VRML would need to meet certain requirements, including platform independence, extensibility, and the ability to function over relatively low-bandwidth situations, like a 14.4 dial-up connection.

The Open Inventor ASCII File Format from Silicon Graphics, Inc. (SGI), was adopted as the VRML standard because it could support complete descriptions of 3D objects rendered in polygon form, including lighting, texture maps, and ambient properties and effects. In addition, the format offered excellent networking support. Gavin Bell of Silicon Graphics was instrumental in adapting the Open Inventor File Format for VRML, and SGI made the format available in the public domain to stimulate VRML viewer development among third-party programmers and companies.

A key decision of those early designers was that VRML shouldn't be an extension of HTML. VRML required more network optimization than HTML, and it was graphically based rather than textual. Besides, HTML was an established standard, and burdening the language with the new VRML standards and issues would impede HTML development. It was also decided that the first version of VRML would not support interactive behaviors, aside from hyperlinking and simple navigation. This was a pragmatic decision, intended to streamline the design and implementation of the new language. More interactivity would be added slowly and intelligently to later versions, but at the time, laying the groundwork and designing a viewer was seen as the important first step.

The first version of VRML allowed for the creation of virtual worlds with limited visual appeal and interactivity, as shown in Figure 9.1 The objects contained in these worlds had hyperlinks to other worlds and/or Web pages, but that was all.

Incarnations of the current VRML specification, 2.0, incorporating ActiveX technology, Java, and JavaScript, allow for richer environments, including animations, motion physics, and realtime multi-user interaction such as chat, teleconferencing, and gaming. Figure 9.2 shows the same rocket file enhanced with 2.0. When a user selects a link to a VRML document from within their Web browser (assuming it's correctly configured with the proper VRML plug-ins), a VRML viewer is launched. VRML viewers are the perfect companion applications to standard Web browsers for visualizing the Web.

Figure 9.1 This shuttle was created using the first version of VRML, 1.0.

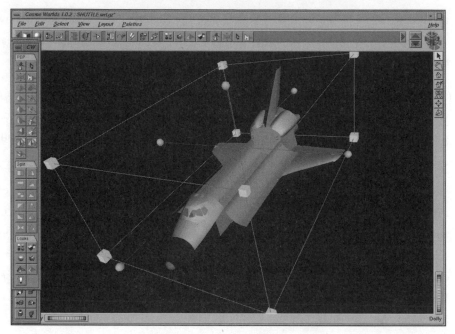

Figure 9.2   The same shuttle from Figure 9.1, enhanced with VRML 2.0.

To learn more about VRML history and programming, and to see what's new in VRML, go to **www.iworld.com**, or check out **www.webdeveloper.com/mayjun96/ duke.html** for Dale Kirby's in-depth discussion with Mark Pesce.

What's It Like In A VRML World?

Like HTML, you navigate VRML through links that connect various servers on the Web, but unlike the text-driven, 2D world of HTML, your navigation takes place in a rich, graphical 3D environment. Like the computer games Doom and Quake, you view the virtual world from a first-person perspective, as shown in Figure 9.3. Like meatspace, you can move left, right, forward, or back. Completely unlike meatspace, however, you can fly through the clouds, swim among the fish in shark-infested waters, and perform many other feats of magic.

Since VRML is so visual, we wish we could take you on a visit to a VRML site. However, since this book is made of paper, we'll have to settle for a short, nontechnical description of a visit to a VRML world. At U.S. Robotics in Skokie, Illinois, Michael Greene works as a multimedia developer and graphic designer. We asked Michael to describe briefly what a typical VRML visit might be like.

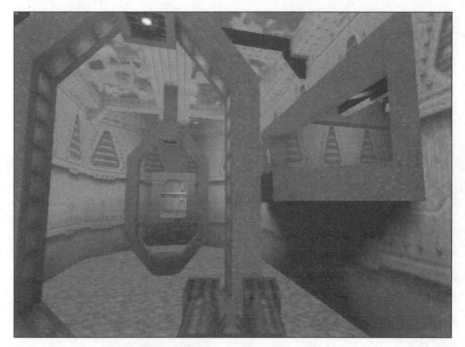

Figure 9.3 Quake uses a first-person perspective to enhance the realistic experience of the player.

Michael Greene Goes Virtual
(Written by Michael Greene for this book.)

Walking around, I notice a mist gathering at the lake. I walk over to the edge and look at the waves. On the horizon, I notice the sun as it begins to set. A bird flies by and I listen as it disappears behind a tree. An avatar approaches and starts to talk to me. We engage in a stimulating conversation about politics and such for a brief while; then I continue to maneuver down the path. Looking over to my left, I see a building with flashing lights and a crowd gathering. It's nighttime, and people have begun to fill the streets. Most just got off work and are looking for a temporary escape from their real lives. I decide that I am not in a "crowd" mood tonight and continue on until I am drawn towards a casino. (See Figure 9.4.) I feel lucky.

Upon entering the glittery casino, I notice a figure strolling out in anger, swearing never to return. I know that he will. We all do. The

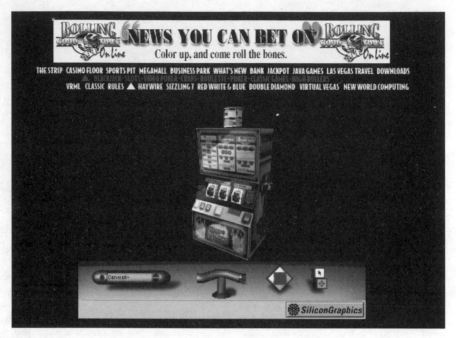

Figure 9.4 Virtual gambling really does exist at Virtual Vegas (**www.virtualvegas.com**).

machine has a way of making you think that you are going to win, and then, before you know it, it's all gone. Oh well, it's just cybermoney. I approach the blackjack table—a shiny crescent shape surrounded by a small gathering of avatars. Behind each avatar is another human, just like me. I cash in 40 cybercredits and lay down the full amount. I also get to cut the deck. A queen and an ace are dealt to me. This must be my day! "Blackjack," drones out the metroid-class avatar/dealer as he gives me a golden 100 cybercredit voucher. I smile and head to the teller's window. I gotta cash out now, because I only have a few minutes to get to work back in real life.

The computer is but a tool, to further develop what we can only dream. VRML could be called the poor man's virtual reality, but it's cool, it's here today, and it doesn't give you motion sickness. What path it takes shall be an interesting subject to follow. I, for one, am extremely interested in watching it blossom into a new medium of expression for the artists and programmers who will create virtual worlds. I'm also interested in how it will manifest itself as a new kind of entertainment for us all; an active kind of fun, not like passive television. Who knows what's next—VRML storefronts are just the tip of the iceberg.

An Interview With The Godfather Of VRML

We recently had a chance to ask Mark Pesce (pictured in Figure 9.5) about VRML as it relates to community. Here's what he said:

Karla & Todd: How do you see VRML changing the way in which online communities exist today?

Mark: Communities today are text-driven; that means we can talk—or at least type—but we can't really experience the "place" that is home. As we move into 3D interfaces, home will become a place as much as it is a voice.

K & T: What do you feel are the greatest strengths of VRML as an interface for social interaction and realtime chat?

Mark: VRML creates a stage where the daily dramas of living can happen; it's no longer just inside your head—your body actually sympathizes with virtual space, and so it feels more "real" to you.

K & T: With VRML, describe how navigation will work within the virtual community framework. Will it be like walking down the street in real life? Will you be about to interact with other Web surfers as they are surfing?

Figure 9.5 VRML mastermind Mark Pesce.

Mark: There isn't any one "right" way that 3D will work for communities; some will structure themselves along lines very similar to the real world. Others will develop complex and bizarre systems, and membership in the community will be equivalent to mastery of an interface.

K & T: Is the average consumer-level computer ready for VRML applications as a regular part of the Internet? If not, what needs to happen to make VRML a normal part of everyday Web life?

Mark: All computers being sold to consumers today can handle VRML; some of the older computers (486s, 68040s) will have a very hard time of it. Now that both browser companies (Netscape and Microsoft) have integrated VRML into their 4.0 releases, we'll see more VRML on the Web; people will get used to having it around.

K & T: What do you feel VRML has to offer online communities that isn't already provided by other applications?

Mark: Once again, I think it offers a place to be; not just in your head, but out in some space that looks tangible, physical, and sensual.

K & T: Please let us know your thoughts about Black Sun Interactive and other 3D community-building applications.

Mark: Black Sun, OZ Interactive, and Paragraph have all been leading the way in the creation of multi-user tools; we'll soon have an interoperable standard— "Living Worlds"—which will allow anyone with a VRML browser to interact in a complex multiuser environment.

K & T: Please tell us where you see virtual communities and VRML in five years.

Mark: VRML will be a basic interface technology in five years—much like HTML. Virtual communities will be driven by narrative and story; you'll go to a virtual community because you like the tale they're telling.

That's Nice, But What Can It Do?

Well, not much right at the moment, but every day brings us closer to practical applications. The problem isn't the technology; VRML technology is in place and improving constantly. The problem isn't bandwidth, either, because VRML documents can be compressed into surprisingly small files, often smaller than graphic files like JPEG or GIF. The reason that most of us aren't zooming around in virtual worlds right now is that the current hardware base just isn't up to the task. As Mark Pesce suggested in our interview, the new Pentium-class PCs (the 200MHz variety with 3D graphics accelerator cards and lots of RAM) can easily handle the most intense VRML applications. Of course, few of us have these powerhouse machines on our desktops today, although we suspect it won't be long before they become standard equipment.

If you're a dedicated Macintosh user, the picture isn't quite so rosy. Although we hear SGI is working on some killer Mac applications, there's very little VRML development going on for the MacOS right now. We sincerely hope to have a different story for you in the next edition of this book.

Many companies already have complex VRML demos and fully realized worlds ready for you to enjoy. They're simply waiting for the home technology curve to catch up. Perhaps within two to four years, a large part of the Internet will be VRML based. But why?

VIRTUAL FILE CABINETS

In the old days, when you needed a document, you or your assistant walked over to the file cabinet, opened the drawer, and retrieved the file with your hands. Today, you may access the company intranet and sift through the directory structure, trying to recall where you put that document in the first place (or worse, trying to guess where someone else put it), so you can open it in a word processor or spreadsheet and print it (so much for the paperless office). In the near future, database management will be conducted in a 3D, office-like, online environment. When you need a document, you'll navigate over to the 3D texture-mapped file cabinet, click on the drawer, and retrieve the file with your cyberhands. Chances are that it will be viewable and printable, without intermediary apps. If you've seen the movie *Disclosure* (based on Michael Crichton's novel and directed by Barry Levinson), you've seen a pretty good interpretation of what a virtual database will probably look like in the not-too-distant future.

In fact, the future may be closer than we think—IBM is experimenting with creating a prototype virtual 3D library front end to a database search engine. And other companies are experimenting with rudimentary VRML databases on their intranets now. Soon you'll be able to apply this technology to your community Web site, allowing easy access to message bases, informational documents, software, and whatever else you have to offer to your visitors.

VIRTUAL MEETINGS

We've talked a lot about chat and social spaces on the Internet. With VRML, chat rooms can literally become 3D rooms (or beaches, taverns, dance halls, or whatever you like). When your group meets, you'll be able to sit around a table with digital cameras and microphones, talking to each other in realtime. It will be just like gathering with friends in your home, except now the friends you get together with can be thousands of miles away.

VIRTUAL SUPERHEROES

Right now, hundreds of thousands of Internet gaming enthusiasts gather to beat the stuffings out of each other in games like Quake. This game is a virtual environment itself, affording the player a remarkable degree of interactivity and full 3D motion. In VRML-designed gaming communities, players will be able to meet before the game, in spaces that simulate taverns, briefing rooms, or the personnel bay of a starship, to plan their strategies, pick teams, or just talk about new game packs or advances in the technology. This will not only provide a richer gaming experience, it will also simplify the process of finding a game in the first place. Whether you enjoy flight simulators, 3D action games, strategy games, or even a civilized game of chess, the VRML environment will greatly expand upon what we do now.

VIRTUAL FRONTIERS

The full extent of VRML's possibilities are still uncertain. We've outlined a few of the more obvious uses of the technology, but let your imagination run wild for a moment. If you're moving to a distant city, you could tour virtual apartments online before deciding which one to move into. You could visit architects to plan home improvements and see the end results (see Figure 9.6) before the contractor even picks up the hammer. You could attend virtual sporting events. You could test drive a virtual car. You could window shop at a virtual mall. Or perhaps you could attend an educational seminar from your home. There are plenty of practical and social possibilities, many of which have yet to be thought of—and we haven't even considered VRML's industrial applications; for example, virtually designing machine tool components to specification, and then ordering them online.

Just because we have to wait until these applications are developed doesn't mean we can't start using the technology now. There are already VRML chat clients and VRML Web sites to check out. You'll need software to take advantage of these sites, so in the next section, we'll look at what's available now.

Figure 9.6 Architects will be able to design blueprints in 3D, while your interior designer decorates the interior—you'll see the end result before the work begins.

So Many Tools, So Little Time

There are many VRML browsers, authoring tools, client and server solutions, and other shiny toys to choose from. Right now, VRML is so new that it's anybody's guess as to what's best, what will still be here in a year, and what will flop. All the same, there do seem to be a few front runners in the field. The folks at Silicon Graphics are taking the lead in application design—so far, their Cosmo Player is the best VRML browser for the home user. Black Sun Interactive's new server technologies are also garnering a lot of attention. Major players in this field are rising quickly, and the great news is that, unlike the early days of the Net when HTML was born, there are so many of us today who are Web-savvy, that really useful VRML applications should develop relatively faster than earlier Web applications did. We fully expect that this chapter will be radically different and probably greatly expanded when it comes time for a second edition of this book.

Let's explore the three main categories of VRML tools: clients, authoring tools, and servers.

CLIENT SOLUTIONS

VRML clients are products that allow the home Internet surfer to access VRML worlds and interact with them. Some of these plug into an HTML browser like Netscape, others stand alone. We'll look at some of the best of the bunch here.

Cosmo Player (Silicon Graphics, Inc)

Cosmo Player is a Netscape plug-in that is compliant with the specifications for VRML 2.0. It allows the user to fully navigate a VRML environment, and allows the option of toggling collision detection on and off, which means that you decide whether to treat virtual objects as solid matter, or as mere scenery that you can pass your avatar freely through. Currently, the Cosmo Player supports the Windows 95, Windows NT, and Irix 5.3, 6.2, and 6.3 platforms, and rumor has it that SGI is hard at work on a Macintosh client (**www.sgi.com**).

Live3D (Netscape, Inc.)

Netscape Live3D adds a high-performance VRML viewer to Netscape Navigator. It also extends Java, JavaScript, and plug-in interfaces within Navigator. This makes it easier to develop distributed 3D applications. Live3D currently supports Windows 3.1, 95, and NT, as well as the Mac PowerPC (**www.netscape.com**).

Passport 2.0 (Black Sun Interactive, Inc.)

Passport 2.0 is a VRML 1.0-compliant browser that makes chat spaces out of VRML spaces, and includes proprietary extensions for Black Sun's Community Server. Passport stands alone, but can also run with Netscape's Live3D, Cosmo Player, or the WorldView Plugins for Netscape 3.0, as well as Microsoft Internet Explorer. Win95 and NT are the currently supported platforms (**www.blacksun.com**).

Community Place (Sony Corp.)

Sony Community Place is compliant with VRML 2.0 standards, and is backward compatible with VRML 1.0 with no apparent problems. It's a browser that supports multiuser shared worlds, text chat, and shared behaviors written in Java. Again, Win95 and NT are the only supported platforms (**www.sony.com**).

ExpressVR (Brad Anderson)

ExpressVR is a Macintosh VRML plug-in for Netscape that supports hardware acceleration in MacOS 7.6. It is not fully compliant to all VRML 1.0 standards, but it's very close. It includes versions for both the 68K machines and the Mac PowerPC (**www.andrew.cmu.edu/user/anderson/vrml/**).

Torch (NewFire)

The NewFire Torch player is still in development, but it will provide a very fast VRML 2.0 engine for interactive games within WRL files, the file format used in VRML. Torch uses a proprietary technology called Visible Scene Management, filtering rich 3D environments to eliminate polygons that are unseen by the user. This can dramatically improve performance in a game. Torch can reportedly increase speed four to six times over that of other VRML players. Keep an eye on this company if gaming is in the future for your virtual community. NewFire intends to support Win95, NT, and MacOS (**www.newfire.com**).

WebSpace Navigator (Silicon Graphics Computer Systems, Template Graphics Software)

WebSpace is part of the WebFORCE software environment from Silicon Graphics. WebSpace Navigator is a point-and-click, standalone browser allowing sophisticated navigation through virtual environments. It was also designed to allow the inspection of 3D product models from online catalogs. This very sophisticated piece of software runs on many platforms: SGI, SUN Solaris, IBM AIX, and Win95 and NT. In the works are versions for Windows 3.1, Mac PowerPC, Digital Unix, and HP/UX (**www.sgi.com**).

WorldView (InterVista Software, Inc.)

WorldView 2.0 is completely VRML 2.0 compliant and acts as a plug-in for both Netscape Navigator and Microsoft Internet Explorer. It supports Microsoft DirectX, including Direct3D APIs, and the JavaScript scripting language, and it features a built-in compiler. If that isn't enough, it also supports Microsoft's Direct Sound Technology. While they are developing a Mac PowerPC version, Win95 and NT are currently supported (**www.intervista.com**).

WIRL (VREAM)

WIRL 1.2 is a VRML 1.0 browser offering rapid access to VRML content in Web-based and client/server applications. VREAM has followed the Netscape marketing model by offering this tool for free. It's both a Netscape plug-in and a Microsoft ActiveX control, and it utilizes Microsoft's Direct3D rendering engine. There's also a VRML 2.0-compliant version as part of VREAM's VRCreator authoring application. Windows 95 and NT are supported (**www.vream.com**).

Internet Explorer (Microsoft, Inc.)

Microsoft's Internet Explorer integrates an add-on module into the browser that lets you explore virtual worlds with your mouse, keyboard, or joystick. VRML support is only available for Microsoft's Win95 and NT platforms at this time (**www.microsoft.com**).

AUTHORING TOOLS

Servers and browsers are great, but most of us won't get very far without authoring tools. It has long been a point of debate between HTML designers whether authoring tools serve any useful purpose. One side claims that a Web author should know their code and be able to construct Web pages from within a simple text editor, otherwise they just aren't very good at it in the first place. Another side feels that this attitude is elitist, and that authoring tools, especially good WYSIWYG (What You See Is What You Get) tools, can be invaluable in speeding up the production process. The third plank, which we subscribe to, agrees that Web authors should certainly know their code, but that authoring tools are essential assistants for preparing complex sites and pages. These tools are also very valuable to the casual home user who wants a home page, but doesn't have time to become fully proficient in HTML.

As it turns out, this debate becomes irrelevant once VRML becomes part of the picture. The complex language of VRML requires a good deal of mathematical prowess, and at least a rudimentary understanding of how programming languages function. Even if you do learn VRML inside and out, an authoring package is an essential tool for developing complex worlds online. Let's look at a few of them.

Pioneer, Pioneer Pro (Caligari Corp.)

Pioneer is a complete package for the Windows platform. This VRML authoring solution includes rapid modeling in perspective space, the ability to manipulate texture-mapped VRML objects in realtime, and also interactive lighting. The Pioneer technology has been licensed by Microsoft for inclusion in a project called "Blackbird," and that means that the technology will probably be an important part of a major piece of Microsoft software in the near future. Pioneer is primarily an authoring tool, but it also has the ability to read and view a variety of VRML files, allowing authors to make use of existing 3D resources on the Web. The Pioneer package is also proficient at testing VRML-specific features such as detail levels, in-lining, and hyperlinks to Internet resources like other VRML sites, HTML documents, and video files. This package supports a multitude of file formats, including JPEG and DXF, and is supported on all Windows platforms including 3.1, provided you are using win32s to enable 32-bit applications (**www.caligari.com**).

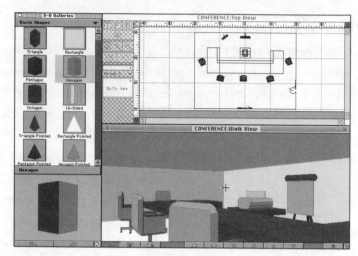

Figure 9.7 The 3-D Website Builder has an easy-to-use GUI interface for quick VRML authoring.

3-D Website Builder (Virtus Corp.)

3-D Website Builder, shown in Figure 9.7, is a WYSIWYG VRML design tool for creating "Virtual Worlds" without programming. Using a handy drag-and-drop GUI interface, this tool lets you build everything from scratch, right down to details like tables and chairs, or you can import 3D modeled objects from other sources. In many ways, this is a scaled-down (but still very powerful) version of their bigger product called Walk Through Pro. (Check out their Web site for information on Walk Through Pro.) By many accounts, Virtus has developed the flagship products of VRML design. 3-D Website Builder is sold as a crossplatform CD for both Win95 and Mac PowerPC, and includes Virtus Voyager, a cross-platform, free-standing browser application (**www.virtus.com**).

Liquid Reality (Dimension X/Microsoft)

Liquid Reality is pretty cool, which is probably why Microsoft acquired this cutting-edge company in May of 1997. A modular and extensible VRML 2.0 platform written in Java, Liquid Reality is both a browser for VRML and a developer's toolkit for creating powerful 3D applications in Java. This application allows the development of dynamically extensible VRML environments that integrate motion, sound, and intelligent behaviors. A neat feature of Liquid Reality is the ability for users to create their own customized VRML 2.0 browser. Using ICE (a 3D graphics library from Dimension X), Liquid Reality isn't just extensible with Java, but it runs on any Java-enabled browser. Wide platform support includes Win95 and high-end platforms like Linux, SGI Irix, and Sun Solaris; a Windows NT version is in development (**www.microsoft.com/dimensionx**).

V-Realm Builder (Integrated Data Systems, Inc.)

A strong competitor in the authoring tool market is IDS's V-Realm Builder. This tool is VRML 2.0 compliant, and it allows for the import of other 3D objects. There are a variety of editors within the program that handle specific tasks like polygon editing. Win95 and NT are supported (**www.ids-net.com**).

THE SERVER

The previous sections are useful if you just want to browse and study VRML environments, but if you plan to administer interactive, realtime VRML content within your community, you'll need to set up a server. VRML files that will simply be viewed by other Web surfers can be placed on any ISP. The WRL files aren't really that different from HTML files; when the browser encounters them, it launches the appropriate viewer.

Interactive VRML applications like chat, however, are another story. At this time, very few ISPs are handling this type of VRML server, so if you're set on being a cutting-edge community with interactive VRML features, you'll need to either shop for an ISP that can fulfill your needs or set up your own server. This is a costly undertaking now, but as with all new technology, the costs will drop as VRML moves into the mainstream.

Unlike browsers and authoring tools, servers require very powerful machines, and consequently expensive ones, to handle the demands that will be placed on VRML environments from a provider's point of view. Also note that at this time, to the best of our knowledge, there are no Mac-based server solutions. Mac users, however, can access VRML environments through their clients (browsers), so you don't have to worry about excluding them when deciding whether to implement VRML into your site.

Community Server (Black Sun Interactive, Inc.)

Community Server incorporates multiuser interaction into a Web site. It can support any VRML-compliant world, and it can add multiuser capability, such as chat, to that world. An evaluation version that allows a maximum of three avatars in a world at any time is available from Black Sun. The software is currently available for Linux, SGI IRIX 6.2, AIX 4.1.4, Solaris, and Windows NT (**www.blacksun.com**).

Worlds Chat (Worlds, Inc.)

Using VRML 2.0, Worlds, Inc. offers a similar environment to Black Sun. Along with offering a chat server, Worlds licenses a browser and authoring tools. Worlds, Inc. also operates AlphaWorld, an interactive virtual community, which is also a launch pad to other virtual worlds, such as Yellowstone Park, Arctic Light, Cyborg Nation, the University of Cincinnati, and more (**www.worlds.net**).

The Next Step

On a flat HTML page, you can display information. To get to more information, you click on a link and move to another flat HTML page. This is the book, magazine, and newspaper model. 3D VRML spaces, on the other hand, allow surfers to "walk" through your site, with visibility in all directions. This fairly profound innovation means that you have at least six 2D surfaces on which to place content, instead of one. At a VRML diner under development that we visited recently, there were three walls lined with booths; each booth featured an old-style table jukebox that you could scroll through to select content. The fourth wall was an ordering counter, where company information and product data could be served. The ceiling provided a link to the site's ISP, and the floor…well, the floor was just a floor. Still, five diverse "pages" of content were available in one room. In many ways, this was more efficient than a single page.

One obvious model of the virtual community is an actual community. By navigating a 3D-modeled town from the outside, a surfer could walk to a town hall to engage in political chat, then go to a theatre to chat about arts and entertainment. After that, the guest could check out some bargains in the various shops, walk over to the neighborhood to visit personal home pages, or stop by the school to download some educational software. Several cities have created virtual city models, the first step in creating these virtual digital cities.

VRML is going to give us a natural metaphor for dynamic interaction that both computer professionals and newbies alike will understand instinctively. We can't tell you today the details of the evolution to come; we'll all just have to wait and see what innovative and imaginative content designers and programmers come up with. Or…maybe you could create that content yourself. Go for it!

Acting Locally

We've studied some history and looked at a range of tools; now it's time to look at a cousin to the virtual community. The *community network* is geographically based, to serve meatspace communities directly. We'll take a little extra space to showcase the community network, because it's different enough from the virtual community that it should be addressed as a separate entity. And don't worry about needing a whole new toolbox; almost every tool that a virtual community uses can be used by a network as well, including VRML.

Part 3

Getting Your Community Off The Ground

Chapter 10

Building An Electronic Village

Chapter 10

- THE ELECTRONIC VILLAGE

- WHY LINK A VILLAGE?

- IDEAS FOR CONTENT ON AN ELECTRONIC VILLAGE NETWORK

BUILDING AN ELECTRONIC VILLAGE

Chapter 10

Geography Is Still Important

We've made the point that communities on the Internet aren't necessarily tied to a physical location, but that doesn't mean that a virtual community can't be based on geography. In fact, geographic virtual communities are a pretty smart idea. As we're about to see, there are many advantages to wiring your town or village into a network to create an *electronic village*. After all, you can't just leave meatspace and live in cyberspace (at least not yet); you still live, work, and interact with other people somewhere in the physical world. Wouldn't it be great to be able to communicate with your neighbor, or your mayor, or that friendly fellow who runs the pizza parlor, as easily as you do with people on the other side of the world? If you suddenly remember at 3:00 A.M. that soccer practice is at 5:00 P.M. this Friday, instead of the usual 6:00 P.M., you can tell the whole team without waking them up, just by sending everyone email. And that's only the beginning.

So What Is An Electronic Village Anyway?

Electronic villages are also commonly referred to as *community networks*. You're probably asking, "Isn't this the same as a virtual community?" Well, yes it is—but with a slightly different twist. The definition approach was really handy back in Chapter 1 when we were trying to understand just what "community" was, so let's try it again. Here's one definition of community network from Mario Morino, a community network evangelist:

"[A community network is] a process to serve the local geographic community—to respond to the needs of that community and build solutions to its problems. Community networking in the social sense is not a new concept, but using electronic communications to extend and amplify it certainly is."

Morino is the founder of The Morino Institute, a nonprofit organization dedicated to the establishment of electronic villages. We're pretty impressed with this institute, and we think you will be also, when you read the mission statement.

Morino's Mission
*(from the mission statement at **www.morino.org**)*

The Morino Institute is dedicated to opening the doors of opportunity—economic, civic, health, and education—and empowering people to improve their lives and communities in the Communications Age. The Institute helps individuals and institutions harness the power of information and the potential of interactive communications as tools for overcoming the challenges that face them.

We are in the midst of a revolution in human communications that is changing how we talk to each other, how we work together, how we create and share knowledge. This revolution is already fundamentally transforming society, and its implications for individuals and communities are dramatic. The most important element of this revolution, and certainly the most powerful, is the new medium of interactive communications, which is already linking millions of people around the globe.

Of course, Mario Morino doesn't have a monopoly on the electronic village. Here are a couple of other knowledgeable voices.

Anne Beamish, Architect And Urban Planner

[An electronic village is] a network of computers with modems that are interconnected via telephone lines to a central computer, which provides community information and a means for the community to communicate electronically.

Douglas Schuler, Author Of New Community Networks

Fueled by rapidly diminishing computing costs and a groundswell of grassroots and organizational enthusiasm, creativity, and hard work, community networks are both a new type of computer application and a new type of social institution. A community network is a computer network system that is developed for use by the local geographical community. They provide a variety of services for the community using a variety of computer capabilities such as electronic forums (or newsgroups), e-mail, and World Wide Web access. Often, but not always, access to the community network is free, for the same reasons that society provides free public libraries, fire and police protection, and public schools. Ideally the community network is run by the community—not solely by an institution or a small group of people.

Everyone Lives Close To Town, So Why Do We Need To Be Wired?

It may seem odd to "wire" a local community. After all, if you need to attend a PTA meeting, the school is probably nearby. Or if you don't know the hours of the local library, you can just pick up the phone and call. What do you need a community network for?

Community networks can serve as an alternative to traditional forums, such as printed newsletters, community-access cable TV, or the local newspaper. It's not about "playing" with computers; it's about people communicating with each other in a new and effective way. Physical communities have been known to thrive when community members become active in virtual space. But community networking doesn't replace face-to-face interaction; rather, it complements it. It's like the old town-hall meeting. If you lived in a small village, you knew everybody and everybody knew you. People talked to each other, and if you needed to research your town's history, or discuss a topic of community-wide importance, or organize a festival, you could do it with relative ease. But if you live in a community with a thousand, a hundred thousand, or a million people, how do you get them all together? That's where a community network comes in.

In the following sections, we'll show you several enterprising communities that have built extremely successful networks, and see how their ideas might be relevant to your own electronic village.

TAKING CARE OF BUSINESS

Economic growth is essential to the well-being of a community. In disadvantaged and rural areas, where civic leaders are hoping to turn the tide of unemployment by attracting new industries into their communities, community networks have been set up to spur growth. A fine example of this is Blacksburg, Virginia, one of the best-known community networks. We'll discuss Blacksburg later in the chapter.

Economic development is also important to healthy urban or suburban communities. To encourage economic development, the Philadelphia LibertyNet, a community network housed at **www.libertynet.org** (shown in Figure 10.1), offers a

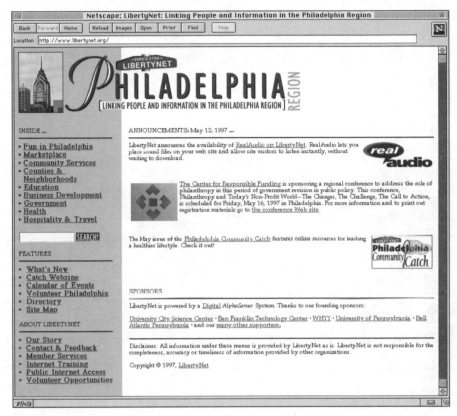

Figure 10.1 LibertyNet provides useful economic and business development information.

wide variety of content, including the Ben Franklin Technology Center, which promotes innovation and business growth in southeastern Pennsylvania by linking entrepreneurs and technology.

Many community networks have been set up to offer career-development services. Charlotte's Web (see Figure 10.2), located in Charlotte, North Carolina, provides many resources for job hunters, including a free job search seminar, a job hunters' support group, and many local job listings.

Of course, sometimes it isn't possible to employ people. That's when motivated individuals seek out ways to employ themselves. In Nebraska, there's a resource that has helped many people change their lives for the better, using both virtual community concepts and electronic village concepts. This program was made possible by the support of the Morino Institute.

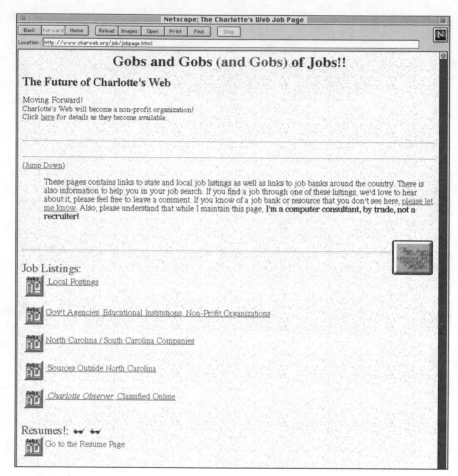

Figure 10.2 Finding a great job at Charlotte's Web.

Success In The Corn Husker State
*(from **www.morino.org**)*

In Nebraska, the Community Networking Institute (CNI) brings together local businesses and service groups throughout the state to help people in rural communities find economic, health, and educational opportunities. A woman in tiny Wallace, Nebraska now teaches graduate courses to students around the world from her home. A rancher in Sand Hills developed systems to manage his herds more productively in collaboration with a colleague over 500 miles away.

According to CNI Director Steve Buttress, "The Morino Institute's partnership and management experience was of tremendous value. They helped us ask the right questions and develop an effective operational plan to meet the needs of local people. Their continuing support in establishing contacts to national resources and in developing educational materials will help assure the success of this ambitious project."

Some Good Ideas For Network Content

The sites in this section had a number of good ideas that could be applied to your community, including:

- Business development information

- Notes from nonprofit organizations, citizen's leagues, and planning committees

- Forums and discussion groups; for example, job-hunting ideas, or support for unemployed, laid off, and striking workers

- Job listings

- Labor news

SHOW YOUR CIVIC PRIDE AND CULTURAL AWARENESS

Civic groups focus on strengthening community bonds and local culture. Communication is essential to realizing this ideal, and a community network can be an invaluable tool to enhance communication.

While some critics see electronic communication as a threat to face-to-face communication in physical communities, proponents counter that many groups are making use of the technology to talk to each other for the first time. Relationships are being built in ways that might never have happened before. This process can be enhanced with "civic maps" that depict promising linkages between people and organizations in the community; a database of "community assets," the basis of civic maps, can be made available online using computer networks.

And what part can CMC play in strengthening the local culture? Incorporating local events and issues, and a collective sense of destiny, the culture of a community can be found in the community members' shared memories. This is something that's been built up over years of parades and festivals, sporting events, poetry readings, and the conflicts and crises that have shaped the community's history. An electronic village can help to chronicle these shared memories, both current and historical, and it can also be instrumental in creating the contemporary events that are becoming part of the culture.

The Electronic Cafe

This is excerpted from Doug Schuler's book, New Community Networks *(©1996 Addison-Wesley ISBN# 0-201-59553-2).*

The Electronic Cafe linked five different locations in the Los Angeles area, including the Los Angeles Museum of Contemporary Art, with family-owned restaurants in Korean (8th Street Restaurant), Hispanic (Anna Maria's), African American (The Gumbo House), and "artsy" beach communities (Gunter's) together into one shared virtual space. Within this space participants could send each other slow-scan images, draw or write together with an electronic writing tablet, print pictures with the video printer, enter and retrieve information (including graphics) and ideas in the computer database, and store or retrieve images on a videodisk recorder that held 20,000 images. This cultural exploration was widely enjoyed by community residents at the same time that it was a pioneer groupware application.

More Good Ideas For Network Content

Here are some of the ideas we've gotten from looking over the sites in this section:

- Forums for ethnic, religious, and neighborhood interest groups

- Support-group information and discussion groups

- Community history and lore

- Recreation and parks information

- Arts events

- Community calendar

WE HAVE SOME LITERATURE WE'D LIKE TO SHOW YOU

Placing information on a network has obvious benefits. First, it can be cheaper than printing a brochure and mailing it, and you can distribute it to many people at once. Second, you can send documents almost instantly; no more waiting for a courier to deliver your portfolio to a prospective employer. And if you're concerned about the environment, remember that electrons are easier to recycle than paper. For example, Figure 10.3 shows the GO Boulder Alternative Transportation Center, which is housed within the Boulder Community Network.

Figure 10.3 The various information readily available at GO Boulder.

Even More Good Ideas For Network Content

Here are some ideas for document-based content:

- "Phone book" of Internet email addresses

- Interactive transportation information such as bus schedules, taxi fares, bicycle paths, and rideshare programs

- Library information and services

- Online databases

- Online periodicals, wire services, and alternative news

- Forums for discussion and debate by citizens on topics of local importance

TIME TO HIT THE BOOKS, VIRTUAL STYLE

We all know that without education, one's opportunities are substantially diminished. Many jobs simply can be unattainable without the right educational background. For the most part, businesses are unwilling to settle in a community with a generally low level of education—and those that do would probably offer dead-end, low-wage jobs. Such a community would also be less likely to initiate, sustain, or expand business ventures. Furthermore, without adequate education, the political process becomes unfathomable, and decisions tend to be relinquished to people who represent interests outside of the community.

It should be obvious that education is essential to develop a thriving community. A community network can serve to facilitate communication among teachers, parents, and school officials, and if the network is linked with a nearby university, it can also help to provide adult education and job training, thereby increasing the community's overall skill sets.

Big Sky Telegraph

(From New Community Networks *by Douglas Schuler)*

In 1988, Frank Odasz of Western Montana University in Dillon, an ex-dude-ranch operator with a degree in Educational Technology, started the Big Sky Telegraph (BST) community-network system with the idea that computer technology could help tame the vast distances of the American West. His first task was to electronically link more than 40 one- and two-room schoolhouses and 12 rural libraries across Montana with microcomputers and modems. Linking these schoolrooms provided a low-cost way for teachers to share information such as subject curricula, to ask questions and discuss concerns with other teachers, and to "check out" educational software in order to evaluate it before purchasing it. The system also offers 600 K-12 lesson plans serving as a "telecurricular clearinghouse" for K-12 projects running on networks all over the world. The system also offers online courses on how to use network and bulletin-board services.

Still More Good Ideas For Network Content

Here are some ideas for educational content:

- Online homework help

- Forums for educators, students, and parents

- Questions and answers on major topics of interest

- School projects (see Figure 10.4)

- Pen pal connections

- Online reading lists and syllabi for self-paced education

- Career counseling, information about choosing colleges, and other planning resources for students

AS THEY SAY IN CHICAGO, "VOTE EARLY, AND VOTE OFTEN"

We live in a democratic society, yet participation in the democratic process is wan-ing. For a community to truly thrive, citizen participation in all levels of

Figure 10.4 At the Seattle Community Network (**www.scn.org**), the B.F. Day School lists Activities and Events, Projects, and more.

decision-making is vital. Increasing participation in local government is a challenge, especially when you're up against all the myriad distractions in our hectic lives. Even little villages in rural America are no longer immune to the hustle and bustle of modern living. Community networks allow a new forum for participation.

Canadians Speak Out

At the National Capital Free-net in Ottawa, Canada, cybercitizens may "cast a ballot" in a number of forums using a system called "VOTE." Using VOTE, network users can read descriptions of current issues, vote on them, look at the vote tally for a particular issue, and add their own comments on local concerns or raise important points to increase community awareness of potential new issues. Now that's democracy!

Since community networks and other computer-mediated systems offer real promise, there will undoubtedly be calls for new approaches to democratic discourse, including calls for "direct democracy," in which citizens actually propose and pass legislation. It will be interesting to see how this plays out in the future.

Yet More Good Ideas For Network Content

Here are some ideas to help your community members contribute to the political process:

- Contact information for elected officials

- Email links to elected officials and government agencies

- Forums on major issues

- Online versions of legislation, regulations, and other government information

- Community action campaigns

Different Networks For Different Folks

After taking a look at how several community networks across the country were constructed, we can only come to one conclusion—they are as varied and unique as the towns and cities they represent. However, we can generally group them into three main types:

- *Governmentally Controlled*—A central administrator manages all content. The end user is considered to be a passive consumer of the information provided. Typically, the available data is an extension of existing printed material.

- *Commercially Controlled*—Many ISPs, and even newspapers and other publishing giants, are getting into the game of developing geographically based content. ISPs benefit from providing community information by attracting people to their Web sites; these systems are usually funded by advertising revenue or strategic partnerships. The Tribune Company, in conjunction with America Online, has launched Digital Cities in several key markets such as Chicago, Orlando, and San Francisco. Positioned as "local content and community specialists," Digital Cities hopes to capitalize on the growing need for local

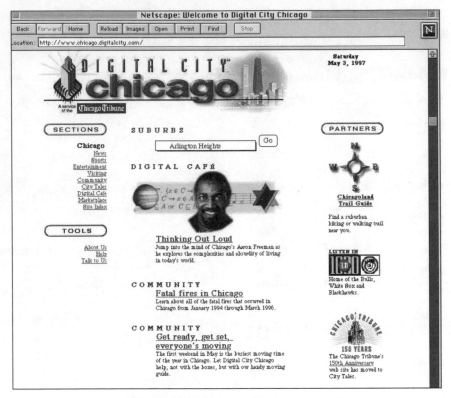

Figure 10.5 Digital Chicago provides an array of local content and interaction.

information and interaction, as demonstrated at the Digital Chicago Web site in Figure 10.5. Although Digital Cities currently focuses on "top down" content, this may not be the case in the near future; soon businesses will be putting up "storefronts." Families and civic groups will likely follow thereafter, thus building content from the "ground up."

- *Community Controlled*—These community networks are grassroots and user-led efforts. The information is created at all user levels, from governmental offices down to the individual; it's not controlled or mediated through a central authority, and the users are responsible for all content. Most community networks are shifting to this paradigm, since it's so open and encourages participation—a real information society. The following section will detail how to initiate and build this type of network.

An Old-Fashioned Community Network Raising

There is a series of steps that you'll have to take to establish a community network. This is no small task, and probably worthy of a whole other book, such as Doug Schuler's *New Community Networks* (mentioned earlier). But if you apply the principles of virtual communities, study other community networks, and follow these steps, you should be well on your way to success.

ASSEMBLING YOUR TEAM

It isn't an easy sell. To get a major community network up and running, you'll need an evangelist to inspire followers and to convert the "techno-heathens." The project evangelist needs to be able to speak in "plain English," not in technical terms. This leader will proselytize the need for the network to people and organizations (including governmental bodies) who may never have touched this type of technology, and who may be resistant to change. Think of the evangelist as a spokesperson. In most major companies, the CEO or president fulfills this role, but that doesn't need to be the case in your project. It really depends on an honest appraisal of your own strengths and weaknesses. If you are the type who can inspire people, do this job yourself, but if not, get someone who can. You'll be glad you did.

Next, the leader needs to establish a core group of members to handle the "mission-critical" functions. One of these members should ideally be the technical consultant; this person will advise the group on the hardware, software, and connectivity issues involved.

Also, a public relations guru would be helpful in taking the evangelist's message and reaching out to the masses, using the local media (cable access, television news broadcasts, and newspaper) to promote the cause. The PR person, as you might guess, needs to be knowledgeable about the fine art of publicity, and hopefully have contacts in local media. You might want to consider rubbing elbows with the people down at you local newspaper or television station (if your community has one) to recruit such a person. Whoever you get, they must be energetic and have a cursory understanding of computers and the Internet.

Get a bean counter—someone with accounting knowledge. This person will create and monitor the budget. An accountant is an obvious choice, but someone with experience in running a small business would likely also fit the bill. Much of what you will be able to do will depend on mustering up grants and/or donations, so naturally, adhering to a strict budget is a must. Computers for servers aren't cheap, and going over budget can break a project like this.

Speaking of grants and donations, a grant writer is a must. Developing grant proposals will most likely be a team effort, but there should be one person with very strong writing skills to actually write the proposals. This person will need to work with all your team members, from the evangelist on down, to understand the needs of the project. Then he or she will need to research the many grant and funding options available. We're going to go into more detail about funding in the next chapter, but while we're on the subject, keep in mind that people who read grant proposals are not very interested in technology, but rather in what the project can do for the community. With that in mind, a grant writer needs to think like the evangelist. It's certainly possible that the evangelist may fill this role.

Public Access Networking
(from www.morino.com)

One of the most compelling aspects of the Communications Age is the way it has inspired grass-roots civic, economic, and public-service efforts across the globe. Public access networking is a profound example of this, where communication and information services are delivered free or at low cost to local citizens. Because these are grass-roots programs, however, there is often little opportunity to share knowledge and experience.

The Morino Institute helps connect these efforts through support of programs like the Ties That Bind Conference, cosponsored with Apple Computer. This kind of knowledge and experience sharing is also the impetus for the Institute's Directory of Public Access Networks, which serves as a resource for community sponsors, public and community service groups, media, policy makers, grant makers and others interested in the emergence and use of public access networks.

You Gotta Have A Plan

This plan is very similar to the planning process discussed in Chapter 3, so we won't reiterate here. However, we again want to emphasize the need for planning—since you'll probably be looking for local, state, and federal funds as well as private backing, you'll need a highly tuned business plan.

Rally The Masses

It goes without saying that you'll need the support of the community to make this project successful. You'll want to make contact with several key players, including local government, the public library, the public school system, and a few well-known business people. Public meetings are also essential. Work with civic groups or your town hall to set up these meetings.

Home Base

A community network typically needs a "home" where it can put down roots and have someone nurture and care for it. We've seen city councils and local governments, convention and travel bureaus, chambers of commerce, universities and colleges, school districts, even local libraries take on the role of "nurturer." The servers and other hardware that make up the heart of the Blacksburg Electronic Village (BEV) is housed on the campus of Virginia Tech. This relationship is symbiotic, as Virginia Tech's students benefit from the learning experience of taking care of the network, while Blacksburg, Virginia, benefits from the community services the network provides. Later in the chapter, we'll take a closer look at BEV.

Choose Your Technology Wisely

Of course, there's more to a community network than hardware, software, and a delivery system, but these technological ingredients are essential. To all but the brightest engineers, networking a community together can seem more like witchcraft than anything else. Fortunately, you don't need a degree from MIT to wire a town, you only need to find the people with the appropriate knowledge. Local ISPs, universities, and businesses can be great places to recruit technical wizards.

The software and hardware you choose will have important implications for you, for your developer, and for your community. Consider your objectives, your interests, and your resources. For example, if you want to have local political issues debated online, you'll want chat applications and a message board. Issues that will have a major impact on the cost (in terms of money, time, and human resources) of your network include:

- Access method (modems and telephone lines, T1 lines, etc.)

- Connection to the Internet (no connection, email only, or direct connection) and with what bandwidth

- Number of simultaneous users

- Type of interaction (text-based, graphics, video, etc.)

Key Questions To Ask About Network Technology And Your Community

As mentioned in the last section, the choice of delivery systems is important. Think about the points in this list while you're making decisions about what type of technology to employ in your electronic village. Needs should dictate what kind of system you choose.

- What kind of community tools do you want to feature? You'll almost certainly want email. What about discussion forums, chat, IRC, database access, voting software, Telnet, FTP, newsgroup access, etc.? A community network can be minimal or it can be complex, but it will be most effective if it meets the needs of the community.

- How many total users will you be serving and how many at one time can you support?

- Will it make more sense for users to access the system through the Internet, a free-net service like the ones that many colleges offer, or a BBS? Internet-based networks are gaining in popularity due to the easy interface of the Web, and with a Web-based community network, the focus can be placed on local information. Members generally must arrange for connectivity on their own, but you could work out a plan with an ISP or a local college or university to provide low-cost access.

- Community-network users come in all flavors: some will have had no computer experience, and some may actually be afraid of computers. It's a challenge to initiate the techno-timid into cyberspace, but these people almost always discover a new sense of empowerment from mastering the technology.

- Some users may have disabilities that make the use of standard computer equipment difficult, and some may not speak or read English. You'll need to carefully consider your user interface to meet the special needs of some communities.

GETTING THE CRITICAL MASS ONLINE

Education is the key. The first challenge will be educating the local government about the Internet and electronic networks, and demonstrating how the technology could be used to provide services to the community. You may encounter resistance from leaders who aren't techno-savvy, but this is where your evangelist steps in. You might also enlist the help of a local computer users group if there's one in your area (and there probably is).

Here are some ideas for educating the general public:

- Visit local community groups and show them how they can publicize their activities on the network.

- Demonstrate to consumers the importance and value of having connectivity within their homes: They can exercise more control over time and information, and their interactions with family, friends, and organizations within the community will improve.

- Show public school administrators and teachers the value of having a network connection within the classroom: Kids with access to technology have automatic access to an immense educational support system. Not only can they get online help with homework, collaborate on class projects, and use writing and language skills, but they'll also be learning essential computer skills as they use the system.

- Introduce the business community to the trend toward electronic storefronts and commerce. Show them how they can reach existing customers more inexpensively and expand their customer base at the same time.

CREATING THE "INFORMATION SPACE"

There's no point in having a network without content, but creating content is a huge job. Why do it yourself, when the very community you want to serve can do it for you? Empower the organizations and individuals who will be gathering on the network to post information and content directly to it. The Seattle Community Network (SCN) (**www.scn.org**), for example, has tried to make this process as painless as possible by providing online forms (like the one shown in Figure 10.6) that allow anyone in the community to become an information provider. These providers are teachers, businesses, and civic groups, among other community members. The SCN has created a "mentor" program with hands-on classes to help local community groups put information on SCN's servers, and guides for authoring HTML are available on the SCN Web site. As a cherry to top their network sundae, the SCN has also created newsgroups and mailing lists to handle questions and provide continuing support.

Let's Visit Blacksburg, Virginia

The Blacksburg Electronic Village (BEV) is in the process of linking an entire town to become a twentyfirst-century telecommunications powerhouse. This Ethernet-based infrastructure has wired businesses, governmental offices, schools, and community groups in such a way that BEV users can interconnect and interoperate directly with any other computer in the BEV network, and they are directly connected to the Internet. No "intermediary" computers are used, as is the case with BBSes and free-nets.

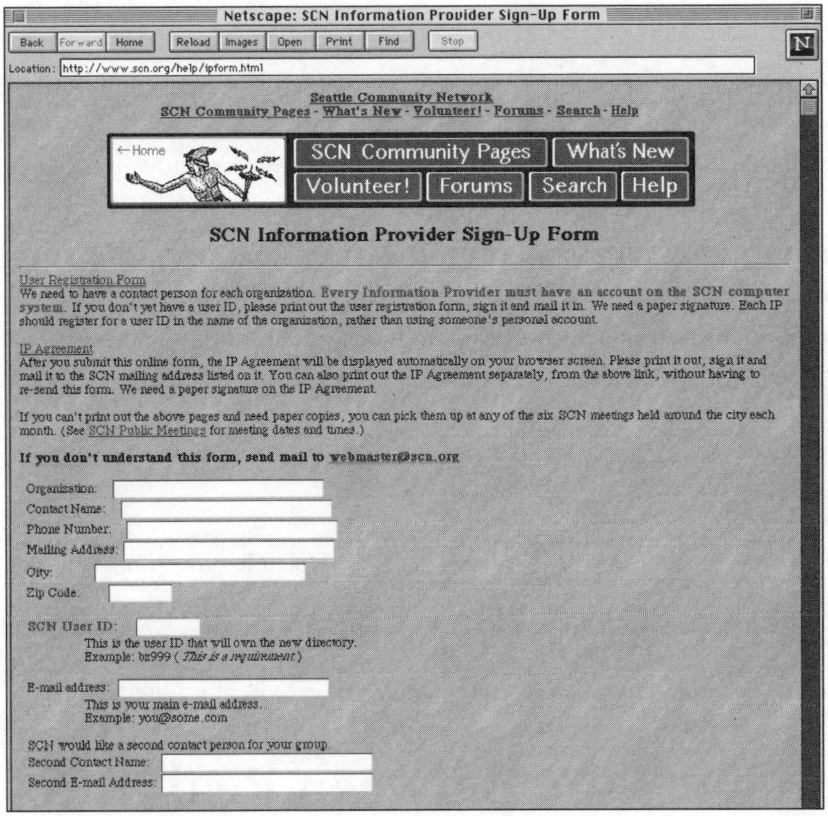

Figure 10.6 The Seattle Community Network form.

Why did this community go through the arduous process to set up this network? Because Blacksburg is located in a mostly rural area, town leaders felt it was essential to have better access to the "information highway" in order to thrive economically. The BEV network incorporates some nifty tools (aside from email, Usenet, and Web access), such as videoconferencing and collaborative "groupware," that make this network truly unique.

EDUCATIONAL USES

Fifth graders use the videoconferencing facility to exchange ideas with students from other countries, such as how to prevent air pollution. Video is also used to create an electronic "field trip" in which students form computer links to remote locations. On one occasion, the children gathered to discuss planetary science.

BUSINESS AND PROFESSIONAL USES

More than a third of Blacksburg's business and professional community are using the network to promote their products and services. For example, restaurants have made heavy use of the network to provide customers with online menus and special coupons. Entrepreneurs who realize the potential of electronic commerce have built new businesses to take advantage of the network. The medical profession is seeing direct benefits as well; using file transfer capabilities, doctors may obtain x-rays, thermograms, and MRI images electronically from the imaging facility. They also have access to information about billing and outpatient status, as well as medical literature databases.

CIVIC USES

BEV includes an "electronic town hall," where people can fill out and file permit applications, pay for public utilities, and send email inquiries to town leaders and agencies. These innovations have dramatically cut costs, and they also make it possible to provide faster, more efficient services to local residents.

Blur The Line Between Real And Virtual Communities

The project evangelist and core committee members should take every opportunity to promote the community network. The BEV Community Network Planning Guide (**www.bev.com**) suggests the following ideas:

- Arrange social events, speakers, and meetings so that online users can meet each other face-to-face.

- Encourage businesses to include URLs and email addresses on traditional advertisements.

- Have online groups participate in community projects and events like clean-up days, Independence Day parades, etc.

- Provide email addresses for all governmental departments to facilitate communication between the citizens and their leaders.

- Have Internet computers available in schools, libraries, and institutions.

- Share stories of how the network has impacted the lives of citizens.

Some Additional Resources

- Community Networking Movement Home Page (**www.scn.org/ip/commnet/ home.html**)

- Center For Civic Networking (**civic.net/ccn.html**)

- Civic Net (**www.tmn.com/civicnet/index.html**)

- The Morino Institute (**www.morino.org**)

- The Organization For Community Networks (OFCN) (**ofcn.org**)

- Community Networking Resource Site (**www.sils.umich.edu/Community**)

- Communet List Serv: Discussion list for community network issues. To join, send email to **listproc@list.uvm.edu** with the message "sub communet first-name last-name."

Are You Up To The Task?

We've given you an overview of what you need to set up a community network, and it probably seems like a daunting task. It requires hundreds of thousands of hours, the cooperation of many people, access to money, and a heck of a lot of research. The good news is that since many cities, towns, and villages have begun undertaking projects like community networks, much of the mystery is being swept away by the information available about their successes and occasional failures. Now, we know a community network isn't exactly the same thing as a virtual community, but we felt the topic still deserved notice, as this kind of online community is part of the future, and successful projects like Blacksburg's contribute greatly to the success of the Internet and the rich content held therein.

Whether it's a community network or a virtual community you're planning, you'll need a little money to get the ball rolling. Follow us to Chapter 11, where we'll look at ways to fund your project with grants and other sources of money.

Chapter 11

Getting The Green For Your Electronic Village

Chapter 11

- FEDERAL FUNDING SOURCES

- CORPORATE GRANTS

- SEARCHING FOR GRANTS

- TIPS ON GRANT WRITING

Getting The Green For Your Electronic Village

Chapter 11

There's A Challenge Ahead

Funding a major project is never easy. Funding a project of $500,000, or $50,000, or even $5,000 is downright daunting. Of course, half the battle is knowing where to find folks who'll give you the money. In this chapter, we'll look at several sources of grant money for your very worthwhile electronic village project, and we'll also share some tips for writing grant applications.

Getting Green From The Federal Government

Though the bureaucracy associated with federal grant programs may seem like a Kafka-esque nightmare, you can, with a little planning (remember those six P's from Chapter 3?), build your electronic village on the public's dime. Don't feel bad; it's your dime, too, and the result will actually benefit the public. Support from outside the community often comes from state or federal agencies. The political climate of Washington is currently in your favor, because developing a thriving electronic infrastructure is being looked upon very favorably by many elected officials. Consequently, there are some available sources of funding aimed specifically at community networking, distance learning, and economic development. However, developing a community network that will ultimately become self-supporting is an enormous plus if you're seeking federal money.

FYI, The TIIAP And The PTFP

Two big grant programs in Washington are the Telecommunications and Information Infrastructure Assistance Program (TIIAP) and The Public Telecommunications Facilities Program (PTFP).

The TIIAP is a highly competitive, merit-based grant program that provides seed money to nonprofit and public sector organizations for innovative, practical technology projects throughout the United States. This program provides matching grants to such institutions as schools, libraries, hospitals, public safety entities, and state and local governments. The grants are used to purchase equipment for computer networks, software, videoconferencing systems, network routers, training, telephone lines, and other products and services essential to an electronic village. For fiscal year 1997, this program has a budget of $21.5 million, and President Clinton has requested $36 million for 1998.

The PTFP awards matching grants to noncommercial organizations for the purchase of telecommunications equipment, with the stipulation that the equipment be used for educational or cultural purposes. The PTFP also provides smaller grants to assist in planning for the purchase and use of telecommunications equipment. The fiscal year 1997 budget for this program is $15.25 million.

While many will apply for programs like these, few will be awarded grants. What the grant committees are looking for are projects that can, over time, become self-supporting. But even if your proposal isn't awarded a cash grant, there are some nice consolation prizes like technical support, in-depth grant application review, and other types of nonmonetary assistance. More information about these programs is available from the National Telecommunications and Information Administration, US Department of Commerce, Room 4096, 14th and Constitution

Avenue NW, Washington DC 20230. The telephone number is 202-482-5802, or you can visit the agency's home page (**www.ntia.doc.gov**) or send email to **tiiap@ntia.doc.gov**.

FUNDING FOR HIGHER EDUCATION

The Agricultural Telecommunications Program provides funding that is only available to accredited institutions of higher education. But don't despair; if you're teaming up with such an institution, your project can benefit from the program, which has a budget of over a million dollars for 1997. The grants are intended to be supplementary moneys, and only 10 percent can be used for hardware. The remaining 90 percent is generally earmarked for human resources.

The guidelines for the 1997 Agricultural Telecommunications Program are not yet available. When they are, they'll be released in the Federal Register and on the program's Web site (**www.reeusda.gov/agtel**). To receive copies of the application submission package when it becomes available, contact the Cooperative State Research, Education, and Extension Service (CSREES) Proposal Services Branch at 202-401-5048 or **psb@reeusda.gov**.

You may also subscribe to a listserv that will notify you electronically when new information is available, such as program guidelines, application packages, and abstracts of funded projects. Subscribers will receive notification of the availability of the information, as well as instructions for obtaining the full documents. To subscribe, send email to **majordomo@reeusda.gov**. In the body of the message type this single line: subscribe atfp.

For more details, contact the Agricultural Telecommunications Program at the U S Department of Agriculture, 14th and Independence Avenue SW, Washington DC 20250, 202-720-6084. At press time, the business contact there is Cathy Bridwell.

While you're visiting the Web site, check out **www.reeusda.gov/fra** to learn about the Fund For Rural America. We learned of this program during our research, and while we didn't have very much information on it during the writing of this book, we were told that it will be of interest to community network builders.

A FEW MORE POTENTIAL OPEN PURSES

There are about a zillion (okay, that's an exaggeration) sources of federal grant money for projects. We can't list them all; in fact, the offices that distribute the grants can barely keep up with publishing them all. We'll list a few more here, and we'll describe the Federal Register's Web site later in the chapter:

- The National Science Foundation, 4201 Wilson Boulevard, Arlington, Virginia 22230. Phone: 703-306-1234. Email for publications and program information: **info@nsf.gov**. URL: **www.nsf.gov**.

- National Endowment for the Humanities, Public Information Office, Room 402, 1100 Pennsylvania Avenue NW, Washington DC 20506. Email: **info@neh.fed.us**. URL: **www.neh.fed.us**.

- Technology Innovation Challenge Grants, Office of Educational Research and Improvement, US Department of Education, Washington DC, 20208-5544. Phone: 202-208-3882. Email: **ITO_STAFF1@ed.gov**. URL: **www.ed.gov/Technology**.

Corporate Grant Providers

The money granted by corporations to charitable organizations in the United States helps to fund thousands of worthwhile causes. Your virtual community could be one of them. Corporations love to be associated with programs that further education, expand cultural awareness, and provide resources to help economically challenged people pull themselves up by their bootstraps. Of course, not every company is interested in every project. If you're wiring homes and schools to provide enhanced educational services, companies like Apple or BellSouth might be interested in hearing from you. On the other hand, if providing shopping services for the elderly is your goal, there are other companies you'd be better off approaching. Not that Apple or BellSouth don't care about the elderly; in fact, we're certain that they do. But corporations focus their philanthropic activities carefully by supporting areas of particular interest, with the goal of aligning their corporate images (and their brand names) with the specific types of charitable services they provide. As it happens, both Apple and BellSouth have keen interests in education.

Feeling Charitable?

It's important to note that, in order for many corporations to consider granting money to your project, you'll need to have tax-exempt status under Section 501(c)(3) of the US Internal Revenue Code.

Here is a short list of URLs for the philanthropic arms of several major corporations. You'll need to sift through the pages to determine whose programs are best suited to your needs.

- Adobe Systems, Inc. (**www.adobe.com/aboutadobe/philanthropy/main.html**)

- Aetna Foundation, Inc. (**www.aetna.com/foundation**)

- Apple Computer (**www2.apple.com/communityaffairs**)

- The BellSouth Foundation (**www.bellsouthcorp.com/bsf**)

- The Ben & Jerry's Foundation (**www.benjerry.com/foundation**)

- Digital Equipment Corporation (**www.digital.com:80/info/community**)

- IBM Corporation (**www.ibm.com/IBM/IBMGives/index.html**)

- Intel Corporation (**www.intel.com/intel/community/corpgive.htm**)

- Microsoft (**www.microsoft.com/giving**)

- Toyota USA Foundation (**www.toyota.com/inside_toyota/toyota_foundation**)

More Opportunities For Funding

What we've listed so far is barely scratching the surface of what's out there. To get the latest information on federal and corporate grants, you'll have to fire up the old search engine on the Internet. But before you do, here are a couple of places where the searching has already been done for you.

Seemingly Redundant, But In Fact Very Useful

It seems odd—a foundation on foundations. But actually, The Foundation Center (**fdncenter.org/2grntmkr/2grntmkr.html**) is an independent, nonprofit clearinghouse of grant information. The Center collects, organizes, analyzes, and disseminates information on foundations, corporate giving, and other related subjects. The Center's resources can be used by grant seekers, grant makers, researchers, policy makers, and the general public. The Center's Grantmaker Information directory contains direct and annotated links to more than 190 grant maker Web sites, as well as to a range of informational materials like program brochures, application procedures, press releases, and more. The annotations, when available, detail the interests of the foundations, as well as any geographic limitations to their grant-making activities. This site also provides a Grantmaker search function. For grant seekers interested in doing funding research online, this tool is invaluable.

LOOKING FOR FEDERAL FUNDS?

The Federal Register (**www.access.gpo.gov/su_docs/aces/aces140.html**) contains announcements of federal grant competitions, funding priorities, and proposed changes in grant regulations. You can search the Federal Register by keyword, like *technology and grants*, or search the tables of contents for a range of dates. Try searching the tables first, by checking the "contents" box on the Web page, and then indicating a particular date or range of dates, noting page numbers for the documents you're interested in. Then search the Federal Register full text or "Notices" for the page numbers. The Register is usually available online on the day of publication.

THE SEARCH IS ON FOR FUNDS AT LARGE

Be sure to use a search engine like Yahoo or AltaVista on a regular basis. We used to dread using search engines, but now we're old pros. We'll share a search tip or two with you. Remember that if you enter words like *telecommunications grants* into a search engine, you'll get every Web site imaginable with either *telecommunications* or *grants* in it. However, many search engines let you put several words in quotes, like *"telecommunications grants"*, which are then searched for as a phrase. This technique will get you fewer hits, and the results you do get will be more accurate.

Also, you might be surprised by the results you can get with some creative wordplay. If you do a search for *"electronic village grants"* you'll get specific hits that may not have been returned under more general searches. Try searching for other keywords too, even if they seem only remotely related to your project. You could find alternate sources of potential funding that you never knew were there.

Avoiding The Technology Pitch

As we mentioned earlier, corporate grants are usually focused in certain areas of interest. Right now, the electronic village is generally not one of them. That doesn't mean that corporate funders won't help you, just that they probably aren't already focused on this kind of program. What do you do? Well, focus on what they *are* focused on. When submitting an application for a grant to fund an electronic village, tailor your description of the benefits of your networking project to the various areas that interest your potential funding partner. This seems obvious, but it can be pretty hard to do. Does your potential grant maker want to assist with education? If so, demonstrate how creating a wired community will improve education. Don't even mention technical stuff, like bandwidth or server hardware, until an officer of the foundation asks for that kind of information. Remember, they don't care what kind of computers you need. They care about what kind of services the community will get.

The Art Of Writing Grant Proposals

If you want a grant, you're gonna have to write a proposal. Most folks find this daunting, even frightening, and we don't blame them. Here's a suggestion: It's important to see your proposal through the eyes of the people who will be deciding whether to fund it. Start by assuming that the reader knows nothing about you or your plan, because they probably won't. To determine if you're getting your message across, ask someone (a friend, a neighbor, or perhaps a relative) who knows little or nothing about your project to read the proposal. If they understand it, you've probably done a good job. If they're unclear about what you're doing, find out what's baffling them and clarify those points.

Most grants are designed primarily for programs that won't be commercially viable, but will serve a community need nonetheless. Even if your project is brilliant and will fill an obvious need, several basic elements must be present in your proposal for it to be worthy of funding. Read your proposal and see if it answers these questions: Will this approach provide a solution to a real problem at a reasonable cost? By what standard will success be judged (in other words, how will you know that the plan is working)? Is the plan making full use of programs that already exist? Will it be a new solution, or will it duplicate an existing program? Does the project serve the public interest? The most important question is this: What community need or purpose will be served, and who needs the proposed program?

As you might guess, we scoured the Web for information, and we found a very helpful page at **www.aspeninst.org**. That's the site of the Aspen Institute, an international think tank in the form of a nonprofit organization. Check them out. It's not just good reading; this Web site contains helpful nuggets of information about grants and grant writing, some of which we've incorporated into the following sidebar.

Talking To Corporate Foundations

We've seen that community networks, or electronic villages, are a growing trend, and that these networks serve to foster economic development. But as we said earlier, the community network arena isn't a well-developed area among private philanthropic foundations quite yet (although there are certainly some exceptions). Bolstering economic development, on the other hand, is very interesting to corporate foundations. So be sure to highlight that concept when pitching to corporate entities.

Foundation officers sometimes join "affiliation groups" organized by the Council on Foundations. These groups focus on such issues as disabilities, the environment, citizen participation, aging, children/ youth/families, income security, film/TV/video, health, women's concerns, immigrants, neighborhoods, and more. Use terms like those when pitching your project.

Finally, foundations have "personalities." Some seek long-term societal impact, while others look for quicker results in the projects they fund. Some prefer dealing with large institutions, others like the grassroots approach. Some may fund the planning stage, while others focus on evaluation. Grant makers in your region probably try to work together to fill each of these niches, meaning that your fund-raising activities will evolve over time.

You Got The Green, Now Get The People

We hope that you've found this information helpful. Of course there's so much more to learn, but once you get started on your money quest you'll discover a wealth of new information along the way. Good luck to you.

Of course, if you're developing a virtual community for profit, this wasn't much help to you. That's why we're including Chapter 13, on the topic of creating a profit center for your community. And, community-network builders might find good ideas in the next chapter. Remember what we said about grant givers being attracted to projects that can become self-sufficient? The information on advertising and revenue generation in the next two chapters may be of great value in attaining the goal of self-sufficiency.

Chapter 12

Growing Your Virtual Community

Chapter 12

- Growth Strategy And Techniques

- Guerrilla Marketing Strategy And Techniques

- Web Advertising

- Using Existing Media

- Networking With Other Communities

GROWING YOUR VIRTUAL COMMUNITY

Chapter 12

It's Like A Real Business

Yes, running a virtual community is a lot like running a business, complete with management concerns, legal issues, technical issues, and the main concerns of this chapter: advertising and promotion. But it really isn't all that hard; in fact, it's kind of fun. Many successful online empires grew from fledgling Internet sites. Get ready to join their ranks.

Five Methods For Growing Your Community

In building community, we see five possible strategic models that can lead to community growth.

METHOD ONE: BE THE FIRST TO MARKET

Yahoo!, created by David Filo and Jerry Yang, leveraged its early market entry by creating one of the most recognized brand names on the Internet.

Yahoo! (yes, that "!" is part of the name) is located at **www.yahoo.com**. The popular search engine began as a college computer project and exploded into a media giant. Filo and Yang, students of electrical engineering at Stanford University, began their Internet guide in April of 1994. Soon they turned their list, dubbed Yahoo!, into a database designed to serve the needs of the growing number of Web surfers, using the software they had written to locate, identify, and edit resources available on the Internet. Yahoo!'s first home was Yang and Filo's student workstations, which they named "Akebono" and "Konishiki." Pretty humble beginnings, don't you think?

In 1995, Marc Andreessen (another genius and the co-founder of Netscape) asked the Yahoo! boys to relocate their search engine and database to the larger servers at Netscape. We all know now that Yahoo! is a big success, but many don't realize how much more than a search engine the company has become. It's now a thriving community with editorials, chat, and threaded discussion boards. As shown in Figure 12.1, Yahoo! offers regionalized information, such as Yahoo! Chicago, which serves to strengthen the bonds that a Net surfer has with his/her meatspace world.

METHOD TWO: CREATE STRATEGIC PARTNERSHIPS

Yahoo! and Netscape. Microsoft and Ziff-Davis. Clnet and Intel. What do these companies have in common? They've joined forces in order to leverage their strengths to bring about something totally new on the Web. Together, Clnet and Intel created the "Screamer," a best-of-the-Web directory that features cutting-edge, high-bandwidth sites. Microsoft and Ziff-Davis produce The Site, a television show and Web site. The opportunities for partnering are endless.

But, why are these examples appropriate for virtual communities? Because there is strength in numbers. So when each party brings its particular attribute to the table, whether it be financial, editorial content, technical expertise, distribution vehicles, or marketing muscle, chances for success grow exponentially. This method is grabbing the attention of the Internet's biggest community builders. For instance, GeoCities is combining forces with ElectricVillage (**www.electricvillage.com**) to link its music content with radio station Web sites that are housed on GeoCities. Richard Rygg, GeoCities' general manager, says in a press release that, "This partnership with ElectricVillage marks the first time that we have been able to

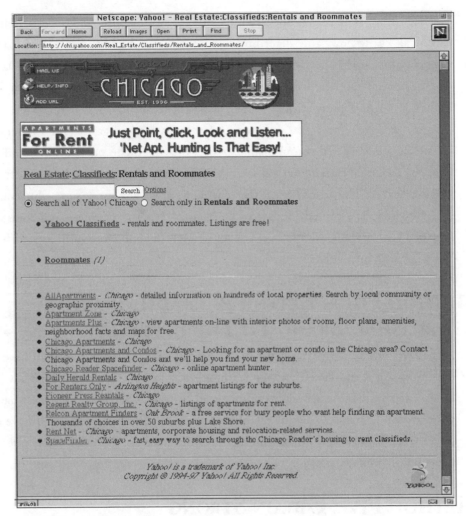

Figure 12.1 Todd is looking for an apartment in Chicago.

share the creativity of our Homesteaders with other sites on the Web. In addition, it provides our Homesteaders with a tremendous opportunity to gain exposure for their wonderful work." Sounds like a win-win situation.

METHOD THREE: USE GUERILLA MARKETING TECHNIQUES

Are you tired of hearing about Howard Rheingold's Electric Minds (**www.minds.com**) in this book? Well, don't blame us; instead, blame the community guru himself. Thanks to Rheingold's aggressive use of guerrilla marketing tactics,

Electric Minds is on the tip of everyone's tongue. He obviously had the experience, technical know-how, and determination to create a highly visible Web-based virtual community, but an aggressive Internet marketing campaign is also a large part of his success. Minds hired the Interactive Public Relations company in San Francisco to post press releases, which were picked up by heavy hitters such as *Advertising Age*, *Wired*, and Ziff Davis's *Information Week* magazine, but even more attention was garnered through smaller sites like the niche publication The Red Herring (political commentary at **www.herring.com/mag/issue36/howard.html**), and e-zines like The Scout Report (Internet news at **wwwscout.sc.wisc.edu/scout**), and Rewired (self-coined journal of a "strained Net" at **www.rewired.com/96/Fall/0911.html**). A lot of buzz on Usenet newsgroups and word of mouth on The WELL didn't hurt either.

METHOD FOUR: EXTEND A TRADITIONAL, ESTABLISHED BRAND TO THE INTERNET

Ziff-Davis did it. *People* magazine did it. So did CNN. What do they all have in common? An established brand name in traditional media. Now, you don't have to be an international megamedia company to do this. What we're saying is that if your group or business has an established presence in meatspace, you'll have an easier time of growing your community in cyberspace, since you probably already have a built-in audience.

METHOD FIVE: OBTAIN STRONG FINANCIAL BACKING

By starting out with strong financial backers, you have a much better chance at "making it." A prime example is iVillage. They've created high profile sub-brands, such as Parent Soup and About Work, on AOL and the Web. But founding partners Candice Carpenter, CEO; Nancy Evans, president; and Robert Levitan, senior vice president had the money—a cool $13 million obtained from venture capitalist Kleiner Perkins Caufield & Byers, along with other partners—and the marketing savvy to do it.

But how are you going to convince a venture capitalist or strategic partner to hand over the big bucks? It's not easy, but Candice, Nancy, and Robert demonstrated that it can be done. First, they emphasized their strengths—Candice had top-notch qualifications in new media at Time Warner and QVC; Nancy had a distinguished management background as the creator and publisher of *Family Life* magazine and as president and publisher at Doubleday; and Robert was recog-nized for his new media entrepreneurial enterprises. Next, they developed a tight business plan, including detailed financial reports and well-thought-out marketing goals. Venture capitalists will examine every detail of this plan, so make sure it's airtight.

We Interrupt This Web Page For A Special Announcement

Web advertising is one of the best ways to publicize your community. Incidentally, it's one of the least intrusive methods to the Web surfer, unlike spam email. Web advertising started when *Wired* magazine launched HotWired (**www.hotwired.com**) on October 27, 1994, complete with 14 charter sponsors. Since then, an entire industry has evolved: There are creative agencies to develop ads, sales representative to sell ads, research companies who measure ad performance, "networks" who aggregate ad buys, software tools to manage ads, industry groups to promote ads—there are even online "auctions" to sell ad banner space. Web advertising produced $157 million in revenue in the first three quarters of 1996, according to the Internet Advertising Bureau (IAB), and revenues will grow significantly in the future (we'll go into this further in the next chapter). Industry analysts forecast that by the end of this year, Web ad revenue will come in at nearly triple the figures seen in 1996.

So you want to get in on the action? Don't fear, you don't need to be a big-budget corporation to advertise on the Web. In fact, many small sites have conducted extremely effective online ad campaigns simply because they attacked the task with creativity and unrelenting perseverance.

ONLINE MEDIA GLOSSARY

Before we get started, let's examine some key concepts you'll need to understand before you start placing online ads. The good folks at Narrowline (**www. narrowline.com**) have a very nice Web site, and some of the following information was gleaned from their online glossary. There's plenty more information there, so be sure to stop by and check it out.

- *Affinity Group*—People with shared interests. People may belong to more than one affinity group. A community of interest is an affinity group with history.

- *Banner Creative*—The term for the finished Web banner, or the artwork that will serve as your banner. We suppose just calling them "finished banners" didn't sound official enough. By the way, "creative" is both singular and plural.

- *Click Through*—A measure determined by the act of a user clicking his or her mouse on an ad banner. Click through is represented both in raw numbers and as a percentage of page *impressions*. For example, if 10,000 users view an ad banner, and 100 users click on it to view the advertiser's information, the click-through percentage is 1 percent. According to Channel Seven (**www. channelseven.com**), a Web site devoted to the Internet advertising community, the industry click-through average is 1.7 percent.

Keep 'Em Honest

Most content sites in which you place advertising will provide you with a "traffic report" of sorts. These reports show aggregate information, such as gross impressions, or the number of times a call to the server was made for the page that an ad banner (namely yours) appears on. Now, how many times have you clicked on a page and then canceled it before the page appeared? See the problem? Gross impression figures must be taken with a grain of salt, because they don't reflect how many times the ad banner was actually seen. The number you want to see is net impressions, but that number is a little harder to come by. So, sites will usually over-deliver with gross impressions instead.

You'll also get numbers reflecting the number of clicks and click-through percentages. These numbers are considerably more valuable because they reflect more accurately the number of Web surfers who actually accessed your information through your ad banner. If at all possible, make sure these reports are reviewed by an auditing service such as I/PRO (short for Internet Pro, a division of Nielson, the TV-ratings people) or ABC (the Audit Bureau of Circulations) to ensure greater accuracy. If the site you're interested in advertising with utilizes one of these services, ask for the report. Content sites hire auditing companies to analyze log reports, so this service won't cost you anything.

• *Cost Per Thousand or CPM*—A standard measure used to compare the cost efficiency of media, such as print, radio, television, and now the Web. The measure is determined by the cost of reaching 1,000 audience participants. As audience segments become more targeted, the cost to reach them increases. CPMs vary widely, depending on the type of site you place your ad on, but, as a rule of thumb, search engines range from $20 to $30 per thousand; general audience content sites range from $30 to $50; and targeted audiences can go as high as $90.

No, We Didn't Screw That Up

"Don't they mean 'cost per million'?" Nope. It's a rather deceiving acronym because of the letter "m." The letter refers to the Roman numeral system where M equals a thousand.

• *Frequency*—The total number of times the same person is exposed to an advertising message. As the number of exposures to a message increases, both the number of people who remember it and the length of time they remember it for increases. Given this fact, frequency is widely considered to be the most important media objective. Compare with *reach*.

• *Hits*—A measure of traffic to an Internet site. The problem with using hits as a measure of site success is that all transactions result in a line in the log file. When a user hits a page with five graphics, six hits are recorded: one for the HTML page, and one for each graphic file sent. This information is more relevant to your IT guru; from a marketing perspective you will be more concerned about *impressions*.

Click 'Em Through To A Targeted Message

Once the user clicks on your ad banner, where should you direct them? "My home page?" you ask. Well, that may seem logical, but dumping Web surfers into your community at the home page may not be the best solution, since most home pages are too generic to deliver a targeted message. From the home page, users must hunt and peck until they find the information they're looking for. Instead, middle pages are the solution for delivering targeted information in a clear and complete manner. Middle pages consist of content tailored to a specific promotion or marketing message. Then you can redirect, or "bridge," the end user to your home page with a clearly marked hyperlink. Middle pages also provide other useful purposes, such as measuring return on investment (ROI) and analyzing Web-site traffic. That can be pretty handy data.

- *Impressions*—Also known as *page views*, the number of times that a banner appears to a viewer.

- *Reach*—The total number or percentage of a defined population group that is exposed to a media schedule during a predetermined time period. Reach measures the extent of the audience exposure of a given media vehicle. Compare with *frequency*.

BEING CREATIVE WITH BANNERS

Until recently, the specifications for banner creative were not standard, making it difficult for advertisers to effectively manage online programs. Online marketing managers were faced with an overabundance of choices regarding width and height, file sizes, and animation looping limitations, and they drove their production teams crazy requesting so many banners for just one campaign! It was clearly an unwieldy system. Enter the Internet Advertising Bureau (IAB), dedicated to maximizing the use and effectiveness of advertising on the Internet. One of the primary directives of the IAB was to define a baseline, voluntary model that would result in standards for banner specifications. The IAB has identified the most commonly accepted specifications for banner ads, as shown in Table 12.1.

Table 12.1 Internet Advertising Bureau ad banner standards.

SIZE (PIXELS)	TYPE
468×60	Full Banner
392×72	Full Banner With Vertical Navigation Bar
234×60	Half Banner
125×125	Square Button
120×90	Button #1
120×60	Button #2
88×31	Micro Button
120×240	Vertical Banner

DOUBLECLICK'S TIPS FOR CREATING EFFECTIVE AD BANNERS

DoubleClick is the largest advertising network on the Web. Globally, they deliver 435 million ad banner creative impressions a month. Later in this chapter we'll look at advertising networks and how they can help you, but first let's look at the banners themselves. We'd like to thank Kevin O'Connor, CEO of DoubleClick, for allowing us to reprint the following ad banner tips.

Lesson 1: Target, Target, Target

In traditional advertising, you want your message to be seen by your target audience (this could be your community's affinity group). You try to select the medium that attracts the audience most similar to the one you are trying to reach. But you don't know for sure exactly who is viewing your ad.

The Web, however, offers the ultimate in accountability. By utilizing the Web's ability to target, you can recognize and reach only your target audience. You can deliver your message to specific industries, include or exclude specific geographic regions or cities, target by user interest, and even control frequency. This eliminates waste and makes your campaign more effective. (See Figure 12.2 for a banner targeted by an ISP.)

Taking advantage of the Web's ability to deliver highly targeted audiences will create one-to-one relationships that will extend and build your brand.

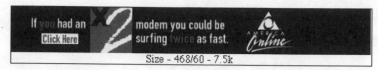

Figure 12.2   U.S. Robotics serves an ad banner directed to America Online users who are surfing the Web.

Figure 12.3   Quicken asks why you're waiting.

Lesson 2: Pose Questions

Don't just make statements or show pretty pictures. Use questions ("Looking for free software?", "Have you seen?"), as shown in Figure 12.3. They initiate an interaction with the banner by acting as a teaser. They entice people to click on your banner. More importantly, they can raise click through by 16 percent over average.

Lesson 3: Bright Colors

Colors affect the eye differently. Using bright colors can help attract a user's eye, contributing to higher response rates. Research has shown that blue, green, and yellow work best while white, red, and black are less effective. Figure 12.4 is in black and white, but the original ad uses neon green to catch your eye.

Lesson 4: Home Is Not Always Sweet

All Web pages are not created equal when it comes to eliciting consumer responsiveness. While the home page often performs very well, a site may have other pages that outperform it. This can vary by advertiser. Certain pages can deliver a more targeted audience than others. By carefully analyzing these pages, you can increase your response by placing your banner on a page that better attracts your target audience.

Figure 12.4   HotWired's eye-catching ad banner.

Lesson 5: Location, Location, Location

According to research, banners that appear when a page first loads are more likely to be clicked on. Negotiate ad placement on the top of the page when buying space. The best possible scenario is having banners placed both on the top and the bottom of a page.

Real Estate Is Everything

When I evaluate a potential Web site for advertising opportunities, I have a list of qualifiers. I feel that the location of the banner is one of the most important items on the list. Most Web surfers are still cruising at a 640×480 resolution, which is a small amount of real estate. You can't expect the end user to view the entire page by scrolling to the bottom of the page. And most don't. Your potential customer will probably be off exploring another page without ever seeing your banner creative, leaving you stuck with the cost of an ad banner that few visitors ever see. So play it safe, and pick sites that place banner advertisements at the top or upper right side of a page, and not the bottom (like the one shown in Figure 12.5).

Lesson 6: Use Animation

Animation can help you catch a user's eye. Strategic use of movement grabs attention more effectively than static banners. Using simple Java or GIF animation can increase response rates by 25 percent.

Lesson 7: Use Cryptic Messages

What did that ad say? What did that mean? Cryptic ad banners help involve a user in the message. Because the "sponsor" of the message is not revealed in the banner, cryptic messages can be very intriguing. (See Figure 12.6.) But there is a downside: Branding is forfeited on the ad. This may not be an issue if branding is not your main objective. Cryptic messages typically increase click through by 18 percent.

Lesson 8: Call To Action

As with traditional direct response, telling consumers what to do helps raise response rates. Simple phrases such as "Click Here," "Visit Now," and "Enter Here"

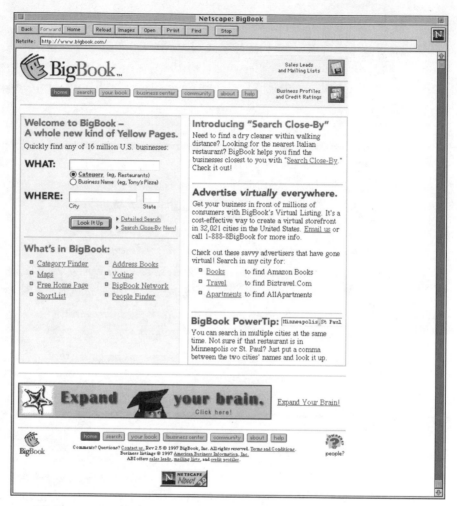

Figure 12.5 BigBook places ad banners at the bottom of its Web pages only.

Figure 12.6 E! Online forfeits brand exposure, but this cryptic ad banner raises curiosity to a level where the end user is compelled to click.

tend to improve response rates by 15 percent. These phrases should be strategically placed in the ad, preferably on the right side, as in Figure 12.7. This is where the eye will be drawn.

Figure 12.7   The Cigar Aficionado captures your attention with a posed question and then requests that you "click here."

 Click Here

According to the IAB's 1997 report, "The Case For Internet Advertising," response rates can increase as much as 44 percent by just providing visual or text cues that a banner leads to more information.

Lesson 9: Avoid Banner Burnout

After what number of targeted impressions does click-through rate significantly drop off? After how many impressions do people start ignoring your banner? Our study concluded that there indeed is a "sweet spot" for user response. After the fourth impression, average response rates dropped to under 1 percent. We call this banner burnout—the point at which a banner stops delivering a good ROI. These findings are incredibly significant. Controlling your frequency extends your reach and maximizes your ad dollar.

Lesson 10: Measure Beyond The Click

Click through is not always the best measurement of campaign effectiveness. It depends on your objectives. If you are simply trying to drive traffic, the click through is great. If you are trying to gather leads, the best measurement is the number of people who clicked through and filled out a lead form. Three percent click through and 80 percent lead fulfillment is better than 10 percent click through and 20 percent fulfillment.

THE NEXT WAVE OF CREATIVE

Many online advertisers are testing Java, ActiveX, Shockwave, RealAudio, and other enhancements in order to differentiate banner creative from static banners or GIF89A animations. Sometimes companies just want to create "buzz." Inventive banners can help do that. Interactive banners that make nifty sounds, or interact with the surfer in ways other than just linking them to another site, help get the netizen thinking about your site, product, or community.

Addictive Ad Banners

Hewlett Packard recently had a banner that didn't hawk a product; it didn't ask viewers to "click here" to register for a giveaway; nor did it offer the reader any slick marketing slogans. Instead, HP simply presented the viewer with a game to play, housed within a standard 468×60 ad banner. It was a nostalgic game that played just like Atari's Pong. HP's creative team developed the game using Java, complete with a computer opponent and an intuitive player interface. Users everywhere reveled in it, sometimes playing for hours. And all the time, the company logo lay subtly in the background, reinforcing the brand name of Hewlett-Packard. Pure advertising genius!

Another exciting development is First Virtual's VirtualTAG technology. First Virtual (**www.firstvirtual.com**) is commonly known for their Web-based secure commerce technology. Now they're incorporating this technology into interactive Web banners. VirtualTAG uses cross-platform multimedia environments such as Java and Shockwave to create amazingly interactive transactional advertisements, all within a standard size banner or "storefront" (as in Figure 12.8). Text fields and forms allow the user to input data. (See Figure 12.9.) A fully interactive selling and transaction tool, VirtualTAG allows users to shop, browse, and buy, arrange for payment through the VirtualPIN, and provide detailed delivery instructions, all without leaving the banner. And all without entering a credit card number. On its

Figure 12.8   At first glance, the Bell Atlantic banner looks fairly ordinary.

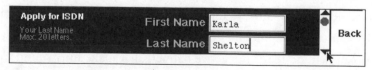

Figure 12.9   Ordering ISDN service through Bell Atlantic's ad banner, using First Virtual's TAG technology.

introduction, the VirtualTAG became the first solution that took full advantage of the Internet's unique attributes by combining advertising, merchandising, and purchasing in one application.

Other new and creative methods of implementing Web advertising are still evolving. Take a look at ESPN's ScorePost (**espnet.sportszone.com**), a Java ticker that scrolls through sports scores. It also rotates ads, like the rotating signage at sporting events. Warner Brothers (**www.warnerbros.com**), AudioNet (**www.audionet.com**), and Gamecruiser (**www.gamecruiser.com**) are selling audio slots for some of their RealAudio programming. Sony (**www.sony.com**) and Berkeley Systems (**www.berksys.com**) are selling "interstitials"—8 to 10 second multimedia "commercials" before, during, and after online multiplayer games.

The Third Generation

Take advantage of the medium—involve your audience with the "Third Generation" of ads that use interactive HTML. Parent Soup's agency, Modem Media, created an innovative ad based on this concept. On first viewing the ad, it appeared straightforward enough. (See Figure 12.10.)

However, upon clicking on the word "Wheaton," a drop-down window appeared with dozens of baby names. Our interest piqued, and we dissected the ad. Lo and behold, the creative team had programmed the drop down window in HTML using the <FORM> tag—the same technique used for creating drop-down "fields" commonly seen in guestbooks and feedback surveys. If you're curious to see how this ad was programmed in HTML, here's the source code:

```
<CENTER> <FORM> <TABLE BORDER="0" BGCOLOR="FFFFFF" WIDTH="470"
HEIGHT="60" CELLPADDING="0" CELLSPACING="0"> <TR>
<TD VALIGN="top" WIDTH="1" ROWSPAN="5">
<A HREF="http://www.lycos.com/cgi-bin/nph-
bounce?KEY[]+ivps7aa11|http://www.parentsoup.com/library/docs/
baby/name_finder.html_QUES_lycos6b">
<IMG SRC="../32497/graphics/htm7aa1h.gif" ALT="Parent Soup"
```

```
WIDTH="1" HEIGHT="61" BORDER="0"></A></TD>
<TD VALIGN="bottom" WIDTH="468" HEIGHT="1" COLSPAN="3">
<A HREF="http://www.lycos.com/cgi-bin/nph-
bounce?KEY[]+ivps7aa11|http://www.parentsoup.com/library/docs/
baby/name_finder.html_QUES_lycos6b">
<IMG SRC="../32497/graphics/htm7aa1i.gif" ALT="Parent Soup"
WIDTH="468" HEIGHT="1" BORDER="0"></A></TD>
<TD VALIGN="top" WIDTH="1" ROWSPAN="5">
<A HREF="http://www.lycos.com/cgi-bin/nph-
bounce?KEY[]+ivps7aa11|http://www.parentsoup.com/library/docs/
baby/name_finder.html_QUES_lycos6b">
<IMG SRC="../32497/graphics/htm7aa1h.gif" ALT="Parent Soup"
WIDTH="1" HEIGHT="61" BORDER="0">
</A></TD> </TR> <TR> <TD VALIGN="top" ALIGN="left" ROWSPAN="2">
<A HREF="http://www.lycos.com/cgi-bin/nph-
bounce?KEY[]+ivps7aa11|http://www.parentsoup.com/library/docs/
baby/name_finder.html_QUES_lycos6b">
<IMG sRC="../32497/graphics/htm7aa1a.gif" ALT="Parent Soup"
WIDTH="82" HEIGHT="45" BORDER="0"></A></TD> <TD WIDTH="257"
VALIGN="TOP">
<A HREF="http://www.lycos.com/cgi-bin/nph-
bounce?KEY[]+ivps7aa11|http://www.parentsoup.com/library/docs/
baby/name_finder.html_QUES_lycos6b">
<IMG SRC="../32497/graphics/htm7aa1b.gif" ALT="Over 40,000
names for babies" WIDTH="257" HEIGHT="18" BORDER="0"></A></TD>
<TD VALIGN="top" ALIGN="left" ROWSPAN="2">
<A HREF="http://www.parentsoup.com/library/docs/
baby/name_finder.html_QUES_lycos6b">
<IMG SRC="../32497/graphics/htm7aa1c.gif" ALT="Parent Soup"
WIDTH="109" HEIGHT="41" BORDER="0"></A> </TR>
<TR> <TD VALIGN="top"><SELECT> <OPTION>Wade <OPTION>Wakefield
<OPTION>Waldo <OPTION>Walker <OPTION>Wallace <OPTION>Walter
<OPTION>Walton <OPTION>Wanda <OPTION>Ward <OPTION>Warner
<OPTION>Warren <OPTION>Washington <OPTION>Watson <OPTION>Waverly
<OPTION>Wayland <OPTION>Wayne <OPTION>Webster <OPTION>Wells
<OPTION>Wendell <OPTION>Wendy <OPTION>West <OPTION>Wetherby
<OPTION>Wheaton <OPTION>Whit <OPTION>Whoopi <OPTION>Wilhelmina
<OPTION>William <OPTION>Wilson <OPTION>Winifred <OPTION>Winona
<OPTION>Winslow <OPTION>Winston <OPTION>Winter <OPTION>Witt
<OPTION>Wolfgang <OPTION>Woodrow <OPTION>Wren <OPTION>Wright
<OPTION>Wyatt <OPTION>Wylie <OPTION>Wyndam <OPTION>Wynn <OPTION>Wystan
</SELECT> <A href="http://www.lycos.com/cgi-bin/nph-
bounce?KEY[]+ivps7aa11|http://www.parentsoup.com/library/docs/
baby/name_finder.html_QUES_lycos6b">
<IMG SRC="../32497/graphics/htm7aa1d.gif" ALT="Parent Soup"
WIDTH="70" HEIGHT="21" BORDER="0"></A></TD></TR>
<TR><TD ALIGN="right" VALIGN="BOTTOM" COLSPAN="3">
<A HREF="http://www.parentsoup.com/library/docs/baby/
```

```
name_finder.html_QUES_lycos6b"><IMG SRC="../32497/graphics/
htm7aa1e.gif"
ALT="…And those are just the W's" WIDTH="206" HEIGHT="13"
BORDER="0"></A></TD> </TR> <TR>
<TD VALIGN="bottom" WIDTH="468" HEIGHT="1" COLSPAN="3">
<A HREF="http://www.lycos.com/cgi-bin/nph-
bounce?KEY[]+ivps7aa1l|http://www.parentsoup.com/library/docs/baby/
name_finder.html_QUES_lycos6b"><IMG SRC="../32497/graphics/
htm7aa1i.gif"
ALT="Parent Soup" WIDTH="468" HEIGHT="1" BORDER="0">
</A></TD></TR> </TABLE> </FORM></center>
```

Where Are You?

Let's say we really liked that ad banner of yours, but we want to visit the site later so we can finish what we're doing now. Be sure to include your site's URL in the design for surfers like us who want to continue to explore the site we're currently visiting—and we'll link over to your site later.

Some of the best ads we've seen include one little word that can greatly enhance click through rates: FREE. Amazing, but true. We suppose we all want something for nothing. Take a look at TurboTax's banner in Figure 12.11. This ad ran during tax time…we haven't heard specifically how high the click rate was, but we guesstimate double digits.

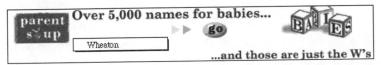

Figure 12.10 This ad for Parent Soup only *appears* to be a standard GIF banner.

Figure 12.11 Free stuff really excites Web surfers.

SO MANY SITES, SO LITTLE TIME

In the old days (about six months ago), advertisers pretty much relied on "traditional" methods of advertising on the Internet. They selected sites (usually just a handful of the thousands of sites available to advertise on) based on the demographics or lifestyles of their audience, and generally ran ads ROS (run of site). There were lots of sites to pick from, ranging from general audience (Time-Warner's Pathfinder—**www.pathfinder.com**) to extremely targeted audiences (Windows95 Magazine—**www.windows95.com**). This "traditional" system was an online advertiser's nightmare, especially from management's point of view. Then, someone built a better mousetrap.

ADVERTISING NETWORKS

As promised, it's time to get back to advertising networks. In 1996, the DoubleClick Network revolutionized how media buyers would purchase online advertising. With ad networks, large groups of Web sites band together to sell advertising as a unit, satisfying advertisers' demands for high-traffic locations and mass audiences. Time-saving advantages to you include:

- Sending out banner creative to one site, rather than many.

- Dealing with one account executive, rather than many.

- Paying one monthly invoice, rather than many. Your accountant will love you.

However, the biggest advantage of employing an advertising network is the ability to target your marketing message. Why is targeting so important? Because you determine *who* will see your advertisement, *when* you want them to, and *where*. Imagine the efficiency (little or no waste) and the return on investment (higher click-through rates). The following sections highlight some of the types of target criteria.

Target By Affinity

Your virtual community is likely to offer services or benefits that would be attractive to a specific audience. Obviously, a community centered on multiplayer gaming will attract a much different crowd than one centered around small-business concerns, parenting, or Pez collecting. Networks can aggregate sites based on interest, such as business and finance, entertainment, travel and leisure, technology, computer and Internet topics, news and information, humanities and culture, or directories and search engines.

Target By Geographic Location

Targeting by geography can be extremely beneficial as well. If you want to create a community for farmers, or city dwellers, or fans of the San Francisco 49ers, then you use advertising networks to target potential visitors by country, state, area code, or zip code.

Another Way To Target

*Many ad networks use computer domain names to figure out the location of a surfer, but this may not be accurate. A computer's IP address may be registered in Dayton, Ohio, but the actual user may be located in Chicago. To help solve this problem, MapQuest (**www.mapquest.com**), an Internet cartographic service, offers "GeoCentric" ad targeting. For example, the Radisson Hospitality hotel group has "geo-coded" all 192 hotels in Radisson's U.S. chain to within a five-mile radius. Now, when a visitor to MapQuest clicks on a city, there's a good chance that a Radisson ad banner will appear. Further, if the surfer selects the lodging link in that city, a Radisson ad will definitely display. To see other examples of unique ad targeting solutions, check out* Advertising Age*'s online site at* **www.adage.com***.*

Target By Domain Type

Targeting by domain type is useful in reaching certain audiences, such as students or government employees. Targeting by domain type recognizes the suffix attached to a user's Internet address. For instance, a user accessing a Web site from MIT (with a suffix of .edu) would be recognized as an educational institution. Suffixes include:

- .com (commercial businesses)

- .gov (government agencies)

- .edu (educational institutions)

- .org (organizations)

- .net (network providers)

- .mil (military)

Some networks also allow you to target by organization type or name.

Target By Keyword

Networks that represent search engines allow you to gather impressions based on a keyword that an end user types into the search string. When the list of "hits" is returned to the end user by the search engine, so is your banner. When we typed "automobile purchase" into the search engine at Infoseek (**www.infoseek.com**), we not only saw a list of sites related to those keywords, we also saw an ad banner for Lexus. We thought that the Lexus looked like a nice car, so we clicked on the ad banner, but it didn't take us to the home page. Instead, we were transported to a middle page (**www.lexus.com/Lscoach**) where we were treated to targeted information designed especially for those who would click on the banner.

Target By Days And Hours

By controlling the specific time of day your banners are displayed, you can promote special events being hosted by your community. You can even select the time of day relative to the user, regardless of where they live in the world. For example, if you're designing a community for insomniacs, you might try having ad creative that only displays between 3:00 A.M. and 5:00 A.M.

Target By Organization Name

You can also target by the specific name of a company. For example, if your community is devoted to high tech communications, you could target employees of powerhouse corporations such as Sun, Silicon Graphics, Microsoft, and Intel. In this very targeted buy, only users in specific companies (or with specific domain addresses) would see your banner ad.

Target By Service Provider

Some networks recognize which ISP an individual is using to connect to the Web, thus allowing advertisers to target members of AOL, Prodigy, Web America Networks, Netcom, and others. If your community evangelizes the greatness of AOL, this is a way to reach others who use this service.

Target By User's Operating System Or Browser Type

Many networks can identify a user's operating system (OS), such as Windows 95, Macintosh System 7, or Unix. Most networks also can identify whether the end user is surfing with Netscape, Microsoft Internet Explorer, or another browser. This may be particularly useful to communities for computer user groups or software developers.

More Information On Advertising Networks

If you're interested in advertising on a network, take a look at some of these sites:

- DoubleClick (**www.doubleclick.net**)

- WebConnect (**www.webconnect.riddler.net**)

- Commonwealth (**www.commonwealth.com**)

- Petry Interactive Network (**www.petrynet.com**)

- CliqNow (**www.cliqnow.com**)

- RealMedia (**www.realmedia.com**)

- ADSmart (**www.adsmart.net**)

ONLINE AUCTIONS

A relatively new variation of the advertising network, online auction houses allow you to purchase inventory where transactions occur through open-bid, outcry auctions. One of the first and most popular is Adbot (**www.adbot.com**), a privately owned, independent company which is a "spin-off" of the securities trading firm, Chicago Partnership Board, Inc. The service is arranged similarly to the networks mentioned earlier by sporting a large number of Web sites grouped by subject categories.

A TIME-HONORED SYSTEM: BARTERING

Bartering is an age-old economic tradition that has found its way to cyberspace. Trading space, or bartering, with other communities or content sites is one of the most inexpensive methods of advertising. The IAB defines bartering as "the exchange of goods and services without the use of cash, i.e., the purchase of media time or space by a media company in exchange for similar time or space in return."

If your community is geared towards golf, you can approach other sites with a golfing orientation about cross-promoting each other with banner ads. However, because this approach can be time-consuming and resource-intensive, you may want to look at banner exchange programs that exist to help Web sites promote each other—with no cash investment! The concept is simple: by joining you agree to display advertising banners for other members, and they agree to display banners for you, as shown in Figure 12.12. You can decide what type of sites to

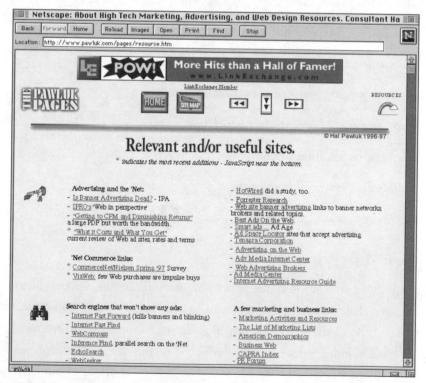

Figure 12.12 An example of deploying a bartered ad using Internet Link Exchange's FREE service.

advertise on and advertise for so you don't need to worry about inappropriate material showing up on your pages. The amount of free advertising you receive from these services is directly proportional to the amount you give to others. The systems automatically display your banner on their network of sites. Most exchange programs even give you access to statistics, as demonstrated by Internet Link Exchange (ILE). Each time the system displays a banner on your site, you receive some sort of "credit." For every full credit your account earns, the exchange system will display your banner on other members' sites. For example, with ILE, if your site displays 1,000 banners, your account earns 500 credits, and the system displays your banner 500 times on other network sites. Your credits will be spent automatically by the system, as long as you have submitted a banner that is approved for display on other members' sites.

Banner Exchange Programs

If you're interested in trying ad bartering, take a look at this list to find the network that's best for your community.

These programs include general audience Web sites:

- Internet Link Exchange (**www.linkexchange.com**)

- Narrowcast Media (**www.narrowcastmedia.com**)

- TradeBanners (**resource-marketing.com/banner.html**)

- Smartclicks (**www.smartclicks.com**)

- Net-On Banner Exchange (**www.net-on.se:81/banner/index.html**)

- Paramount Banner Network (**www.jeopardypro.com/paramount/**)

- Link Media (**www.linkmedia.com/network/**)—free ads for nonprofit organizations

These programs are highly targeted by interest:

- Gamers Banner Exchange (**www.cheatworld.pair.com/exchange/**)

- Mac Web Network (**macinsearch.com/banners/**)

- AfroCentric Banner Exchange (**ethnocentric.com/abx/**)

- Puerto Rico Banner Exchange (**plaza-internet.com/banmat/exchange.html**)

SO YOU WANT TO KNOW MORE

The Internet is packed with resources for those seeking even more advertising and marketing information. Here's a short list of good sites to check out:

- The Best Ads On The Web—Microscope Weekly (**www.pscentral.com**)

- Four Corners Effective Banners (**www.whitepalm.com/fourcorners/effective banners.shtml**)

- Banner Ad Networks & Brokers (**www.ca-probate.com/comm_net.html**)

- Web Marketing Info Center (**www.wilsonweb.com/webmarket/**)

- Cyberatlas (**www.cyberatlas.com**)

- IAB Proposal For Voluntary Model Banner Sizes (**www.edelman.com/IAB/banner.html**)

- Channel Seven (**www.channelseven.com**)

- Interactive Publishing Alert's Online Ad Index (**www.netcreations.com/ipa/adindex/**)

- WebTrack's AdSpace Locator (**www.webtrack.com**)

Guerrilla Marketing

The best thing about guerrilla marketing is that it doesn't cost much at all. Generally speaking, this topic could fill a book, and it did with Vince Gelormine's *Guerrilla Web Strategies: How To Promote And Market Your Web Site* (The Coriolis Group, ISBN 1-883577-80-2). For detailed information, check out Vince's book. Meanwhile, we've gathered a few items that you'll find particularly useful for down and dirty promotion on the Web.

BE THE KING OF THE SEARCH ENGINE

One of the first things you'll do after creating and launching your community is list it in the multitude of search indexes and engines on the Internet. However, you'll want to take a proactive approach in getting the most prominent position possible. Pay close attention here, because truth be told, most sites on the Web fail miserably at getting noticed by search engines. If you follow the advice here, you'll see your URL start coming up closer and closer to the top of the searches that surfers make, and your site will see more and more hits. Many search engines utilize indexing software agents called robots or spiders that constantly "crawl" the Web in search of new or updated pages. Understanding a few basic HTML tags will increase your chances of having your community Web pages noticed.

- Make sure the **<TITLE>** of your document is as descriptive as possible. Search engines like WebCrawler rely heavily on this information. For example:

```
<TITLE>The Pez Dispenser Virtual Community</TITLE>
```

- Use **<META>** tags. These tags, which are placed within the **<HEAD>** tag, allow you to provide detailed information about your community to visiting search engine "robots." The goal? To have your site indexed in a more appropriate manner. Please note that not all search engines use the **<META>** tags. We recommend using two attributes of the **<META>** tag to enhance your positioning within search engines: **description** and **keyword**. **Description** controls what appears in the summary of your Web page. The content of the description should clearly convey what one can expect to find when linking to your site:

```
<META NAME="description" CONTENT="the home page for a virtual
community for Pez dispenser collectors">
```

Keyword allows you to insert "extra" words that describe the content of a particular page. Don't limit your keywords to specifics—if your community is based on tasty snack cakes like Twinkies, you may want to include a keyword like "Hostess," which is the manufacturer of the snack. However, you should keep it honest—you wouldn't include the keyword "music" to attract a snack crowd:

```
<META NAME="keyword" CONTENT="spongy, delicious, yellow, snack cake,
yummy for your tummy, Hostess, flour, sugar, baking powder, salt,
vegetable oil, water, egg yolks, egg whites, cream of tartar, milk,
polysorbate 80, yellow dye #9">
```

- In addition to placing keywords within the <META> tag, sprinkle your keywords liberally within the context of the first few paragraphs of your Web page.

- Use **ALT** tags with photographs, illustrations, and other graphics, especially if you have an image map at the top of your home page. Remember, search engines catalog words, not pictures, but some search engines will index the text within an **ALT** tag. Here's an example:

```
<IMG SRC="images/firstpez.gif" ALT="Photo of the first Pez
dispenser" >
```

- Minimize nondescriptive sentences at the beginning of each page. Some search engines, such as Excite, create their own summary after "scanning" a page. Infoseek, if it doesn't encounter a <META> description, will simply insert the first 200 words of text in its summary. So it's important to carefully craft the introductory text to reflect content.

- Some indexes, such as Yahoo, display information in alphabetical order, so you may want to include a number as the first character in your listing so that your site is cataloged at the top of the list.

META-INDEXES AND RECIPROCAL NETWORKS

According to the WWWlist survey, 92 percent of Web surfers use hyperlinks to connect to sites of interest, rather than typing in a URL. Therefore, publicizing your site through hyperlinks can be extremely effective. Similar in concept to search engines, meta-indexes simply collect hyperlinks into specific categories like chiropractic (ChiroWeb—**www.chiroweb.com**), fraternities and sororities (Greek-Source—**www.greeksource.com**), or metal rock music (Metal Band List—**www. netlab.co.uk/rwoolley/band.html**). Now, if your community was devoted to any one of these subjects, you would want to be in one of these indexes. Too bad someone hasn't created a meta-index of meta-indexes, since you'll probably have to resort to using a search engine to find one.

Reciprocal networks were formed to cooperatively establish links among sites. Not necessarily interest- or audience-based, but nevertheless useful, reciprocal sites can generate a fair number of links to your community. Visit the sites in the next section to learn how to set up these links:

- IlINK Random FREE Link Sites (**www.goodnet.com/~ej77486/linkmeu.htm**)

- PageHost A-Z (**www.pagehost.com**)

- Digiratti (**www.digiratti.com/suckup1.htm**)

- Seeress of the Web (**www.cyberzine.com/seeress/daily.html**)

A mailing list (at **www.turbopromote.com/mail/mailing.html**) is also available to help you establish reciprocal links with hundreds of Webmasters, ISPs, directories, and Web marketers.

Todd And Karla Have Another Way To Link

The Palace User Group mailing list is an excellent resource to network with other Palace-based communities. Recently, a community owner, looking for sites to link reciprocally, posted this email on the list:

"I'm sending this mail to you because we would like to have as much links as possible to other Palaces. So if (and only if) you have a banner available that I could place in a room, please send it to my address with the palace URL and I'll make it a link in our Palace JumpStation."

GETTING THE RECOGNITION YOU DESERVE

There are awards for "Cool Site Of The Day," "Top 5%," "The Net Guide Magazine Award," or even the "Bottom 5%" (which isn't all that bad if it gets you noticed). Getting listed in a What's Cool directory can give your community a significant boost in traffic. Netscape's ubiquitous What's New and What's Cool buttons have probably "made" more sites than any other directory. So, how's your community going to get its 15 minutes of fame? According to our friend Vince at Coriolis, "Make sure your site is cool and then submit, submit, submit." So, where are you going to do this? Take a look at the summary of Hot and Cool sites we've put together for you:

- Netscape's What's New (**www.netscape.com/home/whats-new.html**)

- Yahoo! What's New (**www.yahoo.com/new/**)

- Project Cool (**www.projectcool.com/loindex.html**)

- MecklerWeb's Web Pick of the Day (**www.mecklerweb.com:80/netday/ sotd.html**)

- Spider's Pick of the Day (**gagme.wwa.com/~boba/pick.html**)

- Cool Site of the Day (**cool.infi.net**)

- Computer Life Online's Hot Site of the Day (**www.zdnet.com/~complife/ filers/site.html**)

- Ground Zero (**www.ground.com/zero.html**)

- And, the granddaddy of them all, Yahoo's index of all the Hot and Cool indexes (**www.yahoo.com/Computers_and_Internet/Internet/World_Wide_Web/ Best_of_the_Web/**)

ALL THE NEWS THAT'S FIT TO GROUP

There are acceptable (and unacceptable) ways to advertise your community in Usenet newsgroups. On the acceptable side, if you have a message that is specifically related to a particular Usenet newsgroup, and you want to let people know about it, it's *usually* all right to post *one* notice about it. You can post more, but try to space them out over time. For example, post your notice every other Thursday. Now, the Usenet crowd is generally a persnickety bunch, so try to keep your post relatively hype-free. What often works well is a brief message that includes an email address and URL for people to get more information.

Be absolutely certain that you're posting to an appropriate newsgroup. If you cross-post or post off-topic messages, you will probably be flamed, and your message will be ignored. One way to be certain is to look at a newsgroup's charter. This is the formal declaration of what is and isn't the topical concern of a particular group. It was most likely written when the group was launched, if the group was created in the so-called Big 7 hierarchies of comp.*, soc.*, rec.*, talk.*, misc.*, news.*, sci.*, and humanities.*. Some other groups have charters as well, but not all—and even if they do, they're often one or two lines in length. You can usually find the charter in the group's posts. Newsgroups tend to post Frequently Asked Questions (or FAQ, pronounced "fak") files, and the charter is located therein. In some cases, the charter has been all but forgotten. Charters can occasionally be difficult to locate, so you may have to use your own judgment, and/or ask someone who's been reading the group for a while, whether a particular message would be appropriate.

On the inappropriate side, what shouldn't you do? Well, one of our pet peeves is spamming. Spamming is defined as posting identical or nearly-identical messages (not just ads, although ads are usually what spammers post) to a lot of newsgroups, one right after the other. *Nothing* is as hated on Usenet as spamming. It's extremely rude, and if you do it, you will very likely come to regret it. Another often-practiced (and often-punished) scheme is to send email to large numbers of strangers whose addresses you found in various Usenet newsgroups. In the last year, dozens of people have lost their Internet access after sending thousands of strangers ads for timeshare condos in Cancun or dubious credit schemes; even so, the junk email continues to flood in.

Playing Hardball With The Spammers

Spammers are cowards. They go to great lengths to hide their own email's return path, making them difficult to track; at the same time, they use programs to scan newsgroups, collect the email addresses in all the return paths, collate them, and then bulk mail spam to all those addresses. Most newsreaders (like Forté Agent) allow you to specify a return mail path, so that if you post, say, a long diatribe about why you love lunchboxes, another person can click on your post and reply to you directly through email. This is clearly a useful feature, but it plays right into the spammers' hands. How to beat them? Try a low-tech solution to a high-tech problem.

When you set up your newsreader, you'll be able to specify the return path. Todd's return path is "NoJunk@MyServer.com". (Feel free to use it yourself.) When one of these email-collecting applications comes scouring through his newsgroup, it adds that email address to its list and tries to send him spam, but since that isn't a real address, poof, it goes nowhere! But he still wants legitimate people to be able to email him if they have something to say or share with him about the group's topic. That's where the .sig file comes in. Like most email programs, newsreaders can automatically attach a .sig, or signature file, to his posts. You write the .sig once, and it goes on everything you post. Todd's .sig reads:

ATTENTION: Return path invalid to spoil spam. Email me at Todd@real-ISP.com. (See? Problem solved.) Some folks go a step further and spell out the email address phonetically, and that isn't a bad idea at all. "Todd at real-ISP dot com."

If you want to learn more about Usenet, refer to the official Usenet Advertising FAQ on the CD-ROM.

MAILING LISTS AND EMAIL

We've discussed mailing lists in Chapters 3 and 4 as a tool for you to use in your own community. It is also possible to market your community on mailing lists in other communities.

Mailing Lists

We're listing the URLs for a few nifty sites where you can register your list in an index. People searching for mailing lists of interest to them can then find your list and subscribe to it at these places:

- Liszt: Directory of Email Discussion Groups (**www.liszt.com**)

- Publicly Accessible Mailing Lists (**www.NeoSoft.com/internet/paml/index.html**)

- List of Lists (**catalog.com/vivian/interest-group-search.html**)

- Tile.net Lists (**tile.net/listserv/**)

Also, you can join "new-list," a moderated mailing list all about new mailing lists. To subscribe, send the following message to **listserv@vm1.nodak.edu:** subscribe new-list firstname lastname (where firstname is your first name and lastname is your last name). Don't forget to turn off your automatic email signature when subscribing to mailing lists.

While you're at it, submit a description of your list to "Net-happenings" (**www.mid.net/NET**), one of the easiest ways to spread the word about any new Internet service. Gleason Sackman, the moderator of Net-happenings, operates like this: He reads your description of the service, community, event, or whatever you're offering, and then decides whether or not to post it to his list. His criteria are simple. If you're promoting a new community, Web site, IRC channel, or FAQ, he'll post your message to his list. If you're just trying to sell a widget, he won't. For example, you can promote a new service or an addition to an existing business, but you can't sell anything directly through his list. For details and protocols, access the aforementioned Web site.

Publicize your list's companion Web page. List the page with popular search services such as Yahoo, Excite, and AltaVista. Most search engines contain links on how to register with their particular site.

Don't forget the most basic of all methods, that of issuing a personal invitation to friends, family, and colleagues to access your site and join in on your virtual community.

Email

Because distribution on the Internet is so inexpensive, it's tempting to think of using it like direct mail—to broadcast general advertisements to thousands of people. The problem is that many people must pay for reading their email. Would you hire a promotions director who wants to make collect calls to new prospects? That's exactly the impact you have on customers who receive unwanted email when they have to pay for it. Granted, most folks pay for Internet service by a flat rate, so whether they receive 3 or 3,000 email messages, the cost is the same. But legally speaking, they are paying for access and email is analogous to a collect call.

Email is still a wonderful way to distribute information about your virtual community—provided you're sending to a qualified list of netizens who you are certain want to receive your information. Spamming or posting ads to noncommercial Web sites or newsgroups may generate some traffic to your site; but it also spawns multitudinous flames and alienates many more potential community members than it garners.

Your Web site is an excellent way to get qualified names of prospects interested in receiving information. By including mailing list information, or better yet, including a Java form, folks can subscribe, or ask for information or updates, etc. You can then add them to your mailing list. Just make sure that any mailing list includes instructions on how to "unsubscribe" so that they can remove themselves from the list when they want to. That way you preserve customer satisfaction and still get the advantages of very inexpensive distribution.

Assuming that you are sending email to qualified prospects, you will probably want to look into an auto-responder. Similar to many fax-back services, an auto-responder is a program that will automatically generate a response when an email comes in. This is very useful both for handling information requests and for generating order acknowledgments. When we submit email to a site, the autoresponse gives us the comfort of knowing that the site is handling our request. You can certainly add more information about your community to the autoresponse too, such as a FAQ or notices about upcoming events.

HTML Mail

Netscape 3.0 introduced the capability of sending Web pages, with pictures, color, etc., as email. They call this feature HTML Mail. If you're a Netscape user, you'll want to visit their home page to look into the great ways to use this tool. Just click on the Directory Tab and hit Homepage (or type in **www.netscape.com**). HTML mail is still new, and so far only reaches a limited audience. For example, if you send HTML Mail to Karla, she'll see all the pretty colors and fonts, because she uses Netscape Mail. Todd, however, uses Eudora Pro 3.0, and will not see the pages as email. Rather, the HTML source code is saved to his hard drive and he has to open it in Netscape. In the future, more mail packages, such as Microsoft Outlook, will support HTML Mail.

Karla Says Sign It

It's not uncommon to see mini-billboard signatures at the bottom of email messages these days. These four to eight lines of cyber-schmooze may include URLs, business addresses, and telephone numbers. But …like I said, longer ones aren't uncommon. So, if you want yours to stand out, try to incorporate a bit of your site's personality into your signature. Include the name of the latest cool-site award you've received. Add an occasional testimonial from a grateful site visitor. Highlight a new feature that can be found within your pages. The point is that your email signature is as much a part of your Web site as the actual pages that reside there.

WITH THIS RING, I THEE LINK

Webrings are collections of home pages from around the world. By joining a Webring, you are joining a new kind of virtual community. The Webring provides the Internet with unique Web site organization. It groups together sites by affinity (or any pages at all, if one so desires) by linking them together in a circle, or ring. It's really so simple that it's brilliant.

How Does It Work?

The idea is that once you're at one site in the Webring, you can click on a "Next" or "Previous" link to go to adjacent sites in the ring (as shown in Figure 12.13) and— if you do it long enough—end up back where you started.

It's possible to do this by having each page's owner link their site to the next. However, when a new site joins the ring, someone has to edit their page to point to the new page. Eventually, the ring gets really big and it becomes cumbersome to manage. It gets even more complex when pages disappear and servers go down. (In fact, it's a big mess!) But Webring provides a solution to all that. When you join a Webring, the HTML code on your home page doesn't have to change. Instead of pointing to other sites in the ring, the links point to a special CGI script at **webring.org** that will send people to the next (or previous) site in the ring. Because the central ring database is located in one place, sites can be added and removed

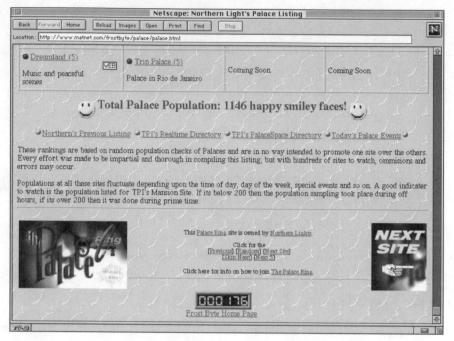

Figure 12.13 The Palace community relies heavy on Webrings to cross-promote sites.

quickly and easily. And because the Webring CGI allows you to continue past sites that are unreachable (for instance, if a server is down), surfers will be able to circumnavigate the ring without any glitches.

There are many types of Webrings covering many topics and genres. The system supports a virtually unlimited number of distinct rings, creating thousands of new virtual communities. And guess what…Webring is absolutely FREE! Webring can be contacted at **www.webring.org**.

AND DON'T FORGET MEATSPACE

If you tell someone that you have a Web site, what's the first question they ask? "What's your URL?" Don't miss a single offline opportunity to promote your site. Include your URL on business cards, stationery, brochures, catalogs, presentation slides and handouts, and in press releases, articles, and interviews. Virtual communities like Tripod (**www.tripod.com**), HotWired (**www.hotwired.com**), and GeoCities (**www.geocities.com**), as well as others, all offer branded items like hats and T-shirts for sale, and they sometimes give these away as prizes to Internet surfers. Every article of outerwear they offer is imprinted with a URL. Even if your community is small, it might be cool to add the likes of T-shirts to your promotional materials.

Be A Publicity Hound

Publicity is not the same thing as advertising. When you advertise, you are buying space to broadcast your message. Publicity, on the other hand, is the art of getting something for nothing. A publicist will write press releases, create media events, organize parties, set up demonstrations at trade shows, and stuff like that. Anything free, media related, and nonpersonal, without cost to your company or organization, is publicity. Let's look first at one of a publicist's most important jobs, writing a press release.

Getting Cozy With The Press

From Vince Gelormine's book *Guerrilla Web Strategies: How To Promote And Market Your Web Site*, we present 10 tips for writing a great press release and getting it noticed:

- *What's the news?* Think about what, if anything, is most "newsworthy" about your site. What value does this information you're offering have, and who is your target audience? Your release must explicitly explain the benefits of visiting "yoursite.com" to just those people whom you're trying to attract.

- *Write a strong lead.* Every press release has a "lead," or first paragraph. You must try to capture the essence of your site in that lead paragraph. How an editor reacts to that one paragraph largely determines whether he or she will read on and become interested enough in your news to consider using it.

- *Don't exaggerate!* Avoid overhyping your Web site—it usually backfires. Don't make claims that you cannot substantiate. If your Web site offers some technical information that auto mechanics might find useful, don't claim that by simply visiting your site, they can throw away all of their parts manuals. For content to be king, it must be real.

- *Describe a viewpoint.* In writing your release, make sure the reader can under-stand for whom you've developed your site—exactly who is the target audience. That way, the editor can decide quickly if his or her publication reaches that audience, and, therefore, if covering your site would be appropriate.

- *Give site examples.* If possible, include some listings and descriptions of the kind of information available at your site. This can be included as part of the press release if it's short, or added as a second document for background.

- *Make a list.* Make a list of those members of the press whom you wish to contact. Don't forget to include local and regional media, business publications, and those trade journals serving your industry. Keep records of your contacts with them in a database.

- *Distribute your news.* Once you're satisfied with your release, proactively send it to the editors on your list. Use both snail mail and email for those editors whose email addresses you know. Do not send unsolicited faxes. Keep your cover message on the emailed releases very brief—no more than four or five lines.

- *Get on the phone.* After enough time has elapsed that you're sure the editors have received your release, give them a call. Don't ask, "Did you get my release?" or "Are you going to publish it?" Instead, explain the gist of the release over the phone, assuming they don't remember it, and try to sell your ideas verbally. If you're successful, then they'll find it in their pile of mail or ask for another one.

- *Make it easy to reach you.* Don't forget to list contact information somewhere in the release. If an editor shows interest, chances are at least 50/50 that he or she will want to contact you. Make it easy for them: list your phone, fax, email addresses, voice mail, even home phone number if appropriate. And of course, list your URL prominently in the release.

- *Follow up.* If editors express mild interest, but put you off, or if they don't return your phone call, then be sure and try again. (Remember, they have real dead-lines, and sometimes can't talk no matter how good your story is.) Be persistent without being a pest. If an editor fails to return three calls or messages, you can assume they're not interested and you should move on.

E-Zines And Other Cyberpublications

Now your challenge is to get Web sites to post your press release or feature your community in an editorial article or RealAudio broadcast. Try some of these sites:

- BoardWatch Magazine (**www.boardwatch.com**)

- Internet Underground Magazine (**www8.zdnet.com/iu/**)

- Magazine of Computer Mediated Communication (**www.december.com/cmc/mag/**)

- Internet World Magazine (**www.internetworld.com**)

- The Net Magazine (**www.thenet-usa.com**)

- Web Week (**www.webweek.com**)

- Web Review Magazine (**www.webreview.com**)

- MSNBC's The Site (**www.thesite.com**)

- C|net and its properties (News, The Web) or C|net Radio (**www.cnet.com**)

- AudioNet (**www.audionet.com**)

- Web Broadcasting System (**www.wbs.com**)

Spotlight On Special Promotions And Events

Special promotions and online events can be instrumental in creating a "buzz" for your community. We have assembled a number of different ideas for you to try. Some ideas will run up a bit of a bill, but others are cheap or free. Whatever your budget is, there's sure to be something you can do that will be effective and reward you in the long run.

SOMETHING FOR NOTHING

People love free stuff! Giveaways to promote your site can represent an investment, such as spending some money on T-shirts and the postage to mail them out. You might also consider content-type freebies, like shareware programs, HTML documents with topical information, or things like that, which can be very cost effective—inexpensive to you, but useful and appreciated by Web surfers.

Something Smells Fishy To Todd

I've always enjoyed keeping tropical fish in spacious aquariums, and it's a hobby that's relaxing and popular. If I were setting up a community for fishheads like myself, I might also want to create an HTML document about fishkeeping. I would include tips on maintenance, water quality, compatibility of various fishes, filters, and more. I would include JPEG format graphics and illustrations, and I would package it in a nice, compact file for easy download. Since this document would ultimately be like a small book, it would prove valuable to newbie aquarists as well as seasoned veterans, and it could be easily read or printed from Netscape. An item similar to this, made for your site, would set you apart, ensure a bookmark from the surfer, and help create return traffic.

PUTTIN' ON THE RITZ

Always a crowd pleaser, special events are fun and bring people together. If you are launching a new Palace site, for instance, you might throw a "Grand Opening Extravaganza." After using the guerrilla marketing techniques we've discussed, you should invite leaders from other communities, in this case, probably other Palace gods and wizards, to attend. You could also invite folks with expertise in your community's area of interest to speak and mingle with guests. Create custom props and avatars to give out. It's just like throwing a real party, only online. Other ideas could include:

- Hosting an Amateur Comedian Night

- Events to celebrate special holidays, like Halloween or Christmas

- A night of free astrological readings (Yes, this really happened, and it was a huge success!)

- A Superbowl party if your members like football

KEEP THE BUZZ THROUGH CROSS-PROMOTION

By promoting events that include other established communities as well as your own (or cross-promoting), you can keep interest in your community alive, infuse it with fresh blood, and develop healthy ties to other communities that may result in valuable alliances. Staying with the Palace example, let's say you cater to aficionados of adventure role-playing games like Dungeons and Dragons with your Palace. You might reach out to other Palaces with a similar theme, and set up a mass online game that would require teams of players to start in one location and adventure through many rooms on several Palace sites, culminating in one team reaching the last room and collecting the prize, which might be special avatars or props. An event like this would be fun, and Palace software, with its whisper modes and other features, would help facilitate this activity quite nicely.

OFFLINE PARTIES

Many communities, like AOL or The WELL, like to bring together people in meatspace. If you can get your community leaders organized (and this is especially true if your community has regional interests), you could rent a small ballroom at a local hotel and hold a party. Why not? A party is fun. The great value of meeting folks in your community face-to-face is probably obvious: You'll help instill deeper commitment to your community by forging deeper relationships between your members.

Also, you might consider a more ambitious plan. You might take advantage of group discounts and schedule for travel, and perhaps schedule a cruise from Florida to the Bahamas. Who wouldn't enjoy that? Of course, we're talking about financial commitment and lots of logistical concerns, so plan early, involve your community in the decisions, and enlist the help of a committee to organize and execute the plan.

A FINGER ON THE PULSE OF THE COMMUNITY

Many virtual communities like to have weekly or daily polls on topics of interest. While the scientific merit of these polls are debatable at best, they certainly are interesting and members enjoy participating. You can pose a daily question like, "Who will be the Democratic vice-presidential choice?" or "Who will Pittsburgh choose in the first round of the draft?" You can employ Java to create either fill-in-the-blank or multiple-choice forms. Then, after a specified time, post the results and discuss them in chat forums or message bases.

HOW MANY JELLYBEANS ARE IN THIS JAR?

Contests are excellent attention getters. You can make a contest out of just about anything. A Palace scavenger hunt could be an ongoing interactive contest idea. You might, if you are so inclined, place a Webcam on a jar of jellybeans and ask folks to guess the number of jellybeans in it. Or you could have a contest to create a new logo for your community's home page.

Don't Be Afraid Of Intimacy

Building "one-to-one" relationships is a major element of any marketing program, but relationships are *the* most important element of your virtual community. So nourish them and help them grow. It's wonderful to see communities come together.

Recently, we watched some heartwarming communication take place online. We'll let the leader of the community in question tell you his story personally:

"Member X is a student at the school I work at. He told me earlier in the week that his mom is ill. Unfortunately, I've learned that her prognosis is not good, as the tumor was cancerous, and is well entrenched in her stomach. They also feel that it has spread to her lymph nodes.

"I will take Member X under my wing, and spend time with him if he feels the need to talk to someone. He doesn't feel comfortable speaking to the guidance counselors at the school. He hangs around my office, as he's really interested in computers, and I'm a computer technician—so I guess he feels like he's on more of an even footing with me.

"I'm sure it would help if folks here were able to lend an ear, if he approaches you. I think discretion is the key here. He's a good kid, and this is no doubt a rough time for him.

"Please let me know if you need any special assistance with him."

Calling All Communities!

Building relationships within your community is important, but so is establishing ties outside of your site. Communities can nurture and support each other. The following letter was sent out to a community mailing list, asking other community leaders and members to please help the sender's cause. Many people mobilized to help this community builder.

Supporting A Support Community

"As some of you know, I am starting support groups at my community. I would like to start a teen support group for kids who need to talk about their problems, but I need someone who is qualified in this area. The groups are self-help, but are headed by someone who is familiar in the area and responsible enough to handle situations. If you or anyone you know would be willing to give an hour of their time each week to helping, please have them contact me. I am also looking for someone to mediate a vets support group. Open House is tomorrow night from 7 to 11 Eastern if anyone would like to come and check the place out."

Show Me The Money

There is a myth and a reality. The myth is that there are millions of dollars to make on the Internet, and anyone can make them by slapping up a Web site. But there are no get-rich-quick, sure-fire, Web-based cash cows. The reality is that you can make money on the Web by providing a community site that generates hits, or by marketing products that people want. It takes time, energy, and dedication, just like any business. You must keep your content fresh, your integrity high, and your nose to the virtual grindstone. If you've leveraged your community properly, by utilizing the marketing and advertising tips from this chapter, you're ripe to start reaping the rewards. At first, like any other business, you goal is to earn enough money to cover costs, and from there to expand into the black. Who knows, you might end up getting rich, but we won't promise that. We will promise that developing a self-supporting community that also turns a profit is a rewarding experience. In the next chapter, we'll look at generating revenue with your community.

Part 4

Management And Monetary Issues

Chapter 13

Cashing In With Your Community

Chapter 13

- SELLING ADVERTISING SPACE

- USING AD NETWORKS

- GETTING A CORPORATE SPONSOR

- ELECTRONIC COMMERCE AND TRANSACTION FEES

- ALTERNATIVE PROFIT-MAKING METHODS

CASHING IN WITH YOUR COMMUNITY

Chapter 13

Virtual Business

With the advent of the Internet, we have entered into a new era of business, and we'd like to make two points about that.

One: In the old days (like the 1980s), starting a business meant taking great risks. If you put up your own capital, you stood to lose everything if you failed. If you didn't have a healthy nest egg to invest, you acquired financing, which might have been an insurmountable uphill battle depending on your situation. Not anymore. Now there is the Internet, which changes all the rules. There are still costs to incur, but those costs are comparatively fractional. Also, you have the luxury of working out of your home, or in your spare time. Don't be fooled; it's still hard work, and there are still risks, but now the playing field is level. In the past, small businesses just couldn't compete with the multibillion-dollar international conglomerate. But on the Web, Joe's Chips can match the professional presentation of Intel with little difficulty. This makes the bigwigs a little nervous. The Internet as a profit medium has brought everyone closer to the tools that can help them realize their personal dreams of success.

Two: In the few short years of commercial Internet development, meatspace models have migrated to the Net. Take *Wired* magazine. That's "old media," made of paper, delivered by snail mail, full of advertising; it's something you pick up, hold, read, consume, discard—and if you did fancy the notion of interacting with it, you had to write a letter. In the beginning, that's what Web sites were: Text and pictures that came over a modem, and when advertising was used, it was applied in old media fashion, just like print ads in a magazine. Then Wired Ventures spawned HotWired. That's "new media:" interactive, dynamic, permanently archived, and full of people and information that's not only consumed by the netizen, but contributed to as well. It's a community. As we've said before, it's the killer application of the Internet, and it's rapidly becoming the standard business model on the Internet. No longer is electronic commerce just about hawking widgets. It's about creating social space.

In the past, there have been gasps of horror at the notion that folks would dare to profit from social space on the Internet. But let's be pragmatic. Creating a virtual community is a vast undertaking, requiring time and energy that, for its creators, costs money and probably takes time away from their regular careers. So developing revenue-generating components for your virtual community makes sense. It needs to be done, and as we'll see, it can be done with little or no cost to the community member, and with very little intrusion. In fact, when you consider the benefits of Internet-based commerce, it can be a plus for a great many Web surfers.

Currently there are five basic models of generating revenue online: advertising, sponsorships, subscriptions, electronic commerce, and let's not forget "other." It's true that "other" seems a bit nebulous, but we'll deal with that later. Any one or a combination of these models can be employed to bring your business into profitability. And as we implied, smart thinking and good timing on your part might result in model number six. For now, let's start with the stalwart favorite, advertising.

Beyond Billboards

We know that banner advertising is the most popular method of distributing ad banner creative. But now most Web sites are going "beyond the banner" with their advertising programs, using every spare electron on the page. It didn't start out that way, though. When Clnet began selling advertising on its pages, the site utilized a banner model of 454×55, later migrating to the IAB standard of 468×60. Then upper management realized that other areas of their pages were important, too; advertisers can now buy "portals," "hot spots," "ad wraps," and "sponsorships." So don't underestimate or overlook ways to implement advertising programs. Maximize every electron—in other words, every square inch of "real estate" is potential advertising income.

The Revenue Explosion

Simba Information, Inc. says that Web advertising revenues will grow to $1.86 billion by the year 2000. Table 13.1 shows how this growth is distributed over the next few years.

Next, you need to decide *how* to sell that advertising. At present, you have three options to choose from: selling space directly to advertisers with an in-house sales team, offering it to advertising networks for resale, or farming it out to an advertising representative.

CASHING IN ON YOUR REAL ESTATE

Setting up an in-house ad sales force is difficult if you don't already have an established brand. Without sales expertise and leveraging capabilities from traditional media, a virtual community faces an uphill battle. However, Suck magazine (**www.suck.com**) overcame the odds. Suck, a cutting-edge digital e-zine with a slant toward community-building, is primarily targeted to Generation Xers. This site started as an underground, anonymous project by several employees of *Wired*. It grew exponentially as the word got out about this biting, often irreverent site.

Table 13.1 Web advertising revenues (in millions), 1996-2000.
(Source: SIMBA, Inc.)

	1996	1997	1998	1999	2000
World Wide Web	$110	$402.4	$913.0	$1,371.0	$1,863.0

Eventually the Suck property was "sold" to *Wired*, who had the marketing muscle to turn it into a revenue-generating powerhouse.

So, if you want to roll the dice and handle ad sales in-house, you'll need a sales team or advertising rep firm to sell the space, a printed media kit for sales demonstrations, a business account for travel expenses, and more. Really, this topic alone could fill a book, so in the next section we'll just touch upon some of the more important items for you to consider.

The most important question, of course, is "What am I going to charge for my ads?" This is a difficult question to answer, since the industry really hasn't been around long enough to have a sense of historical perspective. According to NetGravity, makers of ad management software, your annual ad revenue should equal the number of page impressions on your site per week. In the following sections, we'll describe the various pricing models, and as a benchmark, we'll give you examples of what other sites are doing.

Cost Per Thousand (CPM)

As mentioned in the previous chapter, CPM refers to "cost per thousand," and is the standard in which print advertising sets its rates for publications. As a benchmark, we've listed ranges of prices:

- Search engines: $20-$50 CPM

- Keyword advertising with search engines: $40-$70 CPM

- City guides: $20-$80 CPM

- Top 100 Web sites: $25-$100 CPM

- Small, targeted content sites: $10-$80 CPM

Some of the smaller blue-chip sites we've seen include the award-winning Tennis Server (**www.tennisserver.com**), shown in Figure 13.1, which charges $10 to $15 CPM. Ad packages include rotating banner ads, along with a message sent to 10,000 subscribes in the monthly email newsletter.

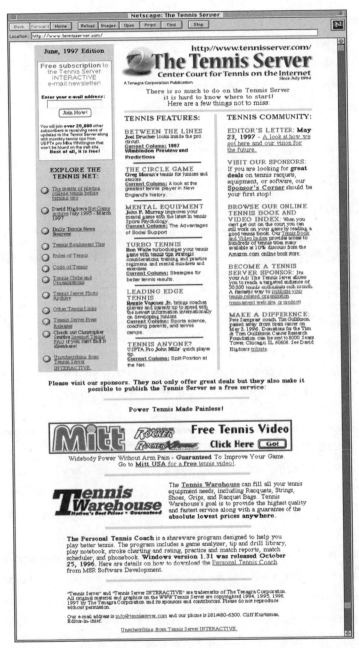

Figure 13.1 A blue-chip Web community sells advertising space on its site.

Click Through

Evan Neufeld, an online advertising analyst with Jupiter Communications, predicts that many Web sites will begin to offer a long menu of pricing schemes that advertisers can choose from by the end of 1997. One of these will be based on click throughs from banners. Sites such as Gigaplex (**www.gigaplex.com**) will charge 75 cents for each click through from a banner; most sites charge between $.40 and $1.00 per click through. Some advertisers, such as consumer-brand giant Proctor and Gamble, *prefer* paying by the click.

Transactional Pricing

Transactional pricing is the new advertising buzz word on the Net. This method accrues fees based on gathering customer leads, purchases, or other actions. It will become more important as "commerce on the Net grows and more sophisticated means of targeting are developed," according to industry executives who recently gathered for coffee at the Ditto Internet Cafe in Manhattan's Flatiron district at the request of *Web Week* magazine.

For more information about what Web sites are charging for advertising programs, take a look at the Ad Resource Web site at **www.adresource.com/whatitco.htm**.

Generate Professional Traffic Reports

*When serving up ad banners, you could take the "easy" approach and hard-wire ads into your Web pages. But you severely limit flexibility by doing so. On top of that, you'll need to create traffic reports for your advertisers. Believe us, that is not a particularly fun way to pass the time. You could write a CGI script to dynamically rotate ads, but you'll still have to generate those reports. Thanks to some helpful hints by ClickOver (**www.clickover.com**), we're presenting nine reasons why you shouldn't use homegrown CGI scripts for banner rotation or traffic reports:*

> *1. Advertisers are demanding. They want reports showing how many times the ad was served (impressions), the number of clicks, and the click-through rate. And they want these reports on a regular basis, online, and probably in realtime.*

2. *Analyzing log files is a drag. Log files, especially if you have an active community, can be megabytes in size. Then you must run the logs through a statistical program like WebStats, before you're even ready to begin analysis. This is a painstaking process. We recommend that you don't try it.*

3. *Preventing overdelivery is hard. Your snappy salesperson sold a contract for 100,000 page views, but because you were too busy supervising the rollout of the Web site redesign, you served up 90,000 of those impressions the first week. Oops. Your client will probably be upset, since they're expecting an even distribution over a four-week period. Monitoring and changing the frequency of an ad in a queue can be a full-time affair.*

4. *Avoiding underdelivery isn't easy, either. Then there's the flip side. How will you handle the same 100,000-impression contract if you mismanage delivery and don't serve enough page views? Talk about having an irate customer! A "make good" is appropriate, but this is only a temporary solution that could eventually turn sour.*

5. *CGI scripts can misbehave. It looks so cute sitting there on your Web server, doling out banners here and there. Yet, as your site grows, so does the source code of this script—and so do the problems maintaining it.*

6. *Web advertising is a moving target. Web advertising is changing as quickly as the Web itself. Keeping up with the demands of the marketplace is difficult.*

7. *Not everyone is a rocket scientist. Managing the whole advertising process can be time consuming. As your advertising volume grows, you'll need to get more people involved in the advertising process. If your Webmaster is the only person who understands your ad management system, he or she will likely become the advertising bottleneck. Your Webmaster probably has a lot of other things to do in addition to managing ads.*

8. *Sometimes, things just don't work under high volumes. Your community is growing. Sometimes, ad hoc solutions just don't scale with the increasing number of ads, pages, and page views you have on your site. They may meet your volume today, but given the nature of the Web, your volume today will not be your volume tomorrow.*

9. *No, really—advertisers can be very demanding. We're serious about this. One advertiser wants run of site, another wants an ad to appear on some pages, but not others. Still another advertiser wants to target ads by domain names, and then there's the one who wants to rotate 10 different ads at the same time. The list goes on...and you're responsible to all of them.*

PROFESSIONAL AD-SERVER NETWORKS

So we've scared the dickens out of you, and you've decided to look for a commercial ad-server solution. What should you look for? Here are four essential features:

- *Online Inventory Scheduling*—Look for a solution that delivers ads to the right place at the right time. You'll want to be able do this in realtime, remotely, if needed.

- *Ad Performance Report Generation on Demand*—Remember those demanding advertisers? Look for a solution that offers timely reports to advertisers and their agencies.

- *Targeted Ad Delivery*—Web advertising is becoming much more targeted, as we mentioned in Chapter 12. Look for a solution that enables you to target to a specific set of customers.

- *Scalable, Distributed Architecture*—A scalable, distributed architecture means a system that can handle the advertising needs of your site, whether you're serving one ad or a million, or whether you have one server or dozens.

Ad-Serving Companies

Convinced this is the right approach? Take a tour through these Web sites; they're the most popular ad-serving software companies on the Net.

- Net Gravity (**www.netgravity.com**)

- Focalink (**www.focalink.com/home/sb/sb1.html**)

- DoubleClick (**www.doubleclick.net**)

- ClickOver (**www.clickover.com**)

- StarPoint Software (**www.starpt.com**)

Going Out-Of-House To Serve Banners

Those advertisers are expecting service 24 hours a day, every day of the week, including holidays! (Remember what we said about advertisers being demanding?) When you consider the costs of the ad-server software and the resources to supervise it, in-house hosting may be more expensive than outsourcing. Some Internet Service Providers are hosting and serving ads as an extra source of revenue. This may be for you if:

- You only want to place ads on specific areas of your Web site.

- You serve less than 1 million page views per month.

- You don't have the technical or management resources to run an in-house program.

- You are experimenting with an ad-based revenue-generating solution, and want to "test drive" the program before you commit.

Ad-hosting services typically charge a nominal one-time set-up fee, and base your cost on the number of ads served to your site. This monthly service fee will be a fraction of the cost of purchasing your own ad banner server, and should quickly pay for itself in increased advertising revenues. Check out the Net Gravity Ad Host Partner Program (**www.netgravity.com/sales/adhostsupp.html#ans**) if you're interested in pursuing this plan.

HOOKING UP WITH AN ADVERTISING REP

An alternative to performing the selling function in-house is to farm it out to an advertising representative. We know many Web sites that are extremely happy with their rep firms. However, we know just as many who are miserable. Why? Rep firms will represent more than one site—sometimes even dozens. The more prominent and profitable sites obviously get more attention from the ad rep, so your community is essentially competing against the other sites that are sold by your rep. This doesn't have to be a problem if you choose your rep carefully. Ask these questions:

- *How many sites does the firm represent?* There is no magical right or wrong answer here. Obviously, the more sites the company represents, the less time they can devote to you individually.

- *Are there any potential conflicts of interest?* If your community is based on golf and the firm represents two other golf sites, your community may not get the recognition it deserves.

- *Are the salespeople trained about the mission and goals of your site?* In order to find the right "fit" with an advertiser, the salesperson must have a thorough understanding of this subject.

- *Are the salespeople familiar with the content and navigation?* This knowledge is essential when sales people are giving demonstrations to potential advertisers.

- *How is the rep compensated?* Most firms take a commission from each sale, but this can vary.

Softbank Interactive Marketing is one of the most notable rep firms in the Internet industry, representing several of the most distinctive sites on the Web, such as Netscape (**www.netscape.com**), Playboy (**www.playboy.com**), and Ziff Davis (**www.zdnet.com**). Their sales professionals are located in major U.S. and European commerce centers. Smaller companies are out there that can serve your needs as well. KMA reps sites such as Addicted to Noise (**www.addict.com**), Save the Earth Foundation (**www.secure.commerce.com/save_earth/**), and Computer Currents (**www.currents.net**). Other firms to consider include:

- WebRep (**wwwebrep.com**)

- Flycast (**www.flycast.com**)

- Burst Media (**www.burstmedia.com**)

- AdNet Strategies (**www.adnetstrategies.com**)

- Venture Online Marketing (**www.ad-venture.com**)

- Katz Millenium Marketing (**www.katz-media.com/millen.htm**)

Maybe You Shouldn't Sell Ad Space At All

No, we're not suggesting that you give it away. Instead, sell it to an advertising network, and let them do all the work. Let us reintroduce you to some of the advertising networks we met in Chapter 12. In addition to buying ad banner programs from these networks, you can also sell them your valuable electrons!

DOUBLECLICK

If you're going to work with DoubleClick, you need to be accepted into the DoubleClick Network. Your site must meet the following network criteria:

- *Number of Available Impressions*—To generate the most revenue for your site, it's important that a minimum of 1 million impressions per month is available to receive DoubleClick ad banners. You'll need to provide them with the actual number of impressions you delivered last month, along with your projections for the next two months.

- *Traffic Acquisition*—Since ad banner availability is relative to your traffic level, they'll need information about any current promotional and marketing programs used to drive traffic to your site.

- *Affinity Group*—In response to market-driven demand for highly targeted editorial content, DoubleClick is currently placing special emphasis on selecting sites in affinity groups. These are technology, business, news, finance, sports, entertainment, health, women's issues, family, and travel.

Upon acceptance to their network, you'll receive a user name and password for your management account. With this account, you can manage advertising on your site through your Web browser. Payments are negotiated on a site-by-site basis. If you're interested in using DoubleClick, contact **support@doubleclick.net**.

WEBCONNECT

WebConnect selects sites on an "as needed" basis. They've positioned their site as an "open" network, rather than "closed." This means that, depending on the needs (affinity group, demographics, geographic region, reach, frequency, etc.) of their clients (advertisers), WebConnect may actually contact your community for a specific campaign. Or you can contact WebConnect at **mail@webconnect.net** to provide them information about your community.

Below, we've listed affinity groups that have been of interest to WebConnect in past campaigns:

- Automotive/aviation/motorcycle/marine

- Banking/financial/investing

- Business-to-business

- Children/infants/teenage goods

- College/Generation X

- Computer

- Consumer

- Crafts/Hobbies/Models

- Educational/edutainment

- Health/Self-improvement

- Home

- Legal

- Medical/surgical

- Men's/Women's

- Music/record buyers/music trades

- News and information

- Pets

- Sports

- Travel

COMMONWEALTH NETWORK

Once you submit your site to the Commonwealth Network (**commonwealth. riddler.com**) for consideration, it will be reviewed by their editorial team, who will evaluate its potential. Unfortunately, a list of criteria is not available.

The Commonwealth Network has an intriguing payment system. Royalties are paid or accrued, as appropriate, from the monthly Author Royalty Purse announced prior to the first day of each month, based upon Unique Host Impressions (UHIs). You are credited with one UHI each time a unique IP address loads a Web page registered with your Commonwealth Portfolio (and containing the Commonwealth HTML Code, properly placed and unmodified) within a 24-hour period. At the end of the month, your total UHIs are divided by the total UHIs generated by the entire Author tier and multiplied by the Author Royalty Purse amount for that month. In other words, your Web site generates a percentage of all of the UHIs generated by all Authors and your share of the Authors Royalty Purse corresponds to that percentage. But there's more...

Bestsellers Model

Bestsellers occupy the ultimate tier in the Commonwealth Network, being a part of a very small and select group of stellar Web sites. If you're a Bestseller Author in the Commonwealth Network imprint, then you've made it. Your first perk: your own editor. Commonwealth will assign an in-house resource to assist you, helping you build your site and your brand. The payout? Bestsellers are the highest-paid tier in the Commonwealth Network imprint. No purse at this level; instead, all royalties, contracts, and license agreements will be arranged on a deal-by-deal basis.

SOME OF THE OTHER NETWORKS

We've just touched on a few networks that will pay you for your space. Other networks to investigate include:

- NarrowCast Media (**www.narrowcastmedia.com**)

- AdSmart (**www.adsmart.net**)

- Petry Interactive Network (**www.petrynetwork.com**)

- Virtual Billboard Network (**www.virtualbillboard.net**)

- The Mining Company (**www.miningco.com**)

- CliqNow (**www.cliqnow.com**)

Before you plunge in, though, we recommend that you check out Mark J. Welch's Web site (**www.ca-probate.com/comm_net.htm**) about advertising networks and brokers. Mark, an attorney who specializes in Internet advertising networks and brokers, lists tons of useful information, including scams to watch out for, things to look for in a contract, and transaction models.

Yoursite.com, Brought To You By...

Selling "advertorial spots" has become a feasible revenue model on the Web. The Microsoft Network (**www.msn.com**), Clnet (**www.cnet.com**), and ZDNet (**www.zdnet.com**) are all teaming up with advertisers to develop sponsored programming. Take a look at Figure 13.2 for Clnet's advertising partnership with Intel. Not only is the Intel brand name prominently displayed at the top of the page, but upon clicking through to the "Screamer of the Week," the user sees a server-push, five-second Intel "commercial," which reads "from the digital frontier Intel brings you…" From what we've seen, sites generally charge $45 to $85 CPM for sponsored content.

Rick Boyce, Vice President/Director Of Advertising Sales, HotWired

"The more deeply you can connect the content and the advertising message, the deeper the communication you can achieve."

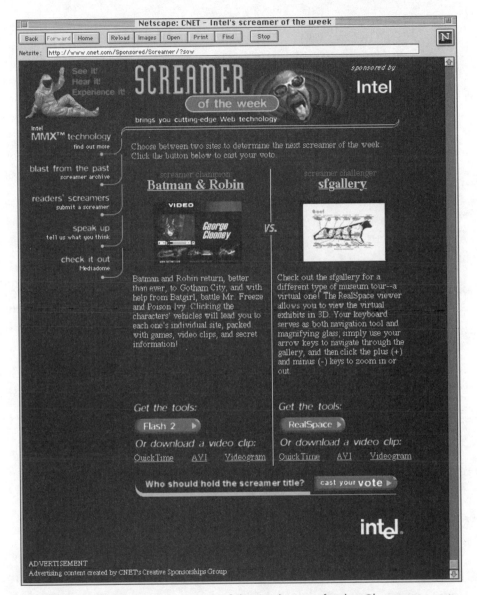

Figure 13.2 Intel sponsors the Best of the Web area for the Clnet community.

Even HotWired, the originator of banner advertising, is combining editorial content and advertising to give its sponsors a "beyond the banner" alternative. Rosalind Resnick, editor and publisher of the Digital Direct Marketing Letter (**www. netcreations.com/ ddm/**), estimates that sponsored areas consist of 95 percent entertainment and 5 percent marketing message, and that sponsored sites are less intrusive than banner ads, with visitors crediting the sponsor with making the content possible.

Jeannine Parker, Executive Board Member Of The Internet Developers Association

"[Sponsored content] is akin to the early days of radio and television— much like The Texaco Star Theater presents…"

The key to a successful program is to make sure that there is a good fit between the content producer and the advertiser. Next, we'll show you how well a relationship like this between two parties can work.

APPLE USERS COMMUNITY

Since April 1990, Adam and Tonya Engst have published the email-based newsletter TidBITS (**www.tidbits.com**) for the Apple community. Although TidBITS began as a labor of love, the Engsts' began to feel the drain on resources as their newsletter grew in popularity and distribution. Eventually, Adam and Tonya decided to look towards a revenue-generating model to cover operating expenses and the income lost while not working at their "real jobs." Since issue #134, in July 1992, TidBITS has been sponsored by a variety of Macintosh and Internet companies such as APS Technologies, Power Computing, and Aladdin Systems, each paying a sponsorship fee to reach a highly targeted audience.

The Price Of Admission (Or, Will People Pay For This?)

Subscription fees are fixed charges (usually monthly) to the user for the ability to participate in the community. To date, however, subscription fees on the Internet haven't been very successful. USA Today Online found this out when they launched their site in 1995. So why have The WELL ($5/month) and the Wall Street Interactive Edition ($19.95/month) been able to pull this off? First, they've clearly communicated (and delivered) a value to the end user. Second, both companies have migrated successful brands to the Web from previous incarnations.

Industry analysts are looking forward to when member fees become ubiquitous in the business-to-business communities. Other types of fees to consider may be:

- *Usage Fees*—Based on the number of "pages" accessed.

- *Content Fees*—For downloading specific information, such as a market research report.

- *Service Fees*—For specialized services, such as a notification service.

Let's be honest, though. It isn't likely that too many fee-based subscriptions are going to work. People pay for computers, modems, telephone service, their ISP, and software, and by now, they're tired of doling out the cash. Many folks consider the monthly payment to their ISP to be their cost of admission to the Internet, and even though that might not always be correct, you aren't going to easily change their minds. Notice, also, that of all the services available online, only one type of service almost universally charges for access: the so-called "adult entertainment" sites. This is partly because many advertisers are unwilling to place their ad banners on sites of this type, and also because many adult content providers consider fees to be the best way to restrict access by minors. Almost every other type of service on the Internet uses a different model to generate revenue, with a few notable exceptions, and there is probably some wisdom in that. Besides, free access helps build traffic, making the advertising model very attractive.

The Community Store

It's the age-old business model, where you have products (or a service) and people give you money in exchange. We don't want to go into too much depth on e-commerce, because that's a topic worthy of its own book; however, we will note that almost all the big Internet communities have "community stores" where you can buy T-shirts, books, hats, frisbees, or even expensive home gyms. Whatever makes sense for your community, you can create an online store to sell it. If, for example, you are a health and fitness community, you might sell related items, such as workout clothing and training equipment.

If you're not into the idea of running a store, you might contract the services of an established company to handle the actual sales, while you receive a commission or a "transaction fee" on the sale. We'll look at one such option in the next section.

Don't want to go to all that trouble? You can still offer the basics, like site-branded T-shirts and hats that, when worn, become free advertising in meatspace for your community.

GeoCities has the right idea. Instead of us explaining it to you, we'll let them illustrate firsthand what they've done in the GeoCities Store.

You Can Get Everything You Want At GeoCities

We've got some of your favorite GeoCities shops, and some new items, all in one exciting place where we promise you'll find a never-ending supply of great items at terrific prices. And it won't stop here; we'll be adding new stores to the Marketplace in coming months to make it even more lively. Be sure to check back often to see all that's new.

Internet Shopping Network is the Web's leading computer hardware and software retailer, with more than 40,000 items to choose from. Full desktop systems to laptops, all kinds of software including downloads, more peripherals and computer accessories than you knew existed. ISN @ GeoCities has it all.

Want to shoot planes out of the sky? Or show your royal flush to the man in the ten-gallon hat sitting across the poker table? Or just spend the afternoon playing games with other folks from around the globe? The best place to indulge yourself is the Marketplace Arcade. We've got seven of the Web's hottest games, and you can play at very reasonable rates. Sign up today and get hooked.

The GeoStore is your specialty shop for being a GeoCitizen. It's stocked with a variety of great-looking GeoCities items, including T-shirts, caps, and the brand-new GeoMousePad. You'll also find books and other items to help you build a terrific-looking site.

Flowers, gifts, and gourmet foods for every occasion…that's what GeoCities Flowers & Gifts is all about. Worldwide delivery for special occasions or just to say you're thinking of someone—all viewable with full-color photographs and easy-to-buy with just a few keystrokes. Plus, if you're on the forgetful side, sign up for the FREE Email reminder service to be notified in advance when it's time to purchase a gift for that pesky anniversary or nephew's birthday.

If you're going to go forward with a store and you plan to conduct actual credit card transactions with your community members, you'll need to use a secure server to give consumers confidence that their credit card data is safe on the Internet. Talk to your ISP about the technology that's available to provide such services.

SPEAKING OF TRANSACTION FEES

As we saw in the previous section, commerce is HOT, HOT, HOT on the Web. And, there are Web sites out there who will pay you for being the catalyst for a transaction between a buyer and a seller—it's like a referral or "finder's" fee for generating the sale.

John Hagell III And Arthur G. Armstrong, Authors, *net.gain*

As virtual communities become a forum for transactions and not simply advertising, the virtual community organizer becomes positioned to charge the vendor a "commission" on each transaction. These commissions now run somewhere between 2 percent and 10 percent of the purchase value. As transaction volume increases, there is the further possibility of virtual communities "squeezing out" traditional intermediaries like retailers and distributors, so that members can deal directly with producers of goods and services. In this case, the virtual community organizer may be able to capture additional revenue by splitting between itself and the producer the margin previously enjoyed by the intermediary.

Amazon.com Books

There are more than 2.5 million titles in the Amazon.com catalog. If you're asking, "What do books have to do with my community?" think about this: your community is probably based on some type of affinity group, like golf, sailing, or online gaming. Whatever the subject, there've probably been a gazillion books written about it. As a value-added service to your community members, you can offer books of interest to them, creating editorial content areas in the process. This is how it works:

As one of the 9,000-plus Web sites that have joined the Amazon Associates Program (**www.amazon.com**), you can feature any of those 2.5 million titles on your Web site. You can even write your own book reviews (or have your members write them) if you like. In essence, you create a personalized Amazon.com "bookstore" just for your community. Amazon.com does the rest. They take orders using secure servers, linked from your pages. They supply, package, ship, and bill the customer for the books. They even handle customer service inquiries. Then, on a weekly basis, Amazon.com sends you an activity report of the sales that were made through your pages.

By providing links to the Amazon.com catalog through their Associates Program, you earn a percentage of the sales made though your site. This is called a "referral fee." How much money are we talking about here? You earn 5 percent of the selling price on books currently in print that are sold at list price. You also garner 5 percent on books sold at discounts greater than 10 percent. There are 1.2 million special order books that fall under those rules, plus a special list of featured books called the Amazon.com 500, which also qualify. In addition, you can earn 15 percent on certain books (about 300,000 of them!) listed in the online catalog. Check out **www.amazon.com** for all the details.

As with everything, there is fine print to read. There are certain situations in which Amazon.com doesn't pay a referral fee. Read that fine print closely on their Web site at **www.amazon.com/exec/obidos/subst/partners/associates/associates.html/6418-8433831-884338**. Or, go to **www.amazon.com** and click on the Associates link.

If you want to find other sites that pay commissions, take a look at Mark J. Welch's page, mentioned earlier. He has put up an index of sites that pay referral fees, including CD Now, CompuServe's Free Outlet, and CD Universe, at **www. caprobate.com/comm_net.htm#_other**.

Other Ways To Generate Income From Your Site

In the beginning, we referred to a nebulous category known as "other." What we call "other" are a couple of ideas backed up by the axiom that "information is power." First, let's look at surveys.

PARTNERING UP WITH THE NUMBER CRUNCHERS

Niche sites typically receive less Web traffic than broader-based community sites, but they have a unique advantage that the niche site can exploit: Nearly every member of a niche community belongs to the same affinity group. For example, if you've dedicated your community to camping and hiking enthusiasts, you may say with certainty that most of your members are actually consumers of outdoor athletic gear, like backpacks or hiking boots. It reasonably follows that niche Web destinations, with their highly specialized and targeted content, can provide exceptional soil in which to plant surveys or other data-gathering tools. You can cultivate information for other companies, or on your own with the intention of selling your data.

Happy Puppy is a site that caters to the hard-core computer gaming and multiplayer gaming community. It's a select audience with a narrow interest, but Happy Puppy has aggressively leveraged this unique feature of their core affinity group. They developed an in-depth, 105-question survey that focused on game player habits. Then they partnered with companies like Simba Information for data analysis and Greenfield for data collection. About 2,200 Happy Puppy community members completed the survey, and were rewarded with an entry into a contest that promised (and delivered) prizes of special interest to the gaming community.

From the survey results, a report was generated containing over 200 data tables; it sells for $2,400 in printed form, or $10,000 on disk. Companies that produce computer games and/or advertising are buying the comprehensive survey. To these companies, the information is valuable, and buying the report is far more economical than undertaking the research and creating one of their own. Happy Puppy then splits the profits evenly with its partners. "Information is power," and it may be especially prudent to approach companies whose products are of interest to your community's core audience and learn what type of information they find valuable. Even a survey of 20 multiple-choice queries can provide data that many companies can use to fine-tune their marketing strategies, and they would cheerfully pay for it.

Remember, this is a win-win situation. You can sell data at a cost that means high profits for you. Companies receive data at a price that represents significant savings to them. The consumer ultimately benefits from companies being better informed of the consumer's needs.

SELLING LEADS

Traditional businesses, such as magazine companies, generate revenue streams by selling lists of its subscribers or its subscribers' profiles to direct mail or research companies. New media companies are beginning to follow in their footsteps. With the data you can glean, theoretically you could also sell "transactional" profiles.

Rosalind Resnick, President, NetCreations

"These days, dozens of companies are peddling electronic mailing lists containing names and addresses of online users for direct marketers to target. By taking a politically correct approach, you generate money from these qualified leads.

"Once you have built up a sufficient list, start informing your industry colleagues that you are the administrator of a list that may have value to them. Explain the mass email option using the 10 cents per name fee, which is fairly standard in the direct marketing industry.

"It should be clearly defined up front that the cybermailing lists being referred to here are built from voluntary submissions. Generally,

these addresses are gleaned when someone enters an online contest, registers software, or partakes in an Internet-related trial offer and give you express permission to send them additional information."

We agree with Resnick that community owners need to be careful with this approach. After all, you're building personal or business relationships, and the selling of sensitive information about your community members may undermine trust. We feel that advertising, sponsored content, or transactional fees are much more viable means of generating income for your community.

It's also wise to note that laws are evolving that regulate the sale or posting of private information. To be on the safe side, not to mention the ethical side, don't sell data about Web surfers without telling them. Tell them that you sell lists, what kind of companies you sell lists to, and offer a way to be removed from lists that you sell. If they opt out, honor that request diligently.

If you are honest up front, you might be surprised by the number of people who opt in. We've seen some sites that go a step further. Some sites will not only tell you that they sell the data they collect, but what type of companies they sell to, *and* let you choose the type of companies you wish to opt out of with a Java applet that offers a list and checkboxes. For example, you can choose to receive targeted mar-keting information from computer companies and from home-improvement companies, but not to receive information from clothiers or financial services. That's good for the surfer, and great for you because now you can sell lists targeted to affinity groups that are already predisposed to respond favorably to the information they receive.

You Got Online, Now Stay Online

Okay. You leveraged your community and sold ad space, and you're pretty pleased with yourself. But this is no time to rest on your laurels. Now you must evolve, grow, create new content, and expand your marketing opportunities; in other words, manage. In the next chapter, we'll look at management, the practices and the pitfalls, as well as the content concerns and legal worries that good man-agers need to be aware of to ensure a long-lived site with a solid base of community members.

Chapter 14

Managing Your Community

Chapter 14

- Community Management

- Selecting Your Leaders

- Legal Issues Concerning The Internet

- Pornography, Hackers, And Censorship

- Your Crisis Plan

MANAGING YOUR COMMUNITY

Chapter 14

A Formula For Formal Management

What exactly will be expected of you, as the manager of your own community? The "official" definition, found in all the academic textbooks, says that a manager will forecast, plan, organize, delegate, control, and evaluate all the tasks and performances of the organization.

But attitudes in modern management theory tend to evolve. Recently, theorists have proposed that management is now a *shared* organizational responsibility. We believe this approach is much more conducive to the community-building process, since most of the control in any community is usually distributed amongst the members. However, many critics of shared responsibility are quick to point out that distributing authority, forming a "flat organization," often stifles the decision-making process.

There are several ways to make decisions. In the traditional setting, strategic or tactical decisions are made by upper management like the CEO, vice presidents, or the directors. However, one must consider two questions about this sort of process: Does it result in good solutions? Is it a fair process? Of course, it depends in large part on the caliber of the professionals involved. But we believe that in a community setting, it's much better for the people who are affected by the decisions to be included in the process of making those decisions. Wow, this is starting to sound like a democracy! As it turns out, many companies are now adopting a community-like paradigm for their operations, based on the wisdom that employees who are self-directed have a higher level of pride and satisfaction, resulting in greater productivity (and higher profits) for the company.

But doesn't this community model of management cause problems? So many people are involved in the process. Does it take too long to make a decision? How do we know how many people to include in the process? Isn't there too much compromise needed? Will it ultimately dilute the solution to the problem? Fortunately for us, some folks in the business world have begun using a process called *formal consensus* to avoid these pitfalls. The Leap Partnership (**www.leapnet.com**), a "non-traditional, strategic, and creative marketing communications agency," is one such company. Tired of the slowness and inefficiency of larger agencies, the founders branched off to launch Leap, a "flat" organization in which all the employees are "partners." They say they're now spending their time actually working for their clients, whereas in their previous jobs, they found themselves bogged down by bureaucracy and having to fight through layers of management to get good ideas advanced.

Take a peek at Figure 14.1 to see how the formal consensus structure works, and then we'll break it apart and see how you can apply it to your own community management strategy. (*On Conflict and Consensus: A Handbook on Formal Consensus Decision-Making*, C.T. Butler and Amy Rothstein. For more information, go to **www.tiac.net/users/amyr/OCAC.html**.)

COMING TOGETHER

In order for formal consensus to work, a community needs a spirit of cooperation, speaking and listening skills, and above all, mutual respect among contributing members. Let's break down the chart from Figure 14.1 and apply it to a hypothetical community problem.

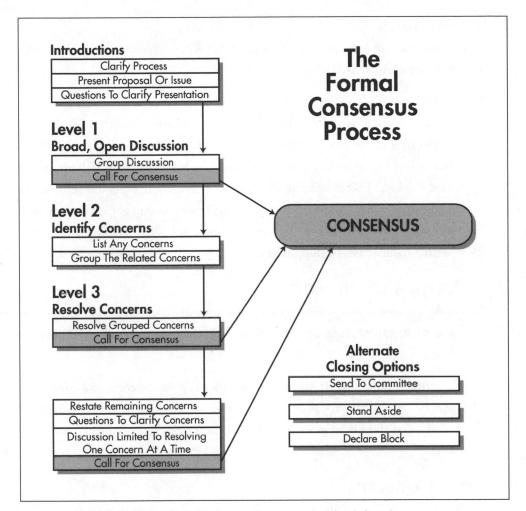

Figure 14.1 The formal consensus structure is clearly defined.

Okay. You've established a community of Pez dispenser collectors, and you all meet on your newly designed Palace site where everyone wears Pez-shaped avatars. Lately, a bunch of ruffians from the Gummi Bear community have been invading your Palace and saying rude things about Pez. What do you do? Well, you could slam down a Draconian fist and tell your Palace wizards to "pin" or "kill" any Gummi promoter than happens by. Or you could try using formal consensus.

Introductions

First, you'd send an email to your community leaders introducing the problem you and your community are facing:

"Dear PezHeads: We have a problem to discuss, and we're going to reach a solution by forming a consensus among our community members. [You clarified the process.] The Loyal Order of Gummi Bears have been running amok in our community, bothering our guests and insulting our Holy Shrine of Pez. [Now you've presented the issue.] We could ban the Gummis altogether. We could continue to warn and discipline the Gummis individually. Or we could negotiate a treaty with the Gummis. [Now you've presented three proposals.] What should we do?" See, it's a pretty straightforward thing to do.

Broad, Open Discussion

By asking for input, you've allowed your community to participate in the discussion and to begin working on a solution. They'll be pleased that their opinion is important.

You'll get many responses. At this point, you ask the group to come to a consensus. The process might be over if everyone can agree on what to do. However, it's more likely that there'll be some argument. It looks like you need to go on to the next level.

Identify Concerns

In the next step, the group needs to list concerns. Pez Lover is concerned about being abused by Gummi Bears, but others are afraid that banning Gummis might lead to difficult relations with other candy groups. Call for consensus again. Be careful not to attack folks with minority views. Everybody's views are important, and it's important that each user knows she's a valuable member of Pez Palace.

Resolve Concerns

Okay, at this stage, it helps to restate the concerns to ensure that everyone is on the same wavelength, and it's also a good idea to encourage questions and comments that will further clarify the issue for the group at large. In the course of this discussion, you discover that Pez Lover doesn't really understand the Palace software features that she could use to protect herself. This new information helps the group to reach a consensus: You, as leader of the community, will instruct Pez Lover in how to "gag" unruly guests, so she can better defend herself. With Pez Lover's concerns addressed, the group decides to extend an olive branch to the Gummi Bears by giving them a gift of special Pez-shaped Gummi avatars. You agree that if the situation improves over, say, the next two weeks, then the Gummis can stay; if not, you may have to come back and reconsider the option to ban them.

Alternatives

If the group remained at an impasse, you could form a committee to reexamine the issue and proposals and reintroduce them to the group at a later time. Another option would be to ask Pez Lover to "stand aside" on this issue, recognizing her concerns but accepting the majority opinion. It's not unusual for decision-making to involve more conflict than agreement, but conflict shouldn't be avoided. Quite the contrary, it should be encouraged. Conflict paves the way to open discussion and clear understanding if it is handled in an even-tempered manner, but it must always be resolved cooperatively.

Managing Your Community Leaders

As the creator of a community, you need to be sure your community leaders remember that they're representing you (or your company) while online. This means it's essential that they be evenhanded at all times in their dealings with members of the community. Conflicts among users will inevitably arise, but it's best if they can resolve these situations amongst themselves, as discussed in Chapter 3. When this isn't possible, your community leaders may need to intervene.

It's very important that your leaders follow a standard set of guidelines when dealing with problems. Document your guidelines, and make them available to all of your leaders through a private, leaders-only mailing list. These structured guidelines will reduce confusion about appropriate behaviors in various situations. In the following sections, we'll discuss some rules that you may want to consider for your own guidebook.

Starring Roles For Your Leading Players

The first issue you'll probably want to address is the function of each of your community leaders. A leader may have a specific role, such as producer, moderator, or support technician. It's important to define each role, much like a job description. At The Palace, Inc., management believes that the "primary directive" of wizards is to "help make the Palace a better place." Since you probably won't want to wear every hat in your community, here are several types of community leaders you'll want to recruit. These roles are not listed in any particular order, and every community won't need every type of leader. As your community grows, you'll come to know what you need for your specific situation.

Chief Executive Officer

This is probably going to be you. This leader manages the day-to-day operations of the community and executes the strategic plan.

Managing Editor (Architect, Minister Of Design)

This will likely be you also, at least in the beginning. This person designs the structure, look and feel, and navigation of the community. For a Palace site, the Managing Editor would coordinate the artwork and site map of the Palace. On a Web site, he or she would make art- or content-related decisions. If your site has a lot of new information to post frequently, this job is very important.

Content Producers (Developers, Staff Writers)

Many of your community leaders will share this job, as will you. You'll want creative and focused people for these duties. Content people manage member and editorial content, like threaded discussions. They write, produce, create, or design content, and they archive content such as chat transcripts, feature articles, news, and press releases.

Moderators (Traffic Cops, Judges, Enforcers, Wizards)

This job is especially important in the chat environment, whether it's an IRC channel or a Palace site. Moderators resolve conflicts and deal with unruly citizens; they also stimulate discussion by offering topics and actively engaging people in conversation.

Customer Service (Welcome Wagon Team, Greeters)

These folks' mission is to reinforce the feeling of community, providing hands-on contact with members to make sure everyone feels welcome. They can host chat events and serve as gatekeepers, and, if a member has problems, these leaders can try to resolve the problems, or, failing that, they can direct the member to the right person.

Programmers (Engineers)

These are the people who create the infrastructure of the community. They work with the ISP to integrate applications into the community toolbox, manage co-located servers, or supervise network and dedicated Internet connections. Keep these folks very happy, for without them, the technical side of your community can go downhill quickly.

Tech Support (Gurus, Troubleshooters)

These people assist members in using the community tools effectively and help users find information.

Marketing And PR Specialists (Chamber Of Commerce)

They implement marketing plans; plan and coordinate special events; create advertising campaigns; and use catchy buzzwords like "leverage," "brand awareness," "strategic positioning," and "target market."

If you're starting from scratch, you yourself will be everything (and more) at first. As you grow, you'll be able to bring in more people to take on specific duties. If you run a small social club on the Web, you might need only a few technical helpers and a bunch of greeters (or wizards); some of these folks will come from the community as it grows. As we've said numerous times, people will want to volunteer to do many of these jobs. On the other hand, if you're starting a community with business in mind, you'll eventually need to hire (and perhaps actually pay) folks for several jobs.

SLICING UP THE POWER PIE

With all those powers and responsibilities to parcel out, you may want to be selective about which people on your team get to fill which roles. It may be a good idea to start new recruits out in your management team with limited authority, and promote them as they're able to take on more responsibility.

For example, you probably don't want your content producer to have the power to ban guests from your Palace site, just as you may not want your customer service folks to be able to upload new Web pages to your FTP directory. Of course, if you cross-train your community leaders and they're truly proficient, you may be able to dispense responsibility and power more liberally.

CONDUCT BECOMING (AND UNBECOMING) A LEADER

How a community leader conducts himself or herself online is a direct reflection on the community as a whole. As we mentioned earlier, it's a good idea (actually, it's essential) that you determine a set of standards for behavior, document them, and make sure that your leadership team is aware of them and can act accordingly.

Of course, situations do arise in which community management personnel don't follow the guidelines. We've talked with several community owners about their own experiences with leaders who've gotten out of line. Here are some situations to watch out for.

Bad Hair Days

All of us have bad days: a flat tire on the way to work, or maybe the cat ate the canary, who knows? It's crucial that your community leaders not let these challenges in their personal lives interfere with their duties online. If they're feeling out of sorts, everyone's better off if they just take a break. One of the worst things to have to do is to explain to a disgruntled user that one of your leaders had a bad hair day, and that's why he acted like a grinch and yelled at people in the discussion forum.

The Guy Who Went Postal

One night a certain well-populated community had an onslaught of members visiting for the first time. Unfortunately, only one leader was on board that evening. The poor guy was deluged—people were asking questions about tech support; they were bickering back and forth; they were pulling pranks. After two hours of this, the frazzled leader cracked and banished everyone from the site. It wouldn't have been so bad if he'd only temporarily deported these people, for a reasonable amount of time like an hour or so. But instead he used the mother of all banishment—a whole year. When the site's producer reviewed the logs the following day, imagine her distress when she saw what had transpired. Not only did it take her quite a while to undo all the "kill" commands, but the damage to the site's reputation may never be undone.

Going On A Power Trip

We've all heard the sayings: With great power comes great responsibility. Absolute power corrupts absolutely. A little power corrupts a little.

It seems that some community leaders feel a sense of absolute power when they see the opportunity to punish a user—maybe even to the point of enjoying it. Be watchful of this behavior.

It can be tempting for a leader, like an IRC Op or a Palace Wizard, to bait an already disruptive user into committing even more heinous acts, be able to inflict even greater punishment, like banishment. We must stress that you should never allow leaders to "toy" with an abuser like a cat with a mouse. Other guests will frown on that, and you and your community will quickly get a bad reputation. All disciplinary actions should be swift, decisive, and totally professional.

Recruiting For The Virtual Community

As mentioned earlier in this chapter, you can recruit community leaders from within your own community. However, if you're just starting out, you probably won't have this pool of potential applicants. Until you do, you'll need to be creative in your search. Try out some of these ideas:

- *Visit other communities. It isn't unethical to "steal" leaders away from other communities, because you aren't really stealing. In Palace communities, for example, a wizard on one site may well be a wizard on many sites; likewise, you may serve as a community leader in someone else's community while you're running your own. In addition, other sites can prove to be particularly fruitful recruiting grounds because there are lots of folks out there aspiring to be leaders.*

- *Contact friends, relatives, or business associates from meatspace who may be eager to participate. Offering the responsibility of community leadership to these people can open them up to a new world of virtual interaction. They'll thank you, and the Internet will be stronger for the quality people you bring in.*

- *Contact civic groups and trade associations for people who have expertise in a specific area. These folks make great moderators for targeted chat events and discussion forums, and their expertise lends credibility to your virtual domain.*

- *Many adolescents perform exceptionally well as community leaders. On Firebird's Forest Palace site, for example, many wizards are under 16, and they do a great job. They can be a wealth of new ideas, and they're hungry to grow and learn in a rich new environment. Post a message at a local high school, or on a teen-oriented newsgroup, to find eager young minds.*

Dissension In The Ranks

You built the community and people came and everything is just cookies-'n'-cream, right? Not usually—it takes work to foster a community. You can certainly encourage free speech, but you probably don't want nasty flame wars. Dealing with a diverse group of people is tough. They'll be chatting along, when suddenly differences arise and conflict ensues. Of course, as we said in our discussion on building consensus, conflict is usually good. Conflict is what we experience through the process of interpersonal discovery. Ever had a fight with your significant other? Of course you have; who hasn't? Usually after a fight you feel closer and have a deeper sense of understanding for each other, right? The Internet is the same way. Sometimes, though, communications break down and someone must intervene. The Electronic Minds model is a great framework for a policy for dealing with potential problems.

The Rules Of The Road

*At the Electric Minds Web site (**www.minds.com**), the moderators typically take a "hands off" approach to conflict resolution. However, when necessary, Rules of the Road are in place to show new users how to deal with conflict. Here they are:*

"We believe that freedom of expression is important and censoring should be avoided when at all possible. We also recognize that tensions inevitably arise online and from time to time inflammatory topics surface. Keep in mind that it is possible to disagree civilly. Hosts will make every effort to deal with these tensions, and encourage all users to participate in conferences and discussions peaceably. We hope that you, our subscribers, will create discussions about appropriate norms. If instances arise where the norms the group creates are not sufficient, if modeling good communication fails, and if email fails, we will pull accounts. This last strategy is something we take seriously and never do lightly—it is because of our commitment to maintaining a community where people can have conversations.

"We provide conferences in the Virtual Community Center to discuss the craft and art of online conversation. We believe in the axiom "tools, not rules," so rather than tell you what to do, we give you the ability to do things, and let you decide how and when to do them. For example, we provide you with the "bozo filter," which you can use to make the words of a specific user disappear from your view without censoring them. Please visit our Help conference to learn how to use this tool and for other information about navigating the Electric Minds interface.

> *"Your messages are your words, and you are responsible for them, as well as your overall behavior as a member of the Electric Minds community. As a member of the Electric Minds community, you agree not to post messages that, or to use Electric Minds to, harass, solicit, threaten, or impersonate any other person or that disrupt the dialogue in the Electric Minds community. In addition, you agree not to post messages that violate other persons' intellectual property, privacy or other rights. Electric Minds reserves the right to remove or hide any message from the site, and to block or terminate any user account, for any reason."*

AGITATORS, MALCONTENTS, AND MISCREANTS

There are a lot of troublemakers out there! But they don't have to be a problem. Most troublemakers start out by reacting to legitimate concerns, but sooner or later frustration takes over. Understanding this may help you and your leaders weed out the "merely fed up" from the true deviants, and take care of potential problems before they erupt.

Here are some truly troubled beings to watch out for.

Psychotics

These folks can be a real pain in the avatar. They enjoy tormenting and threatening others, they use foul language, and they're generally hurtful toward other guests. Interestingly, this type of behavior is one of the easier ones to deal with, since it's so effortless to identify. You'll want to try reasoning with them at first (it's only fair), but if they continue, just kick 'em out.

Rabble Rousers

Folk heros to some and obnoxious jerks to others, these Net citizens have an opinion about everything, will never admit they're wrong, and think you're a moron. Guess what? The Rabble Rouser could turn out to be your best friend. With someone like this providing seemingly endless rants on every topic im-aginable, many Net citizens keep coming back just to read what's been posted by him or her.

However, there can be a downside. If your Rabble-Rousing guest becomes too abusive, it could cause others to make a beeline for the exit. At this point, dealing with this person becomes a challenge. They'll debate you about free speech, individual liberty, and so on, and they might even have a point. But always remember, it's your party and you're in charge.

On the other hand, there might be a silver lining here: If you can convince your Rabble Rouser to accept your vision of community standards and agree to conduct himself or herself accordingly, you might have a great candidate for community leader. Ask the prolific poster to write a weekly column for your Web page and/or newsletter, and then to act as moderator for lively discussion groups. Who knows, this just might be your diamond in the rough.

Political Paranoids

You know them. You probably think they're cranks, but they know you're part of the secret Illuminati, bent on world domination. Furthermore, they know who killed Kennedy, where the alien bodies are, and exactly what's in the tap water. They're usually harmless, even friendly, often fascinating—and from what we can tell, they might even be right. But sometimes their paranoia gets the better of them, and you're left dealing with a unique type of Rabble Rouser. Can you turn them into community leaders? Maybe, maybe not. You'll just have to get to know them and use your best judgment. But remember these words to the wise—if they don't trust you, you can't trust them.

The Mischievous Child

The presence of children online can be a problem. In the freedom of the online environment, kids can act out and be generally obnoxious; after all, naughty words and obstinate behavior can be really fun. Children shouldn't be confused with psychotics. Since you can't physically see that the guest is, in fact, a child, it can be easy to make that mistake.

When a child is acting out, they're typically looking for attention and validation. Rather than being aggressive, try to engage them in conversations about topics that interest them. Make them feel welcome, and in turn they will feel valued. Children usually treat others with respect when they themselves are treated that way.

Breathers

Some folks see these people as perverts, deviants, and just plain rude. Sometimes that's true. "Breathers" refers to people who proposition other members during chat sessions. This can be construed as sexual harassment, and if it gets to that point, don't tolerate it. Usually though, Breathers are harmless and will stop their behavior when asked to. Psychotic Breathers, on the other hand, are persistent and should not be tolerated at all.

New From AOL

Members from America Online bring a different culture with them. For example, on AOL it's considered normal and acceptable to spout questions like these to other members:

* Age/sex check

* Any ladies (or men) wanna cyber?

* Got any GIFs to trade?

Adult fantasy role-playing, which AOL is famous (or notorious) for, is typically harmless fun. It isn't everyone's cup of tea, but we don't think it's inherently unhealthy or unnatural. Out on the Internet, however, AOL conventions are usually considered rude, not to mention rather pointless when you want to stimulate engaging conversation—and not to stimulate something else.

When it comes to the sexually explicit kind of play that some adults like to take part in online, if the community in question is for adults, then let them play. But be sure they understand that they must be respectful of others and stay within the guidelines of the community. On IRC and some Palace sites, users can set up private chat rooms. Consider adding privacy features to afford guests and members a high level of comfort when they talk about sensitive topics or engage in provocative interplay.

Sleepers

This behavior is specific to realtime chat. Sleepers (also known as lurkers) are users who have walked away from their computers without disconnecting from the chat area. Sleepers are completely unresponsive, and for the most part, should simply be ignored.

Four Habits Of Highly Annoying People

There are roughly a billion things that can really annoy the average virtual community leader. Here are four of them.

Flaming

To "flame" is to attack other members with insulting messages. Unfortunately, this behavior is all too common, especially in forums where the topic is controversial and members resort to nasty name-calling. There are a few communities out there that thrive on flames, and there are newsgroups on Usenet that are devoted to flaming, but generally, it's counterproductive. Sometimes, however, it can be part of healthy conflict. Before you intervene, wait to see if the flamers stop on their own. Every situation will be different. Some thick-skinned netizens can take the abuse (a few even relish it), others cannot. It's dicey, and you'll have to play it by ear. Through experience, you'll know when to intervene.

Remedies to consider:

- Send a private message to the culprits, reminding them of the membership guidelines and firmly requesting that they desist.

- Get involved yourself, using diplomatic language to convince the combatants in a flame war to cease the personal attacks and get back on topic with constructive and nonabusive expressions.

Spamming

Spamming is posting or sending aimless messages, or unsolicited commercial messages, repeatedly. Spam is the Internet equivalent of junk mail, and in virtual communities, it is a cardinal sin. Quite simply, there's no justifiable type of spam— ever. Don't tolerate it. Mailing lists are especially susceptible to spammers.

Remedies to consider:

- Keep an eye on your mailing list, eliminating any dreaded spam before it ever gets to your members' servers.

- Filter, filter, filter. Look for classic indicators in the subject line, like "Make $$$ fast!"

- Write a clear policy against spamming.

- Respond quickly to members of your list who post spam without prior permission. Anyone who posts commercial spam is a snert, and they're interested in their own agenda, not in your community. They can go create their own community.

- If the problem continues, promptly unsubscribe offenders from the mailing list, and banish the member from discussion forums or chat areas. Seems harsh? Just remember, they're spammers, and on the Internet, spammers are the lowest of the low.

- If the user persists, as a last resort you can contact the spammer's Internet Service Provider or email host.

The Vigilante

Some folks have trouble staying on topic in a threaded discussion, but that's pretty natural. Then there are the folks who quote an entire post, only to add, "I agree" at the end. That's pretty annoying. But on top of all the rest, there are the vigilantes, members who write long-winded flames about "spelling" or "netiquette." These vigilantes may have good intentions, but nothing starts a flame war faster than public squabbling over petty stuff. To avoid it, establish that only you or community leaders are responsible for regulating behavior. Encourage members to send complaints to you privately for resolution.

Playing Pranks

Members *will* play pranks on each other. Usually, this is harmless behavior, but occasionally, someone gets hurt feelings. We remember an incident where a child was being chased by a wizard through a Palace site because he was wearing a "nude" prop. The kid had been in the "dress-up prop room" and someone used a script to erase his original avatar and then proceeded to change it to a nude woman. He was young and horrified to be a *girl*! Cooties! Naturally, he fled the room. A wizard, who happened to notice this youngster roaming around with no clothes on, yelled at him to take off the avatar; on his failure to do so, the wizard "killed" the child. After the kid returned from his "death sentence," the community leader asked him what happened. Why didn't he take off the prop when asked? The child replied that he did take it off! Unfortunately, he knew only one way to do so—by grabbing pieces of the prop, one at a time, and dropping them as he fled.

In this case, all's well that ends well, but taking just a moment or two to carefully evaluate a situation will help to avoid misunderstandings like this one. Also, the wizard might want to have a stern chat with the prankster, since his actions upset the child, and we expect that you all agree that dressing a child in a "nude" prop is inappropriate.

Virtual Community Standards

Pornography. Why is a discussion of porn relevant to a book on growing virtual communities? Because it's the hot issue throughout all media in discussions about Internet censorship and standards, and it's the impetus for the notorious Communication Decency Act, and it's the emotional button for those who advocate governmental regulation of Web content, as well as for those who champion the tenets of the First Amendment. Although we occasionally hear complaints about the availability of other kinds of information on the web (such as bomb instructions and racial hate propaganda), most of the rhetoric and brouhaha surrounding virtual community standards have been about pornography. It's no secret that Usenet, Web sites, BBSes, and IRC chat channels are loaded with downloadable graphic files of naked people doing naked things. In a civilization as old as ours, this should hardly be a surprise—after all, titillating pictures are nothing new. Yet there's a newly rekindled push to wipe out porn, based on community standards. What are community standards? Well, we've already defined "community" in Chapter 1. Now, let's take a look at the word "standard."

Webster's New Universal Unabridged Dictionary

Standard: 1) An object considered by an authority or by general consent as a basis of comparison; an approved model. 2) Anything as a rule or principle that is used as a basis for judgment. 3) An average or normal requirement, quality, quantify, level, grade, etc. 4) Standards, those morals ethics, habits, etc., established by authority, custom, or individual as acceptable.

Community standards, in the context in which we'll be using the term, refers to the standards by which a community judges the content of material such as books or movies. Since the introduction of the World Wide Web into mainstream society, critics of online content have tried to apply community standards to Web sites. Historically, community standards have been thought to be relevant specifically to the community in which the material exists. Many online activists argue that the contemporary community standards applied in online cases ought to be determined by the online community. This has yet to happen. The laws of communities in meatspace are being applied to cyberspace, yet in the virtual world, unlike its corporeal counterpart, there are no geographic boundaries, no physical proximity of citizens, and no clear-cut governmental jurisdiction.

ACROSS STATE LINES

The real question concerning the Internet and pornography (or any content, for that matter) is who is in charge, and who can apply what standards to whom? You know that as you surf the Web, you may find a link to an adult photography site, and if you follow it, you'll see naked women and men on your computer screen. As impractical to enforce as it may be, looking at pictures of naked women and men might be against local regulations in your small community in rural Mississippi, even though the site originates in New York City. Obviously, one little community can't push its restrictive policy on the rest of the world. Or can it?

United States V. Thomas, 1996

The obscenity prosecution of Robert and Carleen Thomas seems pretty straightforward at first. The Thomases are the system operators of an adults-only, sexually-oriented BBS ("Amateur Action BBS") in Milpitas, California. Not to be daunted by geography, Tennessee prosecutors went after them in a precedent-setting online obscenity case. The prosecution of the Thomases and their "Amateur Action BBS" calls into question the continuing validity of the Supreme Court's obscenity decision in *Miller v. California* (1973). That case has allowed communities to set their own standards of obscenity, but now is being used for just the opposite purpose. It allowed a Memphis prosecutor to dictate the content of a computer system in California.

A Tennessee postal inspector, working with an assistant U.S. attorney in Memphis, joined the Amateur Action BBS and did three things there: he downloaded sexually oriented images; he ordered a videotape (which was delivered via UPS); and he sent an unsolicited child-porn video to the Thomases. The Thomases were then charged with a dozen obscenity counts in a federal indictment.

The indictment included a child-pornography count, based on the unsolicited video, but they were cleared on this count due to the obvious entrapment. At trial, unfortunately, the Memphis jury convicted the Thomases on the remaining 11 obscenity counts, each carrying a maximum sentence of five years in prison and $250,000 in fines.

The Thomases are in appeal as of this writing, claiming that the jury instructions as to "community standards" were incorrect. Their lawyer commented that "this case would never have gone to trial in California."

OBSCENITY

Obscenity on the Internet is a sticky subject. The courts have long held that obscenity is not protected by the First Amendment. After *Miller v. California*, the landmark 1973 Supreme Court case, there's been no national standard as to what is obscene (not that there was any such standard before, either). The Court, in their decision, stated that material is "obscene" if 1) the average person, applying contemporary community standards, would find that the materials, taken as a whole, arouse immoral lustful desire (prurient interest), 2) the materials depict or describe, in a patently offensive way, sexual conduct specifically prohibited by applicable state law, and 3) the work, taken as a whole, lacks serious literary, artistic, political, or scientific value.

If it failed to pass muster on those criteria, the material would be judged obscene, and it would then be constitutional to prosecute someone for distributing it. Ironically, pictures from magazines like *Playboy* and *Penthouse* are never found to be obscene. "Pornography" and "obscenity" are not identical categories, and much pornography is not legally obscene. The ACLU actively promotes the idea that all speech, regardless of content, is protected by the First Amendment. They contend that law is "viewpoint-neutral" and that, in spite of the wishy-washy test for "legal obscenity," all pornography is protected. Beyond this, they argue that failure to protect porn, which may be society's basest form of expression, will foster a political air of tolerance toward the censoring of other types of speech.

GAGGED AND BOUND

Censorship can be an emotional topic, and at some point, almost every virtual community grapples with it. We've seen how some communities handle it already, as in the case of The WELL's philosophy, which stated that you own your words and you take responsibility for them. Sometimes, when the debate over censorship gets heated and objectivity gets lost, we lose sight of what "censorship" actually means. And we often forget the legal meaning of the First Amendment to the Constitution of the United States, which states that "Congress shall make no law abridging the freedom of speech." That means that government may not curtail speech in any way, shape, or form.

Does allowing full-fledged freedom of speech apply to you in terms of managing your own community? Not necessarily. In your virtual community, you may be (if you wish) the final arbiter of the appropriateness of speech, because you are a private citizen with a privately held community. However, be aware that when it comes to issues of libel and defamation, court decisions have thus far failed to establish who is actually responsible for content. Is it you? Or is it the virtual citizen who posted the words? At this point, it's anyone's guess. So be careful. The problem is compounded when you consider that every country, state, and city has its own set of laws and standards. What you say from your apartment in Detroit could have legal ramifications in Mobile, Alabama.

However, the prevailing Internet wisdom is that the free exchange of information and ideas is of paramount importance. It's been said that the Internet sees censorship as a defect and routes around it. This infuriates some special interests because, like it or not, there's really no effective way to stop the free exchange of information from a technical point of view. You can prosecute people, and employ other legal methods to try to control Internet behavior, but the technology will not allow you to police the whole Web. Legal attempts to prohibit so-called "obscenity," like The Communications Decency Act, (see sidebar) have resulted in high-profile court battles, and the dust has yet to settle, nor is it likely to anytime soon. Web-blocking software like NetNanny and SurfWatch, intended to allow parents to block access to pornography from their children, has already failed to provide technological solutions, as software that disables the site-blockers can be downloaded from the Net and used by anyone. You can expect more court battles to begin soon.

Karla Gets Indecent Over The Communications Decency Act (CDA)

*You've probably heard a lot of people in the media discussing the CDA. Or you've seen the scads of little blue ribbons protesting it pasted over many a Web page. I headed over to the Electronic Frontier Foundation's (EFF) Web site (**www.eff.org**) and down-loaded a copy to read for myself.*

The language in the CDA is very vague. Senator James Exon (D-Nebraska), who proposed the bill, uses extremely broad definitions to describe what isn't acceptable. Any material deemed "filthy" or "indecent" would be in violation of the CDA. This could be extended include such content as classic works of literature, medical information, or educational materials on breast cancer or sexually transmitted diseases. Even the King James bible wouldn't be immune! It uses the word "piss"—a word which the Supreme Court has already deemed indecent. Strangely enough, obscenity law considers literary, artistic, or scientific merit, but indecency law does not. But don't take my word for it, read the snippet below:

TITLE V - SEC. 502. OBSCENE OR HARASSING USE OF TELECOMMUNICATIONS FACILITIES UNDER THE COMMUNICATIONS ACT OF 1934.

Section 223 (47 U.S.C. 223) is amended-

"(a) Whoever -

"(1) in interstate or foreign communications-

"(A) by means of a telecommunications device knowingly-

"(i) makes, creates, or solicits, and

"(ii) initiates the transmission of, any comment, request, suggestion, proposal, image, or other communication which is obscene, lewd, lascivious, filthy, or indecent, with intent to annoy, abuse, threaten, or harass another person;

The penalties for violating the CDA are stiff, including jail time and large monetary fines. The EFF believes, and I agree, that it will set off a tidal wave of censorship to "avoid real and perceived liability." Content developers, perhaps fearing prosecution, may opt to remove any "questionable" material.

In June 1996, after a lawsuit was filed by the American Civil Liberties Union and the American Library Association, a federal court issued a preliminary injunction barring enforcement of the law.

Todd Is A Bit Puzzled About Prodigy

Someone posted an anonymous message to a threaded discussion on Prodigy called Money Talk, which covered financial issues. This poster wrote that the securities investment banking firm of Stratton Oakmont, Inc., had committed criminal and fraudulent acts in connection with an initial public offering of stock for Solomon-Page LTD.

Was it true? Probably not. Only Stratton Oakmont knows for sure. Still, they sued Prodigy and on May 24, 1995, the New York Supreme Court ruled that Prodigy could be held responsible for potentially slanderous and libel statements on their online service. Essentially, they were made to be responsible for the words of their community members; since they had editorial control over the message threads, they were found to be liable for the slander (if it was slander).

This sent a chilling message to the online world. First, it bolstered the notion that it is content providers who are responsible for the actions of their customers, and not the customers themselves, thus making the providers actual publishers of information, not mere distributors.

The problem for virtual community leaders is that they can't be sure, when they want to offer a forum for free expression of ideas, whether they actually can offer that, or whether they'll have to edit and censor material to avoid lawsuits. Different court cases have come down with different results, adding to the confusion. It makes you wonder about the true cost of free speech.

Will Your Community Censor Speech?

But what about you? Should you censor? Well, if you expect to include children in your community, it probably goes without saying that you shouldn't allow strong language, sexual imagery, or hateful speech to prevail. We doubt that any reasonable person would object to such a policy. But, if your community caters to adults and say, politics, then censoring speech that supports a position contrary to your own, just because you disagree, will be viewed with scorn. Oh yes, you can do it, but if you want your community to last, don't.

The Arguments For And Against Absolute Freedom

The Palace, Inc., hosts a newsgroup to provide a forum for expressing viewpoints on what constitutes acceptable and unacceptable behavior in social cyberspace. What is offensive? How should it be handled? Should it be handled? Who should handle it?

A vocal opponent of wizard powers on the Palace blasted the readers of the Palace community standards newsgroup with his view of the "fascist" quality of wizards and house rules:

"I did not mean to be petty about my concern for wizardry. Some policing is necessary in any community. Nevertheless, the repressive and idiosyncratic application of wizard power in [The Palace, Inc.'s] Main Palace is inimical to the development of a spirited community behavior. When the history of the Palace is written, the history will have a major blotch. And the current wizards will be remembered as the Thought Police. Or, the KGB. Or, the CIA. Repressive and subversive organizations in any society."

This person obviously feels that they've experienced some censorship. Most likely they were barred from The Main Palace site for behavior that a Wizard considered to be "out of line." Some users have complained that The Palace doesn't offer degrees of control for wizard power; every wizard has all the power afforded to any other wizard. This is seen by many as a flaw in the Palace design, and we agree. The IRC model allows channel ops to assign varying degrees of authority to other ops, and this allows for an evenhanded distribution of power. Perhaps future upgrades of Palace server and client software will allow gods to selectively assign powers to wizards. This would allow gods to keep a handle on inexperienced wizards who sometimes overstep their bounds and try to enforce Palace rules too zealously.

For another point of view, we found a Webmaster and longtime Palace user who disagreed with the disgruntled Palace user:

"Think of the Main Palace as an "athletic or members-only club." Basically, it has a set of rules that its members must follow. These rules are clearly defined by saying "house rules" on sign-on at the gate, or you can visit ***http://newbie.thepalace.com/A600.html#3.8*** *and see the specific listings of these rules.*

"In either case, just as the "club staff" may ask you to leave, so may any of the wizards. Granted, "killing" a user makes a harsher tone than asking someone to leave, but the end result is the same. There are countless other Palaces you can frequent and choose to call your Palace home.

"The job of the wizards on the Main Palace site is to…enforce the rules that the corporation, The Palace, Inc., set forth. The Palace, Inc., is a private corporation, and may set whatever rules it wants on its Palace. Obviously, the choice of the rules, and the ways that they're enforced, has a direct result upon its success as a company, however, (excuse me for being frank) the bottom line is, you have to follow the rules."

The idea that the Internet is the last bastion of purely free expression is central to why many netizens have ventured out into cyberspace. As czar of your own community, you can circumvent potential problems by being very clear when you post your community standards. If you want to forbid profanity, for example, say so right up front; otherwise, when you reprimand a virtual citizen for using strong language, you'll anger more than a few community members.

It's not our intention to scare folks here, but if you're not aware of the potential dangers, you could run head first into a serious legal obstacle. Remember, censorship, obscenity, liability, and standards on the Internet are not about right and wrong, rather they are about the law, which often seems to have nothing to do with right and wrong. The law has yet to catch up with the virtual world, and at the present rate it's unlikely to catch up for a long time. Court decisions in cases covering all aspects of online communications have come down on every side imaginable, so predicting what will happen next is not much more than a dice game. Another word to the wise: Keep yourself informed about law related to speech issues and censorship. The following resources will be able to provide you with excellent resources and current information.

MORE INFORMATION ABOUT CENSORSHIP

Electronic Frontier Foundation (**www.eff.org**)

Why Censoring Cyberspace Is Dangerous & Futile (**www.well.com/user/hlr/tomorrow/tomorrowcensor.html**)

Would-Be Censors Base Arguments On Bogus Research (**www.well.com/user/hlr/tomorrow/cyberporn.html**)

The White House: The Last Stop Before The Censorship State (**www.well.com/user/hlr/tomorrow/clintonveto.html**)

Yahoo Index To Censorship (**www.yahoo.com/Society_and_Culture/Civil_Rights/Censorship/Censorship_and_the_Net/**)

Building A Fort Around Your Community

You've planted a flag, built a town hall, and settlers are moving in. But the Internet is a wild and sometimes dangerous place, and you need to prepare yourself for the dangers that might be lurking out there. You'll also want to be ready for the day when you might need to circle the wagons. Get ready, we're talking legal stuff here.

LAW AND ORDER ON THE NEW FRONTIER

You'll want to contact your own legal counsel, perhaps even keep him or her on retainer, if you plan on building a big community. As we mentioned before, Internet law is tricky and unpredictable. A good and trustworthy lawyer is a valuable asset. Here are a few issues that we thought were important to broach. It's very important to consider ownership and other intellectual property issues when designing your community. Remember, the Internet is relatively new, and so is the body of case law that deals with it. Be sure to interview a prospective lawyer carefully to ensure that they have a keen understanding of this new medium. A good lawyer without Internet experience should tell you up front that he or she lacks the appropriate experience.

Trademark Issues

Before selecting a domain name and an address for your community, and especially before you invest resources in making others aware of your address, you should conduct a trademark-availability search to determine if your address is acceptable from a trademark perspective. Domain names are registered through InterNIC (**rs.internic.net**); however, InterNIC will not test your choice of domain name for possible trademark infringements, so if you have the forms filled out right, you'll get your name regardless of such encroachment. Consequently, you need to be sure you aren't infringing on a registered trademark before you register your name. Consult your attorney if you need help with this aspect. If you do manage to violate a trademark, InterNIC does have a dispute resolution policy in place: They will determine whether your domain predates the trademark, and if it does, you keep it (or sell it, if you choose), but if it doesn't, there are a variety of contingencies that may be enacted. Check the InterNIC Web site for complete details.

Your domain name isn't all you have to worry about. You're likely to use logos, which are also considered trademarks or service marks. Again, it's essential to determine if any marks or symbols you intend to use on your community are, in fact, available for use. To protect yourself in the future, you'll also want to consider filing federal trademark or service mark applications for any existing and proposed marks that you intend to use with your virtual community.

Ownership

Your community has many parts, each of which may be owned by a different person or group. For example, if the room art at your Palace site has been designed for you by various netizens, you'll want to consider who owns that art. Is it yours? Is it the artists? Do you need a contract? It may seem silly to think about, but many of the most successful online communities and Web services started out as side projects or whims, then got corporate sponsorship. If you hit the big time, those fine folks who designed your art, logos, etc., may come knocking at your door demanding cold hard cash. If you've worked this possibility out with them before-hand, and have a contract, then all concerned parties will be better off. It's tempting to scoff at contracts and lawyers. You might be thinking, these are my friends, we can work this out. Don't fall into that trap. Friendship is friendship, business is business, and good contracts will save your friendship if anything ever goes wrong in business.

There are three separate elements that the law firm of Faegre & Benson LLP (**www.faegre.com**) suggests are part of the question of content ownership:

- The content, which refers to the textual, graphical, audio, and other material that is displayed on and used by visitors to your site.

- The "look and feel" of the interface, namely the screens, organization, patterns, operational control features, and the like.

- The coding, which refers to the computer instructions that operate the Web pages, Palace site, or Black Sun chat rooms, and that generate the content and the look and feel.

You'll need to determine who has rights to which elements. The greater the level of ownership you're looking for, the more you'll probably have to pay for it. As a general rule, whoever created the marks, logos, or content associated with your community owns all the copyright to it, unless you have a written agree-ment stating otherwise. Always, always, always (we can't stress this enough), *always* consult a lawyer when dealing with complex or even simple contracts for these rights.

HACKERS

While most incidents of hacking will probably not affect the members of your community as more than an inconvenience, hacking is perceived as being a grow-ing problem. As network security becomes more sophisticated, techniques for locating hackers and tracking their activities have become equally sophisticated. Knowing how to track hackers, implement sophisticated network security, and install firewalls takes a lot of education and experience. Fortunately, the high quality ISP that you chose after reading Chapter 3 already has excellent security, and can provide you with a lot of guidance for additional precautions. If you'd like detailed information about your personal online security, well that could fill a book. This book, in fact: *Web Psychos, Stalkers, And Pranksters; How To Protect Yourself In Cyberspace* by Michael A. Banks (The Coriolis Group, 1997, ISBN: 1-57610-137-1).

You Can Check Your Guests' IPs

With the Palace software, a user may change his or her avatar or nick-name for a number of reasons, many of them perfectly valid. But if they've done so to cause trouble, you can still identify them. If the troublemaker logs on from the same PC as they usually do, a wizard or god will be able to discern the true identity by looking at the IP address of the user. In the Palace client's Input Box (where you would normally type messages), type '**list <name>**. In the log window (see Figure 14.2), you'll see the name of the guest, the domain gateway information, and the IP address.

Despite claims to the contrary, not all hackers do bad things. Many are just looking around to learn or for the challenge of it. However, some hackers cause serious damage to networks. Those who do so with malice are called "crackers," although you might notice that media reports tend to lump all types of hackers together as if they were all the scourge of the earth. While actual hacker damage is relatively rare, hacker infiltration can result in stolen user passwords and other sensitive data. Here's a story about one such incident.

News! Hacker Invades The WELL

Sausalito, California, U.S.A., 1997 Mar 20 (Newsbytes)
By Patrick McKenna

Early this week, the legendary online community called The WELL was hacked by an unknown perpetrator. This latest case involving password theft and some deleted data may have occurred over several months.

According to WELL officials, the incident involved no exposure of credit-card information or copies of documents such as electronic

```
*** ; n Guest 665 mpa183.axionet.com
(207.102.220.183) Guest Generator 1
*** Page from Guest 669 in Firebird's Forest: I
have arrived
```

Figure 14.2 Identifying a user by IP address.

mail. Identification of the problem did send the company into long hours of examining the system and determining exactly what occurred.

Additionally, WELL members have been advised to change their passwords, a task most online services and Internet service providers routinely recommend. In a letter to members, WELL President Maria Wilhelm stated, "This has been one of the more difficult security investigations we've had to deal with in the last several years."

Newsbytes spoke to Saul Feldman, a host of several conferences on the WELL. "This is probably not big news to WELL members," said Feldman. "It doesn't affect me personally. I have changed my password, but go right on with my conferences."

Feldman said The WELL is so highly recognized in the electronic community that the service is a likely target for hackers. "Because The WELL is a liberal sort of place and a lot of people speak out and express their opinions openly, it easily becomes a target for disgruntled people or hackers just wanting to get in so they can say they did," he added.

As mentioned before, not all hackers are bad. This famous post is from a virtual community mailing list in defense of hackers. It has actually appeared all over the Net, and its origin is unknown.

The Hacker Manifesto

I am a hacker, enter my world...Mine is a world that begins with school...I'm smarter than most of the other kids, this crap they teach us bores me...Damn underachiever. They're all alike. I'm in junior high or high school. I've listened to teachers explain for the fifteenth time how to reduce a fraction. I understand it. "No, Ms. Smith, I didn't show my work. I did it in my head." Damn kid. Probably copied it. They're all alike.

I made a discovery today. I found a computer. Wait a second, this is cool. It does what I want it to. If it makes a mistake, it's because I screwed it up. Not because it doesn't like me…Or feels threatened by me…Or thinks I'm a smart ass…Or doesn't like teaching and shouldn't be here…Damn kid. All he does is play games. They're all alike. And then it happened—a door opened to a world, rushing through the phone line like heroin through an addict's veins, an electronic pulse is sent out, a refuge from the day-to-day incompetents is sought; a board is found. "This is it. This is where I belong." I know everyone here, even if I've never met them, never talked to them, may never hear from them again. I know you all. Damn kid. Tying up the phone line again.

They're all alike…You bet your ass we're all alike. We've been spoon-fed baby food at school when we hungered for steak; the bits of meat that you did let slip through were pre-chewed and tasteless. We've been dominated by sadists, or ignored by the apathetic. The few that had something to teach found us willing pupils, but those few are like drops of water in the desert.

This is our world now…the world of the electron and the switch, the beauty of the baud. We make use of a service already existing without paying for what could be dirt-cheap if it wasn't run by profiteering gluttons, and you call us criminals. We explore, and you call us criminals.

We seek after knowledge…and you call us criminals. We exist without skin color, without nationality, without religious bias…and you call us criminals. You build atomic bombs, you wage wars, you murder, cheat, and lie to us and try to make us believe it's for our own good, yet we're the criminals.

Yes, I am a criminal. My crime is that of curiosity. My crime is that of judging people by what they say and think, not what they look like. My crime is that of outsmarting you, something that you will

*never forgive me for. I am a hacker, and this is my manifesto. You may
stop this individual, but you can't stop us all…after all, we're all alike.*

+++The Mentor+++

Mistakes Other Communities Have Made

Managers make mistakes. Even good managers make mistakes. There is nothing
unusual about that—after all, managers are human. Sometimes, though, really
huge mistakes get made. When bad mistakes happen to good managers, the net
result is that you get to read about it and learn from it.

APPLE EVICTS TENANTS OF eWORLD

Even large companies can stumble. Let's look at eWorld. It seemed like a great idea
when Apple first decided to launch their own online service in 1994. The interface
used a "town square" metaphor, with buildings and objects resembling Main
Street, USA, which made eWorld stand out as a well-organized and navigable
community. Its offbeat look and feel, shown in Figure 14.3, helped build a strong

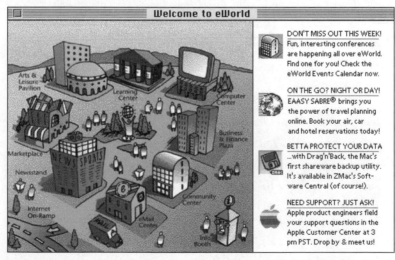

Figure 14.3   The interface of eWorld was charming and built a sense of community.

sense of community. But nearly two years later, Gil Amelio, CEO of Apple, permanently padlocked the doors. How did this come about?

First, Apple could have made some smarter management decisions. Their inaugural strategic mistake occurred when Apple decided to license the software, Rainman, that operates America Online. (See how important it is to select the right tools for your community toolbox?) The AOL software was an albatross. It hung heavily around the necks of the eWorld management team. Apple's promises of cutting-edge tools never happened. Worse, primary bugs in the client software were never fixed.

Next, eWorld didn't differentiate itself from established services such as America Online. Of course, Apple tried bundling the service with its Performa line of desktop products, in the hopes of acquiring home- and small-office users. But users who did log on were faced with "Empty World," rather than a thriving environment. The management team of eWorld did a poor job of "seeding" the community with members who would hang out in chat rooms or post messages on the discussion forums. (Remember the success story of The WELL in Chapter 3?) There's nothing as disappointing to a new member as the feeling that they're strolling about in a ghost town.

Finally, in March 1996, Apple closed the doors to eWorld forever.

After Apple management pulled the plug on eWorld, Apple sent out unclear and often confusing messages. First, they claimed that eWorld was a victim of the Internet, and that it would move most of its eWorld content over to the Web. In a later decision, Amelio decided that eWorld was not a strong, standalone brand, and content would move over to the Apple Internet site in order to "greatly expand Apple's presence on the Web." Did the eWorld community flock to Apple's Web site? That may be debated, but after examining the plethora of eWorld-survivor pages that proliferate the Web, we have our doubts. To this day, hordes of ex-eWorlders post messages in their own Web-generated communities.

Ex-eWorlders Speak Out

"Computer technology has allowed us to form some fulfilling relationships. eWorld supplied a medium for our relationships to

grow and prosper. From the good-natured teasing of Batteredbull and Pupper to the wit of LTG and Cerebral, from the educational discussions with ATooke to the warm, caring, dear friend Joydancer, it has been a grand experiment. It is a community of individuals who have been torn apart by corporate policies. But alas, we all have other lives outside of eWorld that need to come to the front of our consciousness. We are losing the chance to address our relationship imperative, but we will all find another way to keep in touch, because we share that basic need of humans; to interact with others and continue to build relationships."

Yet another ex-eWorlder:

"I cannot tell you what being on eWorld has meant to me. I have made so many friends here, and I hate it that we are losing our home. Some of you have made me laugh, some of you have let me cry on your shoulder, and most of you have just sat there and listened to me vent about one thing or another. There are some of you who have helped me and encouraged me through some very difficult times here lately, and you know who you are, and I can't thank you enough. You have all made me feel as if I belonged, right from the start, and that is not an easy thing to do. You have all touched my life and heart in one way or another, and I will never forget this experience or any of you."

And one final ex-eWorlder:

"It's the end of eWorld as we know it,
It's the end of eWorld as we know it,
It's the end of eWorld as we know it—And I feel fine."

What Is The Lesson?

It really comes down to this: Strategic planning is vital to the growth and sustenance of every community.

ALL'S NOT WELL IN THE WELL

Even the most successful communities have their problems. From an immense article called "The World's Most Influential Online Community (And It's Not AOL)" by Katie Hafner (*Wired*, May 1997), we learned about Tom Mandel. At The WELL, Mandel, one of their most celebrated leaders, was also a huge thorn in their side. Mandel was one of the most prolific members of the online community, and he was extremely outrageous. He hosted a lively and heavily visited forum called "Future." This WELL member was notorious for his love affair online (and off) with "Nana" and for the long, drawn out, painful break up that followed. At the end of his life, he wrote his death tome on The WELL as he was dying of lung cancer. He was a technical guru, a futurist with a heady think tank, who typed over 100 words a minute, posted to every topic dozens of times daily, got in your face, up close and personal, and could attack with animal vengeance. And he was as well-loved as he was hated.

He may have been a loose cannon, but that didn't stop The WELL from adding Mandel to the community's Board of Directors. He had free reign over the servers and archives of The WELL, including the power to "kill" messages and posts, thereby eradicating them from WELL history. Unfortunately, he abused his power, most notably by "killing" posts from Nana as well as others, and when he was informed that he was to be suspended from The WELL for these actions, he permanently erased the entire archive of the "Future" forum and a topic called "Weird" as well.

The damage was done, and there was nothing anyone could do about it. Mandel was removed. The madness ended, and after a few days, his return was negotiated. But he returned to a reduced set of powers, and the threat of permanent excommunication hung over his head until the day he died.

In all fairness to the late Tom Mandel, whose life was rich, vivid, and tumultuous, he was inspired insanity, and despite his near freakish dips into the abyss, he managed to contribute greatly to the mythic legend of The WELL's history. We never knew him, but from what we have learned from the archives, the accounts of his capers, and madness of his darker side, we know he is missed.

What Is The Lesson?

Power must be assigned reasonably with checks and balances in place to stop abuse.

Mayday...We're Going Down...

If all else fails, have a crisis plan ready. Planning for response to crises has a side benefit for management. It poses the following questions: How well are we prepared to deal with this? What can we do to minimize the possibility of it happening?

Policy deficiencies become apparent when you rehearse what you would say after a hypothetical crisis has occurred. When a CEO, for example, realizes that he would have nothing to say about corporate policy in response to, say, a hypothetical workplace violence situation, that realization is likely to result in some changes.

The other advantage of a crisis communication plan is that it buys time for management to formulate a more comprehensive explanation. Remarks made in the heat of battle more often than not will come back to haunt you if you don't know what to say before the crisis ever occurs. Stress reduces your field of vision, and limits the options you are able to perceive. In the midst of a crisis, you simply don't see alternatives that may be obvious in a less stressful planning environment.

PLACE PARACHUTES BY THE ESCAPE HATCHES

What, then, can you do to develop a workable crisis communications plan? Here are some tips that will get you started:

- Have a predetermined plan for your community leaders to contact each other in the event of a crisis. In the meatspace world of telephones and pagers, this is an easy task to accomplish. In fact, it's probably be a good idea for your leaders to have a phone contact list available. But if each of your leaders are Web surfing and has only one phone line at his or her disposal, what do you do?

The Emergency Broadcast System

A close friend of ours, Kelly, is a community leader at a popular digital hangout. One night while "off duty," she received this urgent email message as she was surfing around the Web:

Subject: URGENT!!!!!!

OH NO!! SOMEONE PLEASE COME QUICK!! SOMEONE NAMED 'WHO-AM-I' JUST ENTERED THE WIZARD PASSWORD!!! I DON'T KNOW WHO THIS PERSON IS!!! I WASN'T ABLE TO GET HIS/HER IP ADDRESS!!! HELLPPP…

The ALL CAPS message indicated panic. Immediately, Kelly responded by logging on to the site. Here's a transcript of the conversation (names have been changed to protect the innocent) between herself and the other wizards who rushed to the scene:

***Kelly's Message to "Experienced Wizard": **Everything ok?**

***Experienced Wizard: **heheh. Hi Kelly. Hope you aren't checking out Who-am-i, also :)))**

***Page from Kelly: **I just got an urgent email from "Newbie Wizard"**

***Page from Experienced Wizard: **Hey Kelly, it was just "Undercover Wizard" logging on in disguise.**

***Page from Undercover Wizard: **Yeah, I shoulda warned everyone. I checked in anonymously to see what was up when no wizards were around :))**

This scenario turned out well enough—the "threat" was not real. But what if it had been? How would you mobilize your comm-unity leaders? First, try scheduling regular hours. Obviously if your community is a volunteer effort, enforcing this may prove difficult.

- Another option is to use a tool like ICQ that allows community leaders to page each other while on the Internet. ICQ (I Seek You) (**www.mirabilis.com**) is an Internet application that tells you who's online at all times and enables you to contact people whenever you wish. It's like a pager, but it also performs personal chat and FTP duties for you. When you install ICQ and register at an ICQ server, you receive a unique UIN (User Identification Number). This allows other ICQ users to recognize you when you log on. Once you've registered, you can compile a list of friends and associates, which ICQ uses to find your friends for you. It's a useful tool, and it's free!

- Have a spokesperson ready, and a prepared initial statement for the most probable scenarios.

- Respond promptly; don't stonewall. Even if you find that you're endlessly repeating yourself, respond to all queries.

- Don't speak in absolutes before all the facts are absolutely in. *Do not ignore this warning!* If you do, you'll end up retracting statements later, which damages your credibility.

- Review your crisis communications plan regularly. The news of a traumatic event in another venue can serve as a catalyst for the question, "How would we deal with this?" A 10- or 15-minute discussion among you and your community leaders can help you decide if additions or changes to the crisis communications plan are warranted.

- It's a good idea to have your spokesperson(s) receive some presentation skills training. It doesn't do much good to have a great plan all laid out, but to blow it in the moment of crisis with poor delivery. You want a good public speaker with a friendly outward appearance to fill this role.

I'm All Done, Right?

Are you kidding? You've planned it, you've built it, you've marketed it, and with this chapter, you've staffed it and protected it. You're just beginning! Aside from embarking on the wondrous journey into a long lasting and exciting virtual community, you'll probably want to make some money on your venture. In the next chapter, we're going to look at how to make money with your community. It can be done, and while not every community is going to be as successful as big virtual hotspots like HotWired, The WELL, or GeoCities, many will be, and yours might be one of them.

Part 5

The
Future

Chapter 15

Looking Into The Future
Of Virtual Communities

Chapter 15

- THE FUTURE OF THE INTERNET

- THE FUTURE OF VIRTUAL COMMUNITIES

- THE FUTURE OF HUMAN/COMPUTER INTERFACES

LOOKING INTO THE FUTURE
OF VIRTUAL COMMUNITIES

Chapter 15

The Big, Bright Future

There is a lot of buzz about future technology, and there are a lot of varied visions. If you're a veteran of the computer age, you know that in technological terms, the future appears on store shelves about every seven days. A few short years ago we were all tooling around with 386sx machines at a blazing 25MHz, and those of us who were "wired" could connect at earth-shattering speeds like 2400Kbps. If you can think back to a day when you connected to a BBS at 300Kbps with a Commodore 64, then you are surely a grandparent among cybercitizens. The words you're reading right now were written on May 1, 1997, on an AMD brand 5 x 86 133MHz (roughly equal to a Pentium 90) PC with 32MB of RAM, using MS Word 95. At the same time, Pointcast was downloading news in the background, and something interesting popped up on the screen from PRNewswire.

PRNewswire Report

Intel plans to roll out its first Pentium II microprocessors with internal clock speeds of 233MHz, 266MHz, and 300MHz on May 7. Second quarter pricing includes drastic cuts to Intel's older chip models, such as the 200MHz Pentium, which will drop 48 percent to $257…Advanced Micro Devices Inc. earlier this month unveiled three versions of its new K-6 chip with clock speeds of 166MHz, 200MHz and 233MHz…Apple Computer Inc. this month unveiled a 300MHz PowerMac system

---

Our once mighty PC is a relic! Unbelievable. As we wrote this, a 200MHz Pentium system was top-of-the-line-hardware. When the book went to press, that same system was considered "entry level" and "low end." Now that the book is in your hands, you may be thinking, "How could they compute with such a barbaric system?" Well, we've got news for you: It isn't going to slow down. That's bad news if you're one of the new breed of cybercommandos who thrive on the adrenaline rush of faster and better gear, because you need to keep shelling out big bucks to stay on top of the industry standard. It's a never-ending cycle.

BABY NEEDS A NEW PAIR OF SHOES

They say the coming information infrastructure will provide the neural network that will begin to get the earth to "think." President Bill Clinton has been calling for "a bridge to the twenty-first century," and pushing to "wire" all public schools to the Internet by the year 2000. Grand ideas, and we support them. We love the Internet. (If we didn't, we'd be writing books about tropical fish or kitchen design.) But before we all fall to our knees, dazzled by this bold new era, let's think about something. There are over six billion people on this planet. More than half of them *do not own a pair of shoes.* Think about that. They don't have shoes. Without shoes, how on earth will they get a telephone, a computer, or a modem, not to mention the fundamental knowledge needed to use these things? And what about phones? Of the six billion planetary citizens, only one-tenth of them have a phone. If information and communication are central to the new economy, how can a majority of the world compete?

We may not be able to tell you exactly what will happen tomorrow, but we do know what won't happen. Tomorrow won't bring a golden utopia of high-tech wonder. The Internet is not the panacea that will solve the ills of our society. Don't misunderstand us; the Internet is a powerful tool, and we will all use this tool in our quest for a better future.

But it won't just happen; rather, it will be a challenge. And it's a challenge that we know you are ready to take on. The challenge is to bring distant families closer together. The challenge is to bring educational resources and empowerment tools to people in remote areas. The challenge is to get the whole planet into a pair of shoes, so that we're all ready for the digital revolution (which has already started). The challenge is to celebrate cultural diversity, while avoiding the homogenizing effect of mass media. Let us revel in this time. Let us build communities to strengthen ourselves, our minds, and our human bonds, and to heighten our awareness of each other's trials and tribulations, so that we may work together to rise above them. It is not technology itself that brings the promise of the future; rather, it's the sheer will within us all to work toward that promise.

The View From On High

Remember your first date? How about that first kiss? These events in the lives of teenagers are special memories—rites of passage, all part of growing up. But those moments were often clumsy, and sometimes even scary. Will our braces lock? Will we be in trouble if we get caught? In the minds of some techno-gurus, that's where we are right now with computers and the Internet. We're awkward adolescents fumbling around in uncharted territory. We may think that our shiny new 300MHz PC, with its USR Sportster x2 Voice Modem, 128MB of EDO RAM, and 8MB ATI 3D accelerator card, is some mighty advanced hardware, but just look at it. Can you talk to it in fluent, conversational English? Nope. You still have that antique keyboard and mouse, and an archaic set of commands. Does it anticipate your needs? Not very effectively, if it tries at all. When you think about it, even with your computer, you still have a lot of manual work to do. That's because computer makers are new at this. They've only been at it for a mere half century. They're still learning the ropes, trying to understand the world and its needs. They're still shifting the paradigm.

There are many visionaries out there who are looking toward the future, and we've spoken about several of them already in this book. Let's take a look into the future, and hear what some of those notable thinkers have to say about it.

WHY CAN'T JOHNNY COMPETE IN THE NEW GLOBAL ECONOMY?

Every time you switch on the tube, there's some talking head sitting there telling you about the declining state of education. We're told that kids aren't meeting the needs of the employment market anymore, and there's a lot of finger pointing and blame being cast haphazardly about by politicians, CEOs, education administrators, teachers, parents, and "concerned" citizens. Unfortunately, too many of the solutions involve the redistribution of wealth, or the dismantling of the Department of Education, and very few solutions take into account the real problem: Schools just weren't designed for the new era.

Our public education system was built to serve the needs of the Industrial Revolution, and it functions with a strict hierarchy, approximating a factory model. It was a great system for its time, but the dawn of the Information Age has rendered it obsolete. The emergence of successful new businesses has been accompanied by a shift to flat management and open structures, and contemporary enterprises value creativity and recognize the need to take bold risks. Watch a random sample of MSNBC or CNN/FN and you're likely to hear buzz words like "paradigm shift," which means simply that what we used to do isn't what we do now. There is a paradigm shift happening now, and golden opportunities abound for young people to excel in the new model. There are phrases you hear every day in modern business, like "out-of-the-box thinking," or "well-leveraged in the global economy." The problem is that if we don't redesign our schools to apply cutting-edge business models to education, the only phrase our children will need to learn to survive the paradigm shift will be, "Would you like fries with that?"

Alvin Toffler, Futurist

"I can imagine our entire school system shriveling up. It is a $500 billion-dollar enterprise. By everybody's measure, they are inefficient,

ineffective, and very expensive. When we built that system, it was humanizing and democratic and good. But it's very structure—it simulated the factory. Now they continue to simulate a factory future, but the factories aren't going to be there. So what is going to happen is that these schools are going to shrink in relevance...The single, most important educational gain in America in the last 15 or 20 years has been the fact that 20, 30, or 40 million Americans have learned how to use a PC. Now isn't it amazing? They didn't go to school to learn that. How did they learn? They learned first from pimply faced kids in Radio Shacks, who sold the first machines and said: 'You push this button over here.' Then they brought the machines home and then they played with them and then they said, 'Gee,' they needed to know more, so they called a guru. Who was a guru? A guru was a neighbor or a coworker who had bought a machine one week before them. He was now, or she was now, the expert. What happened was, through an informal process of people-to-people learning, an enormous bank of skills was distributed through our society. No school. Schools didn't matter in that process. Virtually none. That says to me, if we understood people-to-people learning, and distributed intelligence, we could transform and accelerate the learning processes in fabulous ways that have nothing to do with schoolrooms and seats."

HOW MAY I SERVE YOU, MASTER?

How will computers enrich your life in the future? They will not take up valuable space in the corner of the den; instead they'll be part of everything you own. The vacuum cleaner will know when its bag needs changing. The TV will not be a box on the floor; it will be a wall, and it will know what your favorite movies are and will be able to guide you to new movies that you'll want to see. The car will tell you if the tires need to be rotated or if the fuel line is clogged (assuming it even has a fuel line at all). Intelligent agents will not be mere programs on your PC desktop, they'll be inserted into the cardboard that makes up the box of Raisin Bran in your cupboard, and when the box is empty, it will put itself on your shopping list, or just order itself a replacement from the grocer. Don't fear this stuff. This is the future, and despite what you may have learned from watching "The Twilight Zone," these machines are not going to gang up on you and take over the planet. Why is it the future? Because intelligent human interface is what's needed to take technological supremacy away from a handful of geeks and put it into the hands of every last man, woman, and child on this planet. Who has seen this future? Why, Nicholas Negroponte, of course.

Nicholas Negroponte, Founder And Director Of MIT's Media Laboratory

From Being Digital *©1995 Random House, ISBN# 0-679-43916-6*

My dream for the interface is that computers will be more like people. This idea is vulnerable to criticism for being too romantic, vague, or unrealizable. If anything, I would criticize it for shooting too low. There may be many exotic channels of communications of which we may not even be aware today. (As somebody married to an identical twin and with identical twin younger brothers, I am fully prepared to believe from observation that extrasensory communication is not out of the question.)

THE TRIBES ARE GATHERING

They say the world is shrinking, and they talk about the Global Village. Former President George Bush spoke of the "New World Order." But are we becoming homogenized into a one-nation world? Doubtful. The world has been toying with intentional communities and utopias since the dawn of humanity, but with the Internet we've seen the birth of an interesting phenomenon. Communities based on interest and lifestyle, rather than geography, have sprung up, and these communities supersede the geographic structure of our world. Now you can just as easily make a friend in Bombay as you can in Cleveland, without ever leaving your home in Nagasaki. We are forming tribes. *Wired* magazine released a special issue about future predictions, and one author caught our eye. He's the cofounder of Global Business Network and the chief architect of Wired Ventures Ltd. This is one of his forecasts.

Lawrence Wilkinson, Managing Director Of Global Business Network

From "Scenarios," Wired *Special Edition 1.01, p. 74*

The world fragments into a working pandemonium of individuals, organized by jobs rather than geography. Communication is pervasive and focuses on personal empowerment. The Net becomes the chief exchange medium for decentralized work, personal gratification, and global commerce. Physical infrastructure in North America stagnates, while personal spaces thrive. Art and attention are turned inward, as personal expression flourishes in new media and old public spaces crumble. Technology is the global culture. The have-nots become the have-lates. Ethnic or group differences give way to a homogenized patchwork of unbridled individual variety. Europe is wracked with civil strife as its socialistic civilization unravels. Russia rebounds. Japan lags. China and the developing countries become huge flea markets where just about anything goes.

GLOBAL VILLAGE OF THE DAMNED

Political reactionaries and social critics talk about class struggle, about those with wealth versus those without. Fringe radicals, militia nuts, and other extremists rant on about a race war, a class war, or some other apocalypse. These ravings fall largely on deaf ears, but with the increase in global terrorism of late, many people are starting to pay more attention. Information technology and virtual communities play a large role both in fostering fear and uncertainty, and in combating hate and ignorance. Read the words of the colorful and visionary man from Minds.com.

Howard Rheingold, Virtual Community Guru

"In the long term, these information technologies are going to enable us to operate both in a business sense and a government sense in more appropriately smaller units. But the transitions from empires to smaller units is never unpainful (sic) and sometimes downright

bloody. And we have the most well-armed citizenry in history, full of cults with all kinds of nutty beliefs. And if the rule of law breaks down here, it's going to make Yugoslavia look like a picnic. Right? So I can think, 'Gee I'm really worried about the next 20 years.' If we get through it all right, then the next 50 years could be really interesting. When you get a highly disruptive transition that is brought on by the rapid pace of change, it's something to be feared...

"You know, a lot of people believe that the reaction against the Shah [of Iran] and the popularity of the Ayatollah have less to do with true religious belief than a reaction against modernity. And that the speed at which he had accelerated—the Shah—had deliberately accelerated change in society. You know, a lot of old things break down, and people get angry. They lose control of their lives, their families, their kids. Their values, their fate. [They say:] 'Let's get back to the old days, and if we have to kill a million people to do that, let's do it.' And then it happens. So I think those things are in the background to be feared, and if you do fear them and you're wrong, you made a mistake. If you don't fear them and they come and eat you, then you have your children's blood on your hands.... I think it's really important to raise these questions outside the circle of intelligentsia."

BUSINESS AS UNUSUAL

The business community is starting to recognize the power and competitive advantage of virtual communities. Some people, like Howard Rheingold with his Electric Minds community, intend to derive a profit from building a social community. You may be thinking, "this is nothing new, AOL already did that." True, but what AOL actually did was build a behemoth proprietary content network, from which communities serendipitously sprang forth. Not to steal AOL's thunder, though, it's fair to say that when AOL recognized this trend in their own network, they quickly took steps to encourage it, and effectively began setting the standards for modern-day virtual communities.

However, with regard to business, we believe that virtual communities will be influential among all industries, from agriculture to Wall Street to manufacturing. Why? An important key trend has been forecast by John Hagel III and Arthur G. Armstrong, authors of *net.gain* (Harvard Business School Press, ISBN 0-87584-759-5). They say, "…there will be an unprecedented shift in power from vendors of goods and services to the customers who buy them." Therefore, companies that organize communities around these customers will build value, brand, and loyalty, and at the same time, impressive economic returns. The brand AOL sells is AOL, but a business community could just as easily be selling any widget, like cars, toasters, shoes, or pet rocks.

However, businesses will be faced with several challenges during this shift in focus to the customer. First, senior management will need to recognize and understand the shift. Second, organizing and building a community takes resources, time, and money, which some upper-level managers may not be easily convinced to provide. Third, and most importantly, as Hagel and Armstrong have noted, the concept of virtual communities is a "moving target." No one really knows the direction they'll take. One thing is certain: Managers need to remain flexible and focused. If they don't, they'll see the market position of their companies slowly fade away.

Hagel & Armstrong, Authors Of *net.gain*

Virtual communities are a moving target. Organizers who enter with one view of industry structure may find themselves surprised as the virtual ground beneath them shifts in unanticipated ways. Those who keep their eyes (and investments) focused on member acquisition, information captures, and emerging growth opportunities are likely to profit the most from these changes.

It will be interesting to watch the business landscape in the coming years. We'll see markets reshaped, markets expanded, distribution channels rerouted—all as a result of the formation of virtual communities.

Visions Of The Future—We Hope

We're excited and mesmerized by the thrilling prospects of the future and the challenges that we all face there. Since we're determined to be a part of it, we'll share a few of our personal views, not so much from "on high," but rather from somewhere around the middle.

POLITICS AND CYBERSPACE MAKE STRANGE BEDFELLOWS

The digital nation. The new truer democracy. The golden hope of the Internet. They talk about direct citizen interaction with elected officials, and while a lot of it is currently just rhetoric, many elected officials are coming online, putting up Web pages, providing direct access through email, and actually trying to make information technology available to anyone and everyone, regardless of race, income, or anything else. But what about politics in cyberspace? What about government? The Internet knows no political boundaries. Who really governs there? Who will govern there in the future?

Todd Takes Cyber-Politics To A Revolutionary Level

I've heard the idea bandied about in a few corners of the Internet, and it appeals to me as a First Amendment absolutist and as a netizen. It's a notion of government that I think is quite conceivable, albeit maybe impractical in the very near future. Imagine if the denizens of cyberspace all banded together, held a bloodless revolution, and declared the Internet a separate and sovereign state, independent of regulatory control by any one nation or cabal of nations. The Internet could have its own political leaders, its own economy, and its own way of dealing with conflict. I (only partly jokingly) propose we name our new nation The United Peoples of Cyberia. There are no physical issues, and our citizens would enjoy dual citizenship of both cyberspace (with all the rights and responsibilities that would entail) and whatever meatspace nation they originally hail from. It is conceivable that rather than a democracy, perhaps the digital nation might be the first and only stable anarchy. Virtual communities, all with their own independently elected or mandated leadership, would agree by proxy to live harmoniously with one another. Imagine the 700 Club Virtual Community living peacefully with a community established by Howard Stern, or with a society of druids.

ANYONE, ANYTIME, ANYWHERE

The digital civilization. The wired generation. Will it really be an era of haves and have-nots? It doesn't have to be. Today a large segment of our population feels unempowered, left out, invalidated. Why? Because they aren't heard. It's communication that delivers empowerment, which is why the framers of the Constitution gave us free speech and a free press. But speech is only useful if you can be heard, and the freedom of the press is only useful if you happen to own one. The Internet is changing all of that.

Karla Lives A Digital Lifestyle

Today, roughly 40 million people have access to the Internet. Soon, all 6 billion people on the planet will have that access, and they won't even need a computer. You'll be able to send and receive email, access job information, or research a business proposal, much in the same way that you place a local phone call from a pay phone. All you'll need is a PIN number, an email account, and your index finger. We see it beginning already with the proliferation of Internet cafes and Internet kiosks in libraries, but soon (maybe within five years?) Internet kiosks will be as ubiquitous as the corner phone booth is today. Prototype kiosks are displayed at trade shows like Internet World and Comdex, and they're already available in some airports.

In some ways, the future is here today. If you're a laptop or personal digital assistant (PDA) user and you enjoy heart-pounding blues music and zesty Cajun cuisine, head over to The House of Blues, where they have Ethernet ports ready for you to plug into. Soon, no matter where you are or what you're doing, you'll have access to your digital community.

The Civic Center Of Tomorrow

To be able to communicate is to be empowered. For those of us lucky enough to be among the mere 40 million citizens currently online, the ability to participate in communities that ignore political boundaries and geographic limits is tremendously powerful. The virtual communities that we belong to will become our civic centers. In addition, the instantaneous nature of CMC is giving rise to a sort of virtual sub-community that we'll call the "instant community of convenience." These are groups of people who have no knowledge of one another, banding together out of need to improve their condition. These "instant communities" may spawn long-term communities, but they don't need to; often they last just as long as there's a problem that needs solving. This has always happened, but never so easily or effortlessly as with the Internet. Here's an example of one such community from that sage of cyberlife, Mr. Negroponte.

Nicholas Negroponte, Senior Columnist For *Wired*

From Negroponte's column in Wired *issue 4.10, p. 218*

One fine day a young woman went out to buy a car. The dealer convinced her to purchase a Ford Taurus for US$19,500. She said she needed to sleep on it and would come back the next day. But instead of just sleeping on it, she used the Net to inquire whether there were others, near her, who were also considering buying a Taurus. By next morning, she had found 15 people who were. Some email discussion ensued, and she returned to the dealer to say she would take the car, but for $16,500. This was so far below his price that he assumed she had made a mistake. "No sir. I have not made *a mistake," she replied. "I simply failed to mention that I am buying 16 cars, not one." Delighted with the idea of selling in such volume, the dealer promptly sold the cars at her price.*

That is a shining example of an "instant community of convenience." We see this occur from time to time in various online forums, and we will see it happen with greater frequency as the Net continues its exponential growth.

The Tools For The Future

Throughout this book, we've showcased many community tools. What are the next generation of tools going to do? Right now there is a tool called Firefly (**www.firefly.com**) that puts you directly in touch with other cybercitizens based on specific interests like music and movies. It's very likely that long-lasting communities will emerge out of this and similar tools. AOL has certainly spawned its fair share of communities, like the highly praised financial community called The Motley Fool (**fool.web.aol.com**), and iVillage's Parent Soup (**www.parentsoup.com**).

And what about the tools that facilitate the actual act of talking and browsing? Chat has been textual, and now with The Palace, it's graphical as well. Very soon chat will be conducted in realtime video accompanied by full audio. Informational navigation may well take the place of following hyperlinks in a Web browser, as we move toward a 3D interface that looks like the popular action game Quake: you'll travel though virtual hallways past file cabinets, opening doors and drawers to access the data you're searching for. Gone will be the archaic days of FTP sites, Gopher searches, and newsreaders.

Most likely, as the Net begins to settle (not gonna happen too soon), the tools at your disposal will be organized into structured hubs, and you will go to your favorite hub or hubs to complete the task at hand. In the not-too-distant future, you'll do this by just talking. You might name your computer Alice, and you'll say, "Alice, go find information about the annual biker rally in Sturgis, South Dakota, and while your at it, get my email, delete all the spam, and send a message to Todd and Karla and tell them that I never would've believed this possible."

There's A Sucker Born Every Minute

You think this vision of the future is a bit far-fetched? That's what they said about the airplane. "Yeah, but that was different," you say. Well, let's see what some of history's most notorious skeptics had to say:

Some Notable Skeptics

Western Union Internal Memo (1876)
This "telephone" has too many shortcomings to be seriously considered as a means of communication. The device is inherently of no value to us.

Harry M. Warner, Founder Of Warner Bros. Studios *(1927)*
Who the hell wants to hear actors talk?

Thomas Watson, Chairman Of IBM *(1943)*
I think there is a world market for maybe five computers.

Popular Mechanics, *Magazine (1949)*
Computers in the future may weigh no more than 1.5 tons

Sir Richard van der Riet Wooley, Astronomer (1956)
Space travel is utter bilge.

Lee DeForest, American Inventor (1873-1961)
While theoretically and technically television may be feasible, commercially and financially I consider it an impossibility.

Dionysius Lardner, English Scientist (1793-1859)
Rail travel at high speeds is not possible because passengers, unable to breath, would die of asphyxia.

Bill Gates, CEO Of Microsoft (1981)
640K ought to be enough for anybody.

So don't be surprised when your car, or kitchen appliances, or bedroom closets start talking to you in plain English, and actually understand you when you speak to them. When you load a new game, like id Software's Super Quake 7 (perhaps to be released in 2014?), and you put on the special gloves and headset, and climb into the gyroscope, it should not shock you to be immersed in a world where you don't just play, but actually feel the reality (virtually) of the game. You'll not only *want* to play with or against human opponents, you'll *demand* it, and it will happen. And don't be too amazed when a new baby is born in your family, and suddenly you're inundated with greetings and warm wishes from people you'd all but forgotten, because an intelligent agent informed them of your new arrival. Perhaps the future was best forecast by the marketing geniuses at AT&T when they said, "You will."

The Future Isn't What It Used To Be

In the fifties, cheesy B-grade sci-fi thrillers (socially spawned by Red Scare paranoia) warned of impending Martian Invasion. In the sixties, Jane Fonda in *Barbarella* gave us a completely different and thankfully unrealized view, and Stanley Kubrick gave us both *A Clockwork Orange* (a nightmarish vision) and *2001: A Space Odyssey* (a very hopeful one indeed). The seventies gave us a heroic future with the thrilling *Star Wars* (we know it was actually a long time ago in a galaxy far, far away, but it seemed pretty futuristic), as well as xenophobic horror with Ridley Scott's *Alien*. Then the eighties rolled around, ushering in the Reagan Era, and this time Mr. Scott gave us *Blade Runner*, with its media-saturated urban sprawl and ecologically ruined landscape. Terry Gilliam's *Brazil*, where the future was a bureaucratic anarchy, represents a popular future view.

Today, in the nineties, we stand closer to the cusp of the future than ever before, and cyberspace has changed our collective vision. Is Orwell's *1984* coming true a decade and a half late? Frankly, we don't think so. In the first chapter of this book, one of the quotes about community came from Noam Chomsky. It was a cynical and irreverent quote. Ironically, it is Mr. Chomsky's words we will leave you with as well.

Noam Chomsky, Social Commentator And Author

If you assume that there's no hope, you guarantee that there will be no hope. If you assume that there is an instinct for freedom, there are opportunities to change things, there's a chance you may contribute to making a better world. That's your choice.

Well, isn't that the crux of it all. Virtual community should be, and for the most part is, about finding new ways of bringing our world together and working toward a greater future. The technology should be, and one day will be, invisible. It's all about humans, not machinery. Together, we hope, we can build a diverse, exciting, and rewarding cyberspace. A digital society. An electronic global village. Something glorious. Something brilliant. We think you're up to it, and hopefully the information we've presented here will help you on your way. Good luck dear traveler. We'll see you again soon…out there in the ether.

Have a strange day.

Index

Sysop World magazine, 43
System
　administrators, 131
　requirements, 88, 235

T

T1 lines, 85, 88
T3 lines, 85, 88
Tables of Contents, at Web sites, 124
Talk City, 71, 72, 76, 149–150
Talk.com, 29, 76
　chat events, 80–81
TCP/IP, 39
Tech support, 397
　Technical consultants, role in
　　community networks, 295
Technology
　around the world, 434–435
　changes, 435–440
　skeptics, 446–447
Technology Innovation Challenge
　Grants, 310
Telecommunications and Information
　Infrastructure Assistance Program
　(TIIAP), 308–309
Teleconferencing, 259
Templates, animation, 168
TEN, 57.
Tennis Server, rotating banner ads, 368
Terrorism, and the Internet, 439–440
Themes, 187–188
Thomas, Robert and Carleen, 408–409
Thompson, Ken, 46
Threaded discussion groups, 156, 157
　linear threading, 157
Threads, 68–69, 406
　archiving, 83
　message length, 83
TidBITS, 380
Ties That Bind Conference, 296
Tile.net Lists, 348
Time-Warner
　Pathfinder, 336
　Time magazine, 8
Toffler, Alvin, 436–437
Top 5% awards, 345

Torch, 269
Tours. *See also* Sites.
　guided, 242–244
Town hall, electronic, 302
Toyota USA Foundation, 311
Trade associations, 56, 400
TradeBanners, 341
Trademark issues, 417
Traffic
　monitoring, 129
　reports, 370–372
Transaction-based
　fees, 87
　pricing, 370
Transportation information, 290
Travel
　bureaus role in community networks, 297
　Internet Travel Network, 137
　sites, 182
Trial memberships, 192
Tribune Company, The, 293
Tripod, 352
Trivia Module, eaChat, 148
Troublemakers, 402–404
Troubleshooters, 397
Turkette's Frustration, 190–192
Tutorials, 194
TV ratings
　Nielson, 325

U

U.S. Department of Commerce, 309
U.S. Department of Education
　grants, 310
　technological changes, 436
U.S. Games Systems, Inc., 96
U.S. government publications, 111–112
U.S. Internal Revenue Code, 311
U.S. Navy, 38
U.S. Robotics, 260
　Big Picture products, 112
　Towne Square 2000 Palace site, 237, 238, 240
U.S. Supreme Court
　Miller vs. California, 409–410
　obscenity decisions, 408–409

Index